THREE BROTHERS IN A BOAT

THREE BROTHERS IN A BOAT

A True Story of Adventure and Purpose Rowing the Pacific

The Maclean Brothers

CANONGATE

First published in Great Britain in 2026
by Canongate Books Ltd, 14 High Street, Edinburgh EH1 1TE

canongate.co.uk

1

Maps by Ewan Maclean

British Library Cataloguing-in-Publication Data
A catalogue record for this book is available on
request from the British Library

ISBN 978 1 83726 699 9

Typeset in Adobe Garamond and American Typewriter by
Palimpsest Book Production Ltd, Falkirk, Stirlingshire
Printed and bound by CPI Group (UK) Ltd, Croydon CR0 4YY

The manufacturer's authorised representative in the EU for product safety is BGC Sustainability & Compliance, 7 avenue du Général Leclerc, Paris 75014
(gpsr@baldwinglobalconsulting.com)

FSC
www.fsc.org
MIX
Paper | Supporting responsible forestry
FSC® C013604

Contents

Prologue

By Ewan

DAY 083, Friday 4 July

EWAN

My heart stopped as I watched my brother being washed overboard, taken by the sea. Like freeze frames of a motion picture, the memories hang static. Splintered and severed by dark, indifferent water.

The world around me blurred and swung as the wave crashed over us, violently tipping our boat to its side. Yet in my mind, everything was still. I sat there paralysed – just beyond reach – time stretching out to eternity.

Moments ago, Lachlan had stood there. Steadying himself on the handrail of the cabin with his back turned, eyes scouring the looming shapes that raced past. He searched for a sign of yet another eruption, to explode from the depths and crash into the rear of *Rose Emily*. A moment of respite to swing the hatch open and seek shelter in the cabin below. It was his turn to rest. We exchanged no words, for the roar of the storm and the slamming hull was absolute. The red glow of our headtorches seemed sinister tonight – all natural light was gone, for the sky had been consumed by thick cloud some hours before. A cold electric glare from the autopilot screen cast shadows across the deck, dimly framing Lachlan's swaying silhouette.

The wave would arrive without warning, towering high above his head and moving with ferocious speed, unstoppable. A split second later, it would slam into the port quarter where he stood. But I had no time to shout and warn him. No chance that he might even turn his head to face it. Nothing but silence in that haunting moment.

END OF LOG

I remember the adrenaline of the storm and the unpredictable brutality of the waves that had hit. The boat had rolled to 90 degrees twice already that day, which would have kept even the most weathered seafarer from finding sleep. But by then we'd been rowing continuously for almost 12 weeks, resting in short stints and never sleeping for more than a few hours per day. We were exhausted and Jamie was already unconscious when the final wave struck. We were in the jaws of a vast South Pacific weather system, being battered from all sides by relentless wind and swell. My body was bruised by wooden oar handles that had hammered into knees and shins as the boat wrenched about. It'd been some time since I last played rugby, but the physicality of that day felt worse than any game I'd played. We'd been put through the wringer. At least we could see our assailants during the daylight hours. After nightfall, only the rushing and crashing sounds of the thundering sea rang in our ears as seething mountains of water shouldered past.

In those conditions, our options were limited. Overpowered by the rising gale, we had succumbed and turned downwind not long after noon. We were at the mercy of the weather gods, and they would fling us wherever they chose. Oars were all we had to keep our course and, should an emergency strike, we had no sail or motor to help fight against the raw power of the elements. Turning back would simply have been impossible, but stowing the oars and retreating into the cabin wasn't an option either. Keeping the boat from turning side-on to the oncoming waves was vital. And so our fate was sealed: we had no choice but to ride it out.

It was my turn to row alone for a time, as we had done so nearly every night before. That was the pattern we had settled on: row together through the day and for the first few hours of darkness, then split what remained of the night into thirds, rowing alone for three hours each night. There's no easy way to do it, but that seemed to work for us. Lachlan had secured his oars and retreated to the rear cabin, staggering up the deck as *Rose Emily* rolled rail-to-rail. A few seconds later, time would stop. Everything hung in the balance, suspended by a lifeline above four miles of ocean.

Part I

Chapter 1

Where It All Began

By Jamie

Thursday 20 February 2020; 1,878 days to go. My alarm went off. Memories of crashing waves, bagpipes and flares faded away. I was in Glasgow, and the feeling of fresh linen sheets was still novel and comforting on my skin. It'd been 35 days since we landed in Antigua after spending 35 days rowing across the Atlantic Ocean.

We had been participants in the Talisker Whisky Atlantic Challenge, a 3,000-mile non-stop and unsupported rowing race from the Canary Islands to the Caribbean. Our home for the five weeks at sea had been a nine-metre-long, two-metre-wide open-topped fibreglass boat. It had a small cabin at either end, which we crawled into for brief moments of rest. For over a month we lived a life exposed to the elements: a relentless cycle of discomfort and sleep deprivation. Rowing for around 14 hours each day – with four hours of sleep – we were physically and mentally exhausted.

There had been 36 teams taking part in the 2019–2020 race, which set off mid-December and spanned the festive period. I won't ever forget Christmas and New Year spent on a rowing boat in the middle of the Atlantic Ocean with only Ewan and Lachlan for company. The only present we had for one another was a perfectly ripe mango, stowed below deck and forgotten until Christmas Eve. It was the first fresh food we had tasted in more than two weeks. With a set of Highland bagpipes on board, it was ceremoniously piped out of the hatch and onto the chopping board, then devoured by three hungry boys. It was, without question, the best mango of my life.

Even though the Atlantic Challenge is an organised event, once you are over a few hundred miles from land, you are essentially on your own. Quickly one loses sight of the other boats that had initially accompanied us from the Spanish island of La Gomera. Within six hours you won't see another rower until you make landfall in Antigua. If disaster had struck – a medical emergency or a sinking ship – we would have relied on the nearest vessel to come to our aid. Nine times out of ten, this would be a shipping tanker, the scale of which is unfathomable when compared to our rowing boat. Think of an elephant rescuing a mouse in a wave pool, except the mouse is made of glass and the elephant made of steel. It was a situation we wanted to avoid.

Before we even stepped foot back on dry land, we knew life would never be the same. Back in Glasgow, the ocean still filled my dreams, ebbing and flowing with fragmented memories of water and sky. It was visceral, and yet it still didn't feel real. Was it really me on that boat? I felt like I'd changed. I knew I had. But when asked exactly how, I struggled to express it. Maybe the depths of emotion felt in such an intense period of time can never quite be articulated. We lived and breathed the ocean. We depended on it, survived on it, thrived on it. Moments of elation were juxtaposed with periods of despair. It was raw, it was honest and it will stay with me for the rest of my life.

Thousands of miles from land, in the mid-Atlantic silence, I found a clarity of thought that I'd never experienced before. Thoughts came and went like the waves that rolled on by, uninterrupted by the usual distractions of modern-day life. Our existence was unbroken and simple.

Eat, sleep, row, repeat.

We turned to each other for entertainment, having long conversations on anything and everything that came to mind. Topics could last days. All social apprehension or conversational niceties were cast overboard as our sliding seats became our philosopher's chairs, dipping in and out of discussion as the wind whistled by.

The initial idea to row across the Atlantic had formed in unlikely circumstances. As a student, Lachlan's main source of income was as a rickshaw driver in Edinburgh. He would rent a tricycle, human-powered and capable of carrying three people in the back, and ferry (usually drunk) people between late-night establishments until the early hours of the morning. He paid a rental fee for the bike – between £60 and £120, depending on the weekend – then everything he cleared over that was money in his pocket. On one Saturday in November 2017 he sat outside the Three Sisters, one of Edinburgh's slightly stickier establishments, waiting for a job. With him was a fellow driver, Stu. The pair of them had been chatting to a couple who were enjoying a night out and told them about their dual life, which was split between guiding in Alaska and studying in Edinburgh. 'That sounds amazing,' Lachlan said to Stu after the couple returned to their evening. 'I'd be up for something like that one day.'

A few weeks earlier, Lachlan had seen something online about a rowing race across the Atlantic called the Talisker Whisky Atlantic Challenge. A strange-looking open boat, akin to a double-ended clog, had ridden down the side of a wave with four smiling women on board. He hadn't realised that it was possible to do such a thing: 'Why don't we do something like going to Alaska, Stu? We could get there by rowing across the Atlantic.'

Ewan and I had quickly caught wind of the idea, Stu decided it wasn't for him, and, before we knew it, the three of us had made a commitment to one another. We were going to row the Atlantic Ocean. In a matter of months, it became an obsession, consuming every spare minute of every day. It was the thing that got us out of bed. It was exciting and unknown.

Our original motivation was simple: to have a remarkable experience together as brothers. Ewan had moved to Bristol a few years earlier and we hadn't been able to spend as much time together as a family. Taking on a massive challenge like this offered the opportunity to work together on a shared project before life became even more complicated, restricted and busy. It presented an adventure of a lifetime and a chance to push ourselves mentally and physically. To be honest, I think it's rare that people embark on big journeys like this without having thoughts of the prestige it can bring. There were undoubtedly some egocentric reasons for wanting to do it. It was an opportunity to prove to ourselves, and also others, what we were capable of. Growing up around our dad – a world authority in Scotch whisky – had inspired us to want to be the best in whatever we did. But acclaim wasn't our end goal – it wasn't all about breaking records. We were driven by the thought of doing something that we were passionate about, that excited us and fulfilled us on a daily basis. A part of me thought I could achieve that by rowing across the Atlantic, and that this could be my means of creating a small mark on the world, in however small and seemingly arbitrary a way.

The idea of being out there, in the middle of an ocean, at the mercy of the wind and the waves. To be working with Mother Nature to not only survive but to thrive. The excitement of the risk, and the reward of reaching the other shore. The adventure itself appealed a great deal.

The project quickly grew arms and legs. We soon learned about the capacity of a challenge like this to raise a significant amount of money and awareness for a good cause. With no direct link to a specific charity, we met various Scottish-based organisations to learn about the impact of their work. Being aware of how fortunate an upbringing the three of us had, we soon landed on a children's charity, Children First, as one of our charity partners.

Some years back, Lachlan had backpacked around Madagascar, interacting with a small NGO called Feedback Madagascar. The founder, Jamie Spencer, is Scottish and happened to be living in Edinburgh at the time. With only two British employees and a staff of over two hundred local Malagasy, they work hand-in-hand with local communities to help bring people out of extreme poverty. Feedback Madagascar tackles problems around clean water, health, education, livelihoods, human rights and forest and wildlife conservation with a holistic approach – recognising that they are all interconnected parts of one living system. Their clean water projects caught our attention, not only as essential building blocks for life, but as catalysts to help a community develop and thrive.

Growing up, we had all shared a strong spirit of adventure, and sport was rarely far from our daily lives, but we were by no means professional athletes, and certainly not professional rowers. A stone's throw from our family home lay Midlothian Snowsports Centre – Europe's longest dry ski slope at the time. We spent childhood afternoons throwing ourselves off the freestyle jump, and chasing one another down the artificial slopes, less worried about technique than about going as fast as we humanly could. We snapped our thumbs, fractured our arms, and, latterly, on a university trip to the French Alps at the age of 18, Ewan broke his back in two different places. Thankfully his spinal cord was intact and he made a full recovery.

In our mid-teens we also all enjoyed the physicality of rugby, throwing ourselves into it regardless of our average ability. We also climbed every tree within a mile radius of our childhood home, with remarkably few trips to Edinburgh's Royal Infirmary. Our favourites were the large sycamores at the top of the garden, which housed our makeshift tree house and giant swing. We rode our bikes, often uncontrollably, down various areas of the surrounding hills. Lachlan remained interested in cycling throughout university, deciding to bike around the world in stages over the next ten years with a friend. So far they've made it from the Arctic Circle in Norway to the western border of Georgia.

But rowing, other than when faced with faulty outboard engines, didn't appear in any of our lives until a year before our Atlantic voyage. Only one of us, Ewan, had stepped briefly inside a rowing boat before the start of our campaign, and even that ended with an unwelcome swim in the River Clyde.

Our childhoods had been grounded in the far northwest of Scotland in a place called Assynt. Long Easters and summers without Wi-Fi, TV, a landline or mobile signal had driven us to find creative ways to entertain ourselves. We took to the mountains and coastlines of this wild place, finding comfort by the ocean and getting lost among the hills. We gravitated towards the water: kayaks full of holes, and dinghies without a proper rigging. As we bobbed a few hundred metres from the shore, imagining we were 'deep-sea fishing', I can vividly remember looking out to sea and wondering what lay beyond the horizon.

The ocean was our highway to the world. We could leave the shores of this remote corner of the UK and make landfall on any continent on the globe. Were we to attempt it then, aged six, ten and twelve, it would have been a disaster, but a seed had been sown for what might happen if we were to just set off and go.

It was Easter 2003 and Mum had brought us up to Assynt for the school holidays. The bad weather had us trapped in the cottage with only books and playing cards for entertainment. After a few hours and lots of persuasion, Mum agreed to let us take out the boat, as long as we stayed close to the shore. With the weather overcast and damp, we sat as water pooled on the weathered seats of our 16-foot fibreglass boat. She was well loved but required constant bailing to keep the internal water at a reasonable level. The rain gently seeped through my waterproof trousers as I shifted position to keep my legs from going cold. We hadn't caught any mackerel that day and the orange twine from our grandpa's homemade fishing spool was wet and awkward in my hand. Lachlan's line lay tangled in the bottom of the boat while Ewan frantically tried to restart the outboard engine. A southeasterly offshore breeze nudged us further out to sea, and we began to wonder what we should do. The flares in the tackle box hadn't been replaced in a couple of years, and although they probably still worked, it seemed a drastic last measure. With the outboard showing no signs of life, we dug out the oars and attempted to gain some sort of momentum back towards the shore.

Our mission had been simple: catch enough fish to allow us to rebait the lobster pots and have a few left over for a lunch of fried mackerel on toast. We had brought a couple of tins of tuna as backup bait for the pots, just in case the fishing didn't go to plan, but we hadn't anticipated mechanical failures. Ewan and I took turns heaving at the starter line of the engine while the other one attempted to row. Lachlan had sought shelter in the bow of the boat. We were all cold, wet and increasingly hungry. But no one complained. This was exactly the type of adventure we were looking for, and we wouldn't accept defeat.

We had been afloat for a couple of hours, and with no sign of her three sons in the sheltered bay, Mum had become increasingly concerned.

We were getting hungry so Ewan cracked one of the tins of tuna and rationed it out. The oily chunks of fish didn't taste great, but we each scoffed them down as any good castaway would. It felt like we had been afloat for days. We revelled in the idea that our great escapade on the high seas would become one of local legend. The reality was much less dramatic: we were never going to starve nor were we really at risk of being lost at sea, but, as we rounded the headland and rowed into the bay, we triumphantly let out yelps and cheers. With our unbroken voices, it probably sounded more like a gaggle of seabirds, but we felt like great explorers nonetheless.

We could see Mum standing on the jetty, arms folded and head shaking side to side. As we approached within earshot, Ewan shouted to shore: 'Mum, you won't believe it! We thought we were going to be lost at sea and starve so we had to eat one of the tins of tuna to stay alive.' She wasn't impressed. We sheepishly made our way back to the cottage to no ticker-tape parade. The three of us chose not to go out on the boat on our own for the remainder of the holiday.

When we weren't getting lost along the coastline of Scotland's far northwest, the three of us would head inland to the lochs and hills. There, among the bracken and the heather, we'd huddle round campfires, throwing a line into dark brown waters in the hope that a trout might fancy a nibble. Our freshwater fishing tended to be even more unsuccessful than our luck out at sea. Over the course of 32 years, I can count the number of brown trout that I've caught on one hand.

If the trout weren't abundant inland, the midges definitely were. These near-microscopic blood-sucking fiends can be found across the Highlands from mid-May until late September, and they have the capacity to drive anyone mad. To quote from Neil Munro's classic book *The Tales of Para Handy*, 'The Congo's no' to be compared wi' Scotland when ye come to insects.' Akin to a mosquito, but much smaller and certainly more vicious, midges can descend on unexpecting victims in their thousands, nibbling at any exposed skin that's been left unprotected.

I remember on one occasion up in the hills, when a young Lachlan was trying his hand at the fly rod, the midges soon appeared. His casts became increasingly frantic as he attempted to create some sort of disturbance in the air to ward off his tiny pursuers. Angered and agitated, with one almighty cast, he lifted the rod and threw back the line. He felt a sudden tug on the hook from behind. This was swiftly followed by yelps and cries. Ewan, pacing up and down on the nearby shoreline, had been hooked, right through the centre of his nose. As Lachlan wrenched on the rod to try to free the line from what he thought was a fankle in some heather, the hook firmly lodged itself into Ewan's septum. The midges continued to descend. Ewan, grasping the line with both hands, pulled back, f'ing and blazing. To make matters worse, at the time we had an excitable black Labrador called Oscar. Amid the chaos, he responded like any good Lab would, bounding, woofing and jumping with glee. The fishing line, still securely fastened to both Ewan's nose and Lachlan's rod, now wrapped itself around Oscar's leg. You can picture the scene: Oscar, tumbling and rolling, the line yanking and pulling, Ewan screaming, Lachlan panicking under midge attack. Eventually, the line was cut and, with a visit to Inverness Infirmary, the hook was removed by threading it all the way through. We joked that Ewan should now fashion a bull ring as a memento of the experience. He didn't seem too keen on the idea.

Freedom at a young age is a wonderful thing – greater still when it is found in a natural setting. My brothers and I spent years pushing one another's boundaries, in a place that was wild but relatively safe, which helped all of us better understand who we are. We made many mistakes, thankfully none of which had long-term repercussions. Among the hills and coasts of Assynt, we developed an appreciation for our individual limits, learning to place trust in our abilities and in one another. All three of us began to learn what we could achieve when we put our minds to it, both from a personal perspective and as a trio. And, without knowing it, Ewan, Lachlan and I had formed a brotherly bond that would one day help carry us across some of the largest bodies of water in the world.

On that February 2020 morning in Glasgow, I cast aside the duvet and stretched to touch my toes. The muscle tension in my lower back slowly faded, one of the few lasting physical effects of spending so many hours on the Atlantic. I wandered through to the bathroom and caught a glimpse of myself as I slid open the shower door. I looked more tired than I should, having racked up nearly a month of good nights' sleep. There was a deeper fatigue I could feel within my bones. It takes time for the body to recover. There was a look in my eyes that I wasn't quite expecting: that of a man who wasn't quite free. I hadn't realised that I'd already become slightly dulled and muted by a return to the mundanity of everyday life. The appreciation of quotidian luxuries, such as hot showers, that you gain from periods of discomfort is one of the driving forces behind the desire to experience such hardship in the first place.

Looking out the bedroom window, it was an expectedly grey and wet day on the west coast of Scotland. The tenements across the block looked cold, almost despairing, with water dripping down their stone façades as if they were shedding tears. Glasgow can be a fairly miserable place in late winter, with interminable rain and two-thirds of each day shrouded in darkness. It is unsurprising that us Scots tend to turn to the drink for comfort during these cold, short days.

In the kitchen I ground some coffee beans and prepared the cafetière.

I inhaled the rich and fruity smell and remembered how the coffee situation on our Atlantic crossing was a bit of a disaster. We made the fatal mistake of bringing three large tubs of Nescafé Azera instead of individual sachets. Faced with an average wind speed of 17mph, an open teaspoon of powdered coffee doesn't stand a chance, regularly ending up all over the deck instead of in our mugs and caffeine-deprived mouths.

A message on my phone grabbed my attention – it was the group chat with Ewan and Lachlan. This had been our primary means of keeping in touch since we went our separate ways three weeks earlier. I was envious of Lachlan. With no real need to return home until the following academic year, he'd remained in the Caribbean as crew on a yacht in Antigua to make the return voyage across the North Atlantic under sail. He regularly joined our daily calls from a white sandy beach, with turquoise water and palm trees as his backdrop. Mum occasionally joined on the calls. After flying out from the UK to see us arrive at Nelson's Dockyard, she'd decided to remain in Antigua to try to forge a new life for herself in the Caribbean. Even though Mum and Dad were separated, and had been for some time, this was a plot twist that none of us were expecting.

It's no secret that for a large portion of her life our mum has struggled with her mental health. Haunted by depression from before I can remember, her internal battle with this illness has, at times, been very hard to witness. The significant impact it's wrought on her life, with persistent sadness and loss of all motivation, has regularly crushed her self-belief and confidence. As little boys we would try to help, picking daffodils from the nearby forest in the hope that it might bring a smile to her face. On the worst of days, I would wonder why Mum hadn't got out of bed. It wasn't until my late teens that I really began to understand what was going on. This is not to say that she didn't take good care of us. On the contrary, when I reflect upon our childhoods, we were the luckiest three boys alive. Mum sacrificed her career for us, ensuring that Ewan, Lachlan and I were raised in an environment of love, creativity and adventure. No matter how debilitating the depression, she kept the ship steady on its course.

She encouraged music from a very young age, driving us to and from toddlers' percussion sessions in our local church every Saturday. When the time came to progress from triangles and maracas to something a bit more complex, we each had our say. For me it went: recorder, chanter, then full Highland bagpipes – a set of which made their way onto the Atlantic boat so many years later. Ewan chose the violin and then guitar, and Lachlan opted for the piano and accordion. It can't have been a very relaxing end to Mum's week, particularly having to sit in on group violin lessons for a bunch of six-year-olds. I believe Mum always had hope, and possibly still does, of her own trad boyband. Judging by our musical prowess, or lack thereof, this may have to remain a bit of a dream.

Our dad is one of those larger-than-life characters. A charismatic storyteller, you'll often find him sitting by the fire, a dram in his hand with friends gathered round. He's a writer by trade, but with a passion for Scotch he's built a career for himself in the world of whisky. It's far more than just a job, it's the person he chooses to be when no one else is around. He's done what so many people strive and fail to do with their lives: he's taken a passion and turned it into a career. He probably isn't aware of it, but this alone is the greatest lesson he could have ever taught my brothers and me.

Dad is a maverick. A rebellious hippy turned Highland gentleman, he's a slight romantic who has a soft spot for tales of the high seas. To Mum's dismay, he's a big kid at heart – the fourth brother, but one that was old enough to buy us paintball guns, knives and the occasional bow and arrow. Having spent some formative periods of time living on the Isle of Arran on the west coast of Scotland, he developed a passion for boating and the sea. His love of which was no doubt passed down to the three of us.

No matter who you are, what you do or where you come from, the door to his flat is always open, and there'll be a dram to be shared beside the fire.

None of us foresaw the impacts that an ocean crossing would have on family and friends. In the lead-up to our Atlantic row, Dad was visibly stressed, but Mum surprisingly relaxed. At the start-line in La Gomera she helped us clean the boat, polish the hull and portion out our snack packs. She was upbeat, energetic and even nonchalant. This should have been a red flag. Once we had departed and as the weeks went by, her communication became more frantic and disjointed. By the time we were two-thirds of the way across, the penny dropped: the severe stress caused by having her three boys in one boat, unassisted and alone in the middle of an ocean, had pushed her to breaking point. She had been forced into a state of manic paranoia.

The realisation was devastating. Many people subsequently asked us what the most difficult part of our Atlantic row was. We usually reeled off something about the waves, the wind or the discomfort. But, in truth, none of those came close to the feeling of helplessness and guilt we all felt for our mum's situation.

The thoughts of what this journey had done to our loved ones left a bittersweet taste in our mouths. On the second-last night of the crossing, amid the lonely darkness of a solo shift rowing, I felt confused and conflicted. I imagined stepping off the boat into the arms of one of the most important people in my life and not really knowing who that person had become. Only on one other occasion had I witnessed first-hand the change in a person's character as they move into a state of mania. Thoughts race, sleep no longer matters. Impulsive behaviour kicks in with a lack of social judgement and an inability to assess what is reality and what is not. Their altered state of mind can be so out of character and unpredictable that they can temporarily cease being the person you know and love. The uncertainty circled back and forth in my head all night. Who was it we might now meet on the shores of Antigua?

Reflecting on those strange moments at sea, I stirred my morning porridge. Mum was still in Antigua and showed no signs of returning to the UK. She had made the decision to give this new life a go and I admired her for it. Thankfully the mania began to subside and it seemed that the sun and sandy beaches were doing her some good.

I had taken a year out of art school to do our Atlantic row. The plan was to return the following September, complete my final year, and then continue along the lengthy process it takes to become a qualified architect in the UK. But my heart was never truly in it. I've always made sense of the world around me by making things with my hands, whether it's building, carpentry or cooking. I've learned to trust my ability to create something physical that other people can appreciate and enjoy. I've never really known what I wanted to do with my life. I still don't. Back then, in February 2020, I was unsure what the next couple of years might bring. Ewan's sabbatical had come to an end and he'd returned to his work in England. Lachlan bobbed off the coast of the Caribbean, and I sat in my flat in Glasgow reflecting on the adventure of a lifetime. It all felt quite strange. We had learned so much from our time at sea, and, despite the differences in distance and circumstance, there was an underlying certainty that connected us all. The sense of purpose we each got from the campaign was unparalleled by anything we had ever experienced. Although the crossing was arduous and difficult, it was fulfilling beyond measure. All the time, we knew that our efforts were working towards a greater mission of creating positive change through our charity partners – we had raised over £200,000 for children in Scotland and clean water projects in Madagascar. There was something in this combination: doing something you love in the service of others.

The first question you get asked after a trip like this is, 'What next?' There is a pressure to be able to spout out the next perfectly formed idea that's bigger and better. I can't remember how we responded to this question when it was asked by an interviewer a few minutes after making our first wobbly steps on Antigua's solid ground. I can only assume that it was, as is usually the case, an inaccurate prediction of what was to come.

The Maclean Foundation had been forming in our minds during the 35 days, nine hours and nine minutes prior to stepping foot on the pontoon in Nelson's Dockyard. We had achieved something that to us, only one year prior, had been incomprehensible. We had crossed an ocean and reached new continents under the power of our oars. Our perspective on what we were individually and collectively capable of had completely shifted, and we were curious to see how far – how much further – we could go. For the three of us, the charitable aspect of the crossing had given it a greater purpose, one that would last far beyond the medals and applause. We wanted to continue working together to create more positive ripples in the world through compassion and the spirit of adventure. It wasn't for many months, and after a global pandemic, until the idea flowered into a charity that was registered with the Official Scottish Charity Regulator. Combining passion with purpose, the charity's focus is the provision of clean water, continuing the work that was put into motion on the island of Madagascar through our Atlantic row. Back then, and without us really knowing it, the seeds for an even greater ocean adventure were being sown.

Chapter 2

Return to the Source

By Lachlan

Sunday 20 March 2022; 1,119 days to go. The straps of my accordion bag dug uncomfortably into my shoulders as we marched, three astride, up the four-by-four track. Though it was officially the start of spring, the ground crunched underfoot as we broke through newly formed ice. A pink sky hung overhead as clouds soared from right to left. We were safe down here in the glen, but there was serious wind on the peaks and cold air tickled our noses on every inhale. The snow-capped Grampian mountains lined either side of the gulley like bodyguards.

It was a momentous day. Ewan had completed 30 loops around the sun – and what better way to mark his birthday than meeting some friends from Braemar at Allt Scheicheachan bothy near Blair Atholl. Armed with whisky and instruments – accordion, guitar and small pipes – we were ready for some tunes with a few drams.

I'd last seen Jamie and Ewan together in Ranomafana, Madagascar, after three weeks of visiting clean water projects, before they were packed like sardines into a public bus and set off for Antananarivo, the capital. Rows for three were packed with five or six as luggage was lashed to the roof. It was the first leg of their 72-hour journey home: three buses, two taxis, three flights and a tram. Their suntans had almost completely faded in the six weeks that had passed, but they both seemed upbeat. I'd been lucky enough to stay out there, avoiding the tail end of a dreich Scottish winter. They had that slightly unhinged energy that Scots get when they wake up from a long winter sleep. Months of vitamin D deficiency were finally coming to an end.

We'd reflected during our time apart, but it was the first time doing so collectively. It was cathartic, like pressing a release valve on a pipe. We walked and we talked. For us, the best meetings never happen within the confines of a meeting room, and definitely not through a screen. It's when we're doing something: up a hill or on water.

We spoke of our experiences out in Madagascar that were etched into our collective memory. It had been one of those trips that felt important in the moment. I can't pretend to have had a life-changing experience – a moment in time that's transformed my view of the world in some profound way. But I have had experiences that have influenced the decisions I've gone on to make, altering my course through life over time. This journey to Madagascar was undoubtedly one of those. Something shifted in the weeks we were there. We saw something that couldn't be unseen or forgotten about.

The purpose of our trip was to visit water projects we'd funded through our Atlantic row. Conversation cast back to the village of Mahavelo, not far from the Indian Ocean in the southeast. It had been an early rise to get on the road out of Vohipeno, the nearest large settlement. As the glow of sunrise filled the sky, we left the town behind us. Lush green paddy fields tiered open plains on either side, separated by red walls of clay. A line of young men wielding long-handled spades walked out along a mud path bordering their field. This would be their workplace until sunset, expertly sculpting the paddy field by hand. Our transport was on the back of three 125cc dirt bikes with three of Feedback Madagascar's borehole technicians, Vasil, Boniface and Elise. Roads turned to tracks which turned to paths as we got further into the countryside.

One of the elders from the village, Pierre, and the schoolteacher, Sandrine, welcomed us and led us through the cluster of clay houses with thatched roofs. A little boy, barely five, passed us leading four horned zebus: the Malagasy cow. With a flick of a wrist, he slapped one of the beasts on its upper stomach with a thin stick. The boy gave out a high-pitched 'Eh!' It wasn't enough to cause pain, but plenty to remind the beasts who was in charge. I thought about myself as a four-year-old boy, barely out of nappies and too scared to go upstairs on my own, let alone herd cows.

Turning a corner in the path, we rounded the final house in Mahavelo to reveal a huddle of about 30 people, adults and children, standing around a green picket fence. Mango and lychee trees lined the small winding path that snaked down; chickens trotted ahead. The crowd watched as we approached, smiles beaming. The fenced area was carpeted with plants and shrubs, bordered with half a dozen brick pillars. The centrepiece was a grey tap with a horizontal wooden handle. It was the first borehole we'd seen in the flesh that we'd funded through our Atlantic row.

Not far away, I noticed a rectangular bamboo structure. It must have been 20 metres in length and a few metres wide. Inside I could see hundreds of little black socks. It was the village's tree-nursery, and the black socks were home to hundreds of saplings – mango, lychee, eucalyptus and coffee – which were watered from the borehole.

We were there for the opening ceremony. As the baton of conversation was passed between the elders of the village, my gaze was transfixed on the small tap at the centre of our huddle. Coming from Scotland, a place that enjoys bountiful clean drinking water, it was difficult to get my head around. I was so used to flicking on the tap each morning – to drink a glass of water, to brush my teeth, to shower or go to the toilet; to clean my clothes, my dishes or the floor. It was so normal, just something I expected in life, that it was difficult to really see its importance – let alone imagine a life without it.

The borehole in front of us would serve this community of about two hundred people for 70 years, all going well, through careful monitoring, maintenance and water testing. All in, it had cost £6,000. As little as £30 was enough money to give each villager clean water for a lifetime. The scale of the impact on the community was impossible to quantify. The sad reality is that dirty water impacts children most. In

2016, UNICEF estimated that at least a quarter of under-five mortality in Madagascar was due to water-related diseases. Sickness often takes kids out of the classroom, and drinking dirty water can cause developmental issues – both physical and mental – which might last a lifetime.

That's only the beginning of the rippling effects. Parents' focus is taken away from their livelihoods and financial security, and turned towards collecting and boiling dirty water and looking after sick children – if they're not sick themselves. The job of collecting dirty water traditionally falls to the women and girls of communities, worsening inequality. In many parts of southeastern Madagascar, economic deprivation and the need for firewood drive people to cut down trees, leading to deforestation. The people can't be blamed – I'm sure I would do the same if it put food on the table for my children.

We'd heard all of this before the trip and could reel off the positive impacts of clean water. But, in a sense, we didn't truly know anything. Until that point, our understanding of the water issue was theoretical. It was something we had read and been told about by other people, but it wasn't something we had seen for ourselves.

Two days prior, we'd met a family living illegally in the rainforest. It had been a shocking example of the other side of the coin: a life without clean water. A young mum, I would guess in her early thirties, was cooking a wild tuber, described to us as hafy, that had been gathered from the forest. Though it offered little real nourishment, it gave a false sense of fullness. She had five children, ranging from a newborn up to a ten-year-old. The children's limbs were skeletally thin, but each of them had pot-bellies protruding from their t-shirts. Only afterwards did someone explain that the children were in a constant battle with the tangle of intestinal worms, some longer than large earthworms, that lived in their bellies, acquired from drinking dirty water, which were sapping any nutrients from their food. The children's eyes were opaque, their gazes distant.

As the ceremony at the borehole came to a close, a gesture of thanks in the form of locally made rum was offered to us. Though it was sincere, I couldn't help but feel uncomfortable. It didn't seem right that we were being thanked. Feedback Madagascar had done the hard work of installation. The money was thanks to the many generous donors to our Atlantic campaign, and our only role had been in asking for it.

You don't need to look far in a place like Madagascar to see the lasting impacts of colonialism. Part of Madagascar's legal system is still conducted in French, despite only a minority of the population speaking the language. In recent years, opportunistic foreign countries have been extracting natural resources with no consideration of the local economy or natural environment. Non-governmental organisations march in to 'save lives', investing vast amounts of money into schemes that are top-down and short-sighted: vast tree-planting projects done in the name of carbon 'offsetting' . . . but the trees are dead within a few years because nobody's looked after them. We'd already seen a brand-new borehole in a village – which probably cost £50,000 to install – that sat unused, the white concrete pump stained red from dangerously high iron levels in the water. The intent was there, but it lacked the follow-up.

The thought of supporting another ineffective NGO was the last thing we wanted. That's why we'd partnered with Feedback Madagascar. 'Grassroots' is a bit of a buzzword these days, but Feedback Madagascar is that in its truest sense. One of the charity's foundational principles is that the Malagasy people are the key to resolving the challenges they face – hence the charity being run by the team of 250 local staff. Their work is focused around communities living on the fringes of one of Madagascar's last remaining rainforests. Over the last 30 years, they've partnered with over 540 such communities – roughly a population of 500,000 people. In supporting people to lift themselves out of poverty and co-create viable alternatives to forest exploitation, Feedback Madagascar works to protect and restore the natural environment. Despite being economically poor, Madagascar is rich in terms of biodiversity due to having evolved untouched from the rest of the world for 88 million years. A staggering five per cent of the world's species are found on the island, and 85 per cent of plants and animals are endemic to Madagascar. The charity works across multiple sectors, but clean water is one of their core activities in bringing communities out of poverty and protecting biodiversity.

We stood beside the tap as the villagers returned to their homes. Vasil, the head of the water team, gave some context about the village. Shortly before the village had made their request, a woman was filling a bucket at the river's edge. As she scooped the muddy water, there was a sudden white wash of commotion, a frenzy of splashing and struggle, as something grabbed her leg in the water and started pulling her deeper under. She fought with all of her might to reach the shore. The people heard the woman's screams and started wading out into the water. But it was too late. The woman, a mother of three, was never seen again. It wasn't the first time the crocodile had taken someone from the village, but it was hopefully the last.

I looked over to the murky river meandering nearby and tried to take in what Vasil was telling me. Sickness and cutting down trees were comprehensible to me, but this was not. A small group of children formed beside the pump. They watched us, curious about these strange visitors that had come to see their village. They were bright-eyed and curious, in stark contrast to the children in the rainforest. The new pump had been used to fill three different buckets in the time we'd stood there, and a young girl was washing clothes nearby.

As we climbed the final mile to the bothy, conversation wove itself back to an all-too-familiar topic: our next big fundraising challenge. We'd made a pact in Madagascar that we wanted to try to raise £1,000,000 for clean water projects following the launch of The Maclean Foundation later that year. Taking on a huge physical challenge was the best way we knew to raise a considerable amount of money, and we couldn't ignore the fire that rumbled within each of us. The Atlantic campaign was the hardest but most fulfilling thing any of us had ever experienced. It had given us a taste for getting stuck into a huge, multifaceted project, surrounding ourselves with great people, and setting all sights on an ambitious fundraising target.

We'd discussed a number of ideas. The endurance tricycle was a forerunner: designing and building a three-person bike to cycle around the world. We'd even kicked around the idea of taking our instruments with us, busking as we went. The idea quickly fizzled out. What it had in adventure appeal, it lacked in seeming like a jolly, and we didn't think it would be a good fundraiser.

The race across the Atlantic had been the perfect entry point into the sport of ocean rowing. Though the actual row was unsupported, the race offered a framework and a support network to make sure we were doing it safely: kit lists, timelines to hit, people to call up. It was an inroad into a tightly knit community of like-minded people. The race organisers, Atlantic Campaigns, had recently initiated another race in the Pacific that we'd eyed up, starting in Monterey and finishing in Hawaii. But the idea hadn't stuck. It would have felt like trying to recreate our experience on the Atlantic. We didn't think it was big and audacious enough for us to raise considerable amounts of money.

As we approached the summit that we'd been steadily climbing, Jamie stopped. 'What about a full Pacific row . . . a non-stop and unsupported crossing?'

Little did Jamie know, but this had crossed both Ewan's and my minds already. 'Yeah, I was looking at that the other day,' I replied, stopping beside him. 'I don't think a team's done it non-stop and unsupported. But it's a fair old distance. You'd be talking five or six months at sea.'

The idea struck a chord.

There are a few different options available if you want to row the Pacific. Our small amount of research had suggested that going east to west was possible due to prevailing wind and current. This would mean continuing our loop around the world from the Atlantic crossing. We agreed that not crossing the equator to avoid the Doldrums – a belt of calm, windless water near the equator that's famous for trapping sailors – would be preferable.

We shared what little research we'd done. The journey spanned 8,000 to 9,000 miles of some of the most remote ocean on the planet, equivalent to travelling from Scotland to Western Australia. The fastest-known time, set at 159 days, was held by a maverick of the ocean-rowing world, Fedor Konyukhov, a Russian adventurer and priest. Other attempts included the legendary Coxless Crew, a team of six women who completed the full Pacific, east to west, with a couple of stops along the way. John Fairfax and Sylvia Cook, an American couple, had completed the crossing with stops in the 1970s after a year at sea. Fairfax had been attacked by a shark halfway into the journey and was unable to row for over a month. Though a handful of solos had completed unsupported crossings, including the remarkable Roz Savage, there was no precedent for teams doing the same. Chris Martin and Mick Dawson had come close in 2009 by rowing the North Pacific from Japan to San Francisco but had to stock up with food. As a solo rower, you can fill the bow cabin with provisions for the journey. As a team of two or more, you need to leave space in both cabins to sleep, and you also need to take a lot more food. It wasn't clear whether a non-stop and unsupported crossing would be possible for a team of three.

'Half a year at sea, shark attacks, treacherous weather and a high chance of failure. Sounds great, doesn't it?' I said with a smirk as I pinpointed the roof of our refuge for the night. 'Maybe that's an idea for the backburner?'

As we strolled down the final mile of track, conversation moved on to other things. But there was something about the idea that had captured our imaginations. It was the thing we thought about as we lay in our beds at night, sat on the toilet or stood in the shower. It niggled at our minds, like something stuck between our teeth. No matter how hard we tried to forget about it, the idea wouldn't dislodge. The flint had produced a spark.

Chapter 3

Early Headwinds

By Ewan

You may think rowing across the Atlantic would have cured me of any desire to repeat that kind of experience again.

I'm sure that's the point for some. A last hurrah before real adulthood begins, or an attempt to satisfy the pangs of midlife wanderlust on the road to finally becoming a more responsible human being. It often goes as follows: you suffer through the thing, stagger back onto dry land, briefly consider getting 'HOLD FAST' tattooed across your knuckles as a memento, reconsider, and then happily settle back into normality with a newfound appreciation for bed sheets, dry socks and the miracle of a hot shower.

For a while, this was certainly my reality. But as more time passed, I started seeing those memories through increasingly rose-coloured glasses.

As it often seems to do, life slipped back into its usual rhythm. The sabbatical I had taken to row across the Atlantic came to an end, and I returned to the southwest of England to continue a career as an engineer at Dyson. Work deadlines. Life admin. Grocery shopping. Domestic mundanities that feel mildly irritating – unless you've spent weeks on end using a 'bucket toilet' in the rain while the entire world pitches beneath your feet. Even the restrictions that Covid brought to our lives felt less restricting compared to 35 days at sea in a small rowing boat. Maybe it was good practice.

Every so often, I'd get a flash of our existence out on the Atlantic. Not the discomfort, exactly. More the odd freedom of it. Out there, your body is trapped in a relentless routine, but your mind has been freed from thousands of tiny decisions. Your mental bandwidth isn't occupied by the same daily drudgery that we get caught up with on land. You don't need to remember to put the bins out or buy more dishwasher salt. There's a strange clarity of thought there, where the distractions of modern life are muted. I remember standing in a supermarket aisle one evening, confronted by a wall of breakfast cereals and feeling somewhat overwhelmed. On the ocean, your food options are whatever you packed into the lockers many months ago and can still vaguely tolerate. On land, there are 14 different varieties of granola and a man beside you earnestly comparing the protein contents.

Post-Atlantic, I was struck by the chatter of life's decisions, a sort of tyranny of choice. I felt the clamouring attention that society demands from us at every waking moment more keenly than I had before – the kind that fractures focus and draws you away from what matters.

I tried to rationalise my thoughts. On land you get to stop what you are doing and go for a walk. You can collapse on the sofa and watch TV with someone you love. You can happily lose an evening at the local pub with friends. You can choose your own discomforts. Small, ordinary, optional ones. Like 5k runs or wearing slightly damp jeans that you were sure had been left out drying for long enough. And in those moments, the whole idea of rowing across an ocean seems, at the very least, rather unnecessary.

And yet.

Somewhere in the background of all that normality, a feeling refused to budge. Not a dramatic epiphany or a lightning-bolt moment. More like a pebble in my shoe. Small enough to ignore but irritating enough that I couldn't stop noticing it. At first, I tried to pretend it wasn't there. I would be in a meeting at Dyson, nodding at a slide deck about product requirements and resource plans, and my mind would drift. Not to holiday fantasies or dinner plans, like a normal person's might, but to the Pacific. To the idea of it. To the sheer absurdity of it. It would occasionally surface on group chats between my brothers and me, casually dropped into a passing comment and then discarded for how ridiculous it was. But I'd later catch myself doing calculations about average speeds, imagining weather patterns between distant islands. I would be happily going about my business when the distant relative whom I hadn't seen for years would appear, or the chatty mechanic who worked at the MOT garage, or the greengrocer near Dad's flat, and the inevitable question – 'What's next?' – would come up. I'd mumble through an answer about 'adventures closer to home', and watch the interest drain from my questioner's eyes. Eventually, with as much sincerity as I could muster, I simply started telling people that I had decided to become a postman, which swiftly closed down the conversation. Apparently, this was a trick used by people who worked for the Ministry of Defence if they wanted to limit enquiries directed towards them, or so I had been told. In any case, it seemed to do the trick. And as the conversation floated off onto some other topic, a part of me would be left thinking of the great expanse of water between South America and Australia, and I'd hope the distant look in my eyes wouldn't betray me.

I started to realise that rowing across an ocean had completely rearranged my sense of what's normal. The impossible now felt like it could actually be achieved, if only it could be broken down into lots of smaller, manageable tasks. Maybe many of the limits in my life were in fact self-imposed? Once I'd noticed that, it became a hard thing to un-notice.

But there was another part to it too. Ever since Madagascar, some aspects of ordinary life had become slightly harder to take at face value. The contrast was more difficult to ignore. We could busy ourselves with the usual small concerns of a comfortable life in a developed country, while elsewhere something as basic as access to clean water still shaped the course of a person's entire existence. At the same time, the direction of things seemed to be narrowing, not widening, with international aid in retreat and conflicts breaking out. That made the feeling sharper, not weaker. If we were going to do something difficult again, on a similar or greater scale, I felt it ought to be in the service of something that mattered beyond the three of us.

Eventually it was Jamie who put together a tentative slide deck one spare afternoon, entitled *One Hit Pacific*, casually saying, 'Here's one for the Pacific,' as he nonchalantly sent it into our group chat. We'd been batting various fundraising ideas back and forth for weeks in a fairly non-committal fashion, but getting something on paper – or on screen – seemed to solidify things. Gradually, without any grand announcement, the unimaginable idea stopped being a ridiculous hypothetical thing and began to resemble some semblance of a plan.

The Atlantic had given us a rough point of reference, which was useful mainly because it supplied the shape of an ocean-rowing campaign, and that was enough to make clear that the Pacific would be something else entirely. For the Atlantic, we had bought a third-hand boat, done the refit ourselves, and had little to no money set aside for things like PR, social media or fundraising initiatives. It was an annual race, too, so much of the infrastructure already existed and many of the costs were simplified or shared. Through necessity, we had done everything as frugally as possible. Even then, by the time we'd added up the boat, training, equipment, food, communications, shipping and the rest, the cost had run to somewhere in the region of £125,000 – all of it needing to be covered by corporate sponsorship, secured through months of graft.

The Pacific would demand all of that again, only on a much larger scale and without the comfort of an established framework around us. It was at least three times the distance, with many more months at sea, more food, more preparation, more moving parts and, inevitably, significantly more sponsorship money to raise. And if it was going to work as a fundraiser, not just an adventure, we would need to think not only about crossing the world's largest ocean, but also building a campaign big enough to carry the cause with it.

There wasn't a fully formed plan at this stage. It was more like a shape in the fog. We couldn't discern the whole thing yet, but could tell it was there, drifting somewhere in the distance.

Wednesday 28 September 2022; 916 days to go. Before long, we found ourselves on a flight to the Netherlands to visit a world-renowned boatbuilder by the name of Mark Slats. We told ourselves it was just a 'research trip', although probably knew better before we even stepped foot on the plane.

If you've never seen an ocean rowing boat before, you might assume they're like normal rowing boats, just a bit bigger. Perhaps with a cabin for sleeping in. Maybe a deck chair. Something tasteful. But an ocean rowing boat is less a boat, more a tiny, stubborn, floating survival raft with oars attached. It's part lifeboat, part campervan, part science experiment, and part psychological endurance test. Everything about it is designed around one basic truth: you will be stuck on it for months and the ocean will attempt, each day, to make you regret your life choices.

The third-hand boat that we had used for the Atlantic, which we'd sold to raise funds for charity after the row, had done its job. But the Pacific was a different beast entirely. More miles. More time at sea. More weather. More everything. And if we were going to do this properly – if we were going to build a campaign around raising a million pounds for clean water projects – then we needed a boat that could take a beating and wouldn't be the point of failure in our outlandish plan. And the rumours of what Mark was building in Holland, his entirely new approach to these unique vessels, seemed to potentially fit the bill.

We met Mark at his gym in the small town of Wassenaar, just north-east of The Hague; a small, brightly lit studio space with a line of well-kept rowing machines and a kitchenette for making espresso, only a few doors down from his home and boat workshop. The proximity felt like a clue in itself. An entirely intentional efficiency. I've come to learn that Mark's life is organised around removing excuses. He's been alone at sea for months at a time, breaking multiple records in sailing and ocean rowing, but in person there's none of the theatre you might expect from someone with that sort of background. He carries himself like someone who has spent a long time doing hard things without an audience.

Mark is touching six foot seven, which means you don't so much shake his hand as step into his gravitational field. He's something of a legend in the world of ocean rowing. The kind of person whose name makes other rowers' eyebrows lift in awe, but also maybe fear. He's done things alone that most people would struggle to do with a full crew and a healthy tailwind. And he's also sailed around the world twice after paying for a yacht with the prize money from a kickboxing competition that he entered entirely on a whim. He makes you immediately reassess what you've been doing with your weekends.

What struck me most wasn't some dramatic tale of storms and survival (although he has many), but the mundane brutality of his routine. Because of a pact made with his wife, he gets up in the middle of the night to train, sometimes as early as 3 a.m. On weekdays he has to be finished with his training by 8 a.m. so that he can do his share of the childcare for their one-year-old son. It's an arrangement that sounds almost comically gruelling, and one which he follows six days a week alongside running five businesses: his boatbuilding company, a boat chartering business, a speaking and adventure brand, a construction company, and a small property business. But it also explains a lot. Mark isn't just a man who can suffer. He's a man with drive. A man that doesn't shrink away in the face of a challenge. And a man who makes pretty much everyone else look like they're training for a Sunday morning lie-in. And we knew he'd approach our plans for the Pacific with the same laser focus. If Mark didn't think it was possible, it probably wasn't possible. By that point he'd rowed the Atlantic twice and was preparing to do it a third time, as if rowing across an ocean was something you fit in between going to the dentist and popping to the shops.

Alongside Mark was Dick, the naval architect and designer behind his boatbuilding operation. In any normal setting, Dick would be of fairly average stature. But stood beside Mark, he somehow seemed shrunken. Mark fills a room with unbridled Dutch confidence, whereas Dick hovers just to the side with dark brown hair and the sort of quiet, focused attention that makes you feel like he's measuring the world in millimetres. He's not shy exactly, rather just tuned to a different frequency; the kind of man who doesn't waste his words. But when he does speak, it's with analytical precision.

We soon learned that designing boats went back a few generations for Dick. He joined his father's naval architecture business in the mid-1980s. His family history, somewhat unsettlingly given the potential danger of the Pacific, goes back to coffin-making. Dick's father had learned to build things from his grandfather, a funeral director, who constructed coffins before turning that same craft towards wooden boats. I couldn't help but wonder whether Dick viewed ocean rowing boats as simply a more athletic version of the old family trade. If you asked him anything technical – hydrodynamics, structural limits, failure modes – he'd answer as if he'd already run the conversation in his head. His gaze would narrow slightly, then he'd answer the question we probably should have asked instead, and then two more we hadn't even thought of yet – all delivered in his calm, matter-of-fact tone and no-nonsense Dutch accent.

They were the perfect duo. Part practical, part obsessive. These were people who cared about the details, knowing all too well that the ocean is an unforgiving critic. A loose fitting, a bad seal, a cheap component: you don't really notice those things in the marina. You notice them at 3 a.m. in the middle of a storm, when you're tired and wet and the waves are trying to flip you over.

They walked us through the concept, the vision, the differences between their boats and what we were used to. There was no macho bravado. Just practical confidence and a clear desire to make things better. And this was best exemplified with their approach to manufacturing.

Our previous boat, like most composite boats, had been made in a traditional way: fibres and resin worked into a mould by hand and cured at room temperature. Skilled, yes, but also relatively old-school.

More artisan than aerospace. Mark's boats were something else. He described a process that sounded, frankly, more like building a Formula One car than a rowing boat. Parts were formed in a giant autoclave – a huge high-pressure vessel used in advanced composites, the kind of thing you associate with jet wings and high-end racing technology. This meant a boat with an ultra-lightweight, precision-moulded carbon-fibre construction, and an unparalleled strength-to-weight ratio. In practical terms: something far lighter and stiffer than the fibreglass ocean rowing boats we were used to. Less weight to drag across the ocean, less flex in the structure, and a hull that could take a great deal of punishment. The manufacturers working with Mark seemed mostly from the world of sailing, where the technological arms race had been accelerating for years, and the boats were nearly unrecognisable from only a few decades ago. The ambition, Mark explained, was to take that level of modern engineering and apply it to a sport that had, until recently, been using far more traditional methods. Ocean rowing boats had evolved, but slowly. Mark wanted to catapult things to a whole new level. That ambition translated into more than just a sleek shell. Bulkheads ran through the boat like ribs, stiffening the structure and dividing it into watertight compartments from bow to stern. Those sealed spaces would hold our food, equipment, supplies and spares for months at sea. Our old Atlantic boat had weighed around a tonne before loading. This one, before all the food and gear went aboard, was closer to 270 kilograms.

As he talked, I could feel my engineer's brain light up, which is always a dangerous thing. Engineers love a good solution. We also love to underestimate the chaos of real life. But still, there was something hugely compelling about the idea of a boat that was designed with such care and attention, and the almost romantic ambition of creating the fastest ocean rowing boat ever made.

Although getting across the Pacific in one piece was the main priority, if we didn't make it to Australia in less than five months, we'd likely run out of food. So the boat had to move quickly through the water, even when it was packed with mountains of freeze-dried meals. Mark estimated that it would be possible for him to build a carbon-fibre boat that was less than a third of the weight of our previous fibreglass boat, despite being the same length. It wouldn't be much heavier than the three of us put together. All considered, we should be able to move the boat fast enough through the water to reach Australia before our food ran out – at least by Mark's worst-case estimates. One hundred and twenty days was the number we were working with, give or take maybe 20 days of leeway. The boat would be able to carry that amount of supplies, but without much room to spare.

There were design improvements, too. The front of the boat, known as the bow, was shaped with a wave-piercing nose, helping it slice through the water, and there were small wings that extended out of the sides down the length of the rowing deck, to help deflect water rather than let it hit the hull and then splash over the rowers. Drinking water was stored in a low central tank after it had been produced with a desalinator (a device which removes the salt from seawater), which was both more practical than having loose containers on deck and better for the boat's centre of gravity. The rowing positions were spaced further apart as well, reducing the chances of oars clacking together when two of us were rowing in rough water – a small irritation that becomes wildly disproportionate after enough repetitions. It was a keen balance between comfort and performance. Because if you can't sleep, you make mistakes. If you can't repair things easily, you waste energy. If your boat layout encourages chaos, you live in chaos. Mark's design prioritised better storage, top-spec electronics and equipment, and improved layout. Things that wouldn't make life exactly easy, but at least slightly less ridiculous. Even more reassuringly, it was designed to self-right even if one of the cabins filled with water during a capsize. These were not simply cosmetic refinements.

We asked, as you'd expect, an endless number of questions. How does this fail? What happens if that breaks? How would you repair that at sea? How do you access this? How do you seal that? What about salt ingress? What about contingencies? What about the things you only discover after months of being smashed by waves the size of buildings? This would be the first boat of its kind, and we would have to trust it with our lives.

Dick and Mark, true to form, met every question without flinching. We'd ask, 'What happens if this leaks?' and Dick's brow would furrow slightly in concentration, as if he could see the water path in his mind. Then he'd start talking about tolerances, interfaces, and the sort of things you don't realise you need to care about until you are a thousand miles from land, doing repairs in the dark with a headtorch after two months of living like a bedraggled bilge rat.

And then we came to our own prerequisite. One that really mattered to us: we wanted to be part of the build. Not because we fancied ourselves as amateur boatbuilders, but because we knew what it was like out in the middle of an ocean. Things will inevitably go wrong. That's not pessimism, it's pragmatism. And when they do, you need to understand the boat inside out. Where the weak points are, how it's put together, what you can bodge, what you absolutely cannot bodge.

But it was also more than that.

Paying some money and collecting an immaculately polished thing a few months later felt too transactional. This wasn't meant to be a simple product purchase. It was meant to be an adventure. Being involved in the build felt like the beginning of that story. The first proper step into the unknown. And for the three of us this had become a non-negotiable, long before setting foot in Mark's workshop.

After the meeting, we left and wandered down the road to a café, as if we were just three ordinary blokes deciding what we were going to have for lunch. The one-way street was cobbled with a chevron pattern of brown bricks, which ran around the banks of a long pond stretching between the boat workshop and the café. We sat outside with coffees in front of us, watching the quiet suburban life pass by, contemplating what we had learned.

There was one glaring problem, which we'd been skirting around for weeks: a boat built by Mark was clearly the safest and most plausible option for us to get across the Pacific without stopping, but we simply didn't have the money to pay for one. The initial payment alone was nearly ten thousand pounds, and that was only the start. The boat itself would ultimately cost more than ten times that amount, while shipping, equipment, communications, food, contingency and everything else around the campaign was still largely unknown – and likely significantly more expensive than it had been for the Atlantic row. Between us, we could perhaps scrape together enough to secure the build slot – through every penny we could lay our hands on: the meagre flat deposits; the proceeds from selling anything with a vaguely respectable resale value; pretending overdrafts were a sort of flexible budgeting tool – but we had nowhere near the amount required to fund the whole thing, nor pledges from sponsors to help towards it.

And to make things harder, our open-ended 'research trip' had been met with a deadline. We had a decision to make and needed to give an answer there and then. To secure the build slot, we had to make an initial payment within a matter of weeks, and we had to go back and shake Mark's hand in good faith that we could come up with the rest of the cash over the coming months. He could fit our boat into his busy schedule by building it concurrently with his own. Miss that slot, and we wouldn't get a boat until the end of 2024, after Mark's other commitments were done.

From our research on route-planning, one thing was clear. It was crucial that we avoided the cyclone season on the Pacific, and because it could take several months to complete the crossing, this gave us a narrow weather window to hit. If we missed this build slot, it wouldn't just push back the start of the row by a few months, it would mean delaying by an entire year, which would mean we wouldn't set off into the Pacific until 2026, at the earliest. Three and a half years felt like a long way off. And the truth was that this was not just a question of weather or logistics. In reality, there were a particular set of circumstances that made the whole thing conceivable: our energy, our appetite for risk, our relative freedom, the rough alignment of our lives at the time. Realistically, there was a finite window in which a row like this felt possible, and we knew it might close if we did not act.

The cost of an ocean row is such an impossible barrier – in many ways the campaign to the start-line is the hardest part. It's either an enormous personal cost – far more than we could ever afford – or a relentless challenge in raising finance through corporate sponsorships, or both. From where we were at that moment, sitting outside a café in Wassenaar, we had neither. We'd need to put everything we had into the campaign, emptying our bank accounts to secure the build slot, and then quickly bring sponsors on board before the costs became unmanageable. *If we managed to bring sponsors on board*, I should say. It felt, objectively, quite irresponsible.

And yet, sitting there, it seemed like the decision in front of us wasn't really about the boat at all. It was about committing to the project as a whole. It was about living an adventurous life. It was about seriously trying to make a difference to people's lives through our charity. Commissioning the boat would be a line in the sand. A point of no return. A statement, both to ourselves and to the world, that we were serious. That we were doing this. In earnest. Properly. With all the fear and responsibility that came with it.

And so we decided to go for it. We committed to the plan. We shook Mark's and Dick's hands, bid them farewell and stepped back out into the quiet Dutch street to make the journey home. We had a slot with our name on it. A payment deadline to hit. A problem that we now owned. And in our minds, there was no going back.

Of course, after the initial high of committing to something expensive with nowhere near enough money and an imminent deadline, reality kicked in. The next phase of our lives became an endless stream of outreach. Emails. Instagram chats. LinkedIn messages. Pitch decks attached. Covering notes rewritten a hundred times. Follow-ups that felt increasingly like we were talking into the void. Polite, hopeful, slightly desperate, and trying not to sound like we'd sent essentially the same message to 30 other people over the past week. We'd try short and snappy approaches. Then long, thoughtful ones. Then short ones again. We tried photoshoots with the products sold by the companies we were reaching out to, posing with them on the boat. I only hope they received a few laughs before finding a digital dustbin somewhere, because we rarely heard back from the people we sent them to.

It was a long series of dead ends, raised hopes, and disappointments – one of which I couldn't help feeling foolishly responsible for.

We had made many attempts to reach out to Steven Bartlett. At the time, Steven was a Dragon on *Dragons' Den* and the creator and presenter of the popular podcast, *Diary of a CEO*. He was involved in many companies: some of his own, and plenty more as an advisor or investor. But the reason he mattered to us was because of his role in a campaign we'd been following closely. Earlier that year, an endurance athlete called Russ Cook had run the entire length of Africa and raised over £1 million for charity in the process. Steven had seemingly helped make it happen.

Russ, better known as 'the Hardest Geezer', had set off with very little money relative to what the whole trip would cost. Enough to cover his first two weeks on the road, and not much more – pretty bold for a journey that would take nearly a year to complete. And yet the campaign had quickly snowballed into something enormous. From what we could tell, Steven had made timely introductions at the critical moment, unlocking a couple of make-or-break partnerships – namely Huel (a huge nutrition brand) and PerfectTed (a fast-growing energy drink start-up). They were the sort of companies that could take on some of the logistical strain and give the story the momentum it needed.

We were in a similar situation. We had big ambition. A huge charitable fundraising goal. A project that would live or die on whether we could build the right partnerships. And Steven seemed to understand our world: the blend of madness, storytelling, and the commercial reality of a major endurance campaign. So we tried. Countless times. We sent messages on Instagram. LinkedIn. Emails to the various companies associated with him. Decks sent into the ether.

But nothing came back. No response on any front. And then, in a moment of desperation, I spotted something on LinkedIn. Steven had made a post, and a stream of comments had started to appear. Scrolling through the comments, I noticed a reply to one of the messages from Steven himself. He was apparently keen to hear more and had left a crucial piece of information: none other than a contact number to reach him via the mobile messaging app Telegram. I had a direct line for him. And it felt like discovering a secret passage – the sort of thing you'd find in a spy film.

I downloaded Telegram, having never used it before, and messaged the number. I then did what any sensible person does when trying to impress a famous entrepreneur: I put together a few short sentences by way of introduction, attached a PDF with an absurdly formal name ('The Maclean Brothers – Pacific Row Introduction'), and then shamelessly added a YouTube link which explained what we were up to, all the while trying not to feel like I was someone sliding leaflets under a door.

Then we waited. A day or so later, a response came. And I'll admit: my heart rate rose in a way that was completely disproportionate to what was, objectively, just a notification on a phone. The reply opened with: 'Hi, Ewan! Nice having you here!' which is not, in fairness, a sentence I've ever heard another human being say in real life. But we were deep in sponsorship mode, where a response of any kind felt like progress. It was warm and polished. The continuing message was full of the right kind of encouragement. It called our plan 'awe-inspiring' and 'deeply meaningful'. He asked what I currently did. The cadence felt close enough to Steven's public voice. Had we finally reached him?

Looking back, there was a clue sitting right there in the profile picture. It was Steven Bartlett all right, but it was the kind of Steven Bartlett photo you'd expect to see in a glossy magazine. Studio-lit with a white background. Almost airbrushed in appearance. Plenty of people use professional headshots for these sorts of things, sure, but it did have a faintly suspicious vibe to it. If you typed 'Steven Bartlett headshot' into a search bar, it's probably the photo you would see smiling back at you.

Then again, I don't exactly have a bank of studio-perfect portraits of myself, ready to deploy on my social media channels. So, at the time, I concluded that successful people probably just have better photos for their profiles than me, and carried on. I replied, explaining what I did for work, and added a bit more context around the project. Why we were doing it, what the goal was, what we were trying to achieve. The account responded with exactly the kind of congratulatory language you might expect from a supportive high-performance podcast host.

But then the cracks started to show. 'By the way,' an aside came through, 'there's something new I've been working on in the digital space. I haven't made it public yet but I definitely will soon. Have you heard of digital assets?' In hindsight, there were clearly some obvious red flags in this message, and I probably should have ended things there. But I was desperate. And we'd been at this for months. I was in that strange mental state where you've sent so many messages into nothingness that even a vague, ominous 'maybe' starts to appear like a door opening.

So I replied politely with something non-committal and hopeful, the way you might speak to someone when you're trying very hard not to scare them off.

And then the whole thing came toppling down. 'When I say digital assets, I'm actually referring to crypto, like Bitcoin Eth and Xrp. The markets are doing really well and it's not too late for you to get on board. This is one of the best times to build a legacy, earn money from your passion, and utilise the opportunities presented.'

And in that precise moment, it became quite clear that we were not talking to Steven Bartlett. We were talking to someone impersonating Steven Bartlett, with the lure of a shiny headshot hoping to catch fools such as us. When you put it like that, it does seem pretty obvious.

It was almost funny. Almost. Because the feeling beneath it wasn't humour. It was frustration and fatigue of being repeatedly led down paths that went nowhere. Messages unanswered. People being enthusiastic and then vanishing. Leads that turned out to be scams. Sometimes you just didn't get a reply. Sometimes the person you were trying to reach was, understandably, busy living their own life. But that whole Steven Bartlett incident captured our quest for sponsorship perfectly: the chasing, the hoping, the brief spikes of excitement, and the constant need to brush yourself off and try again.

Friday 24 January 2025; 68 days to go. It's easy to look at things in hindsight and view them through a lens of possibility, seeing past all of the uncertainty. At this stage, however, it's important to remember that we were attempting something that had never been done before. That was exciting, but it also carried with it some risk. A number of those who had tried to cross the Pacific by oar had been rescued after capsizing or being hit by cyclones, or physically collapsing. A few solo rowers had managed the journey after many months at sea, but around half the recorded attempts had resulted in either a recovery or a resupply. There simply wasn't a precedent for a team to go the full distance non-stop and unsupported. Viewed through the eyes of a potential sponsor, it was a huge bet for anyone to make. The stakes were high, and for many it was too hard to see beyond that.

Although we'd raised a little over £200,000 for two charities through our Atlantic row, we didn't have any experience with fundraising on the sort of scale we were now talking about. Our primary bargaining chips to bring sponsors on board were exposure, positive brand association and philanthropy, which we used to try to garner support. But we couldn't exactly guarantee any of those. Which made the sales pitch all the more challenging.

By this stage, our best estimate on the total cost had reached £360,000, roughly broken down as follows:

- Boat, spares, equipment and trailer (£150,000)
- Shipping, transport and logistics (£50,000)
- 18 months training and team wages (£50,000)
- Food, medical and miscellaneous (£30,000)
- Media, PR and fundraising activities (£80,000)

It was an absolutely eye-watering amount of money, and put the fear into all of us. We poured every waking moment into trying to chip away at the mountain that lay before us. And, occasionally, our days didn't end in disappointment and growing anxiety. Occasionally our efforts paid off.

One of our major partners, who had believed in the vision from the start, was an entrepreneur and philanthropist called Mike Bain. He had helped to get the project off the ground and made the initial boat payments possible, stopping us from defaulting on our promise to Mark in the Netherlands. Beyond the financial support, he had passed our sponsorship decks around, hoping to get a bite from his network. After a few months, he invited me up to the Scottish town of Banchory, near Aberdeen, to meet some of the investors in his whisky business. It wasn't going to be the standard pitch, however: we were going mountain biking.

I arrived first thing, having taken some time off work to drive all over the country for various row-related engagements and training sessions. I'd taken the car 14 hours or so from the southwest of England all the way to the far northwest of Scotland, then back down to Edinburgh, and finally to Banchory. The grey drizzle welcomed me as I arrived at the muddy gravel carpark to meet our mountain-biking guide, who was unloading e-bikes out the back of a large panel van. Three of Mike's investors pulled up in a shiny rental car that looked slightly out of place amid the puddles and potholes. They had flown in from Hong Kong and Majorca for a short visit, and this activity had been slotted into their agenda between various meetings and facility walkarounds.

Almost immediately it was clear that a muddy day out on the trails hadn't been part of their original plan. The outfits of the gentlemen stepping from the rental car were more appropriate for a lengthy board-room session than being caked in muck and grime in the Grampian mountains. No waterproof jackets in sight. One chap wearing light brown suede loafers and immaculate cream chinos. Far from ideal.

Whether it was the mountain-biking guide who was supposed to have brought suitable kit, or the investors' packing list that had been missing a few essential items, I wasn't sure exactly where things had gone wrong. But to make matters worse, Mike had been called away on last-minute childcare duties, and it suddenly dawned on me that this entire activity had likely been orchestrated for the sole purpose of giving me some airtime with potential sponsors, whom I'd never met. As it was, they looked understandably more concerned with getting through the ride without ruining their outfits than assessing whether three Scottish brothers rowing across the Pacific was a prudent investment to make.

I shook hands and said a few polite hellos, waiting to see if a bag full of Gore-Tex layers might be offered to them for the ride, but none materialised. I could see eyebrows being raised as the mud-splattered bike frames, suspension forks and nobbly tyres gave everyone a clue as to what we were about to embark upon.

Mercifully, I had just been on a training weekend up north. I had a car full of rowing kit with me: waterproof trousers, jackets, even a few extra pairs of trail-running shoes. They would be a little ill-fitting and slightly smelly, but it meant I had enough options to offer to the smartly dressed gentlemen. The loafers and chinos would be saved. Crisis averted.

For the next hour or so, we rode through the hills and the heather, enjoying the ancient Caledonian woodland and visiting the historic buildings hidden among the estate. When the moment felt right, I explained our plans for rowing across the Pacific. It's hard to gauge exactly how someone is reacting when you're clinging on to a set of handlebars, slightly out of breath and trying to avoid ending up in a bush halfway down some slippery slope. In any case, there were plenty of questions, which I dutifully answered, trying to make it all sound as exciting as possible. After the ride and a quick bite to eat, the gentlemen were ready to continue with the rest of their plans for the day. I sent one of them a pitch deck and was told it would be given further consideration, and then I set off down the road again to return to the day job down south. If nothing else, it had been fun to do some exercise that was different from the usual slog on the rowing machine.

I came away from the biking day feeling that it had been a hugely generous introduction, but was unlikely to be the start of anything concrete. Not because of any lack of goodwill or interest, but because support for a project like ours was hard-won, and most conversations didn't lead anywhere.

Sponsorship is a world full of polite maybes. Of people who mean well but are busy. People who like the idea but can't make it work.

People who think they can help but don't follow through. People who genuinely want to be involved but are constrained by budgets and boards and timings. And many, many more who never respond.

But then, amid all that, there are the ones who do show up. The partners who believe in the vision, who take a chance on you, who see value not just in the story but in the mission behind it. Without them, none of our ambitions would have been possible. Not the boat. Not the shipping. Not the media and PR support. Not the logistics. Not any of it. This project only happened because a handful of people chose to believe in what we were trying to do. And we'll be forever grateful that they did.

Just when I had nearly given up hope, I heard from one of Mike's investors from the mountain-bike ride, Kai Einheuser, the director and co-founder of M Yachts, who eventually became one of the main sponsors for the row. The funds were make-or-break for the entire project, which was hanging by a thread. Without them, I honestly don't know how we would have continued. You never know when these things might work out. You just need to keep trying. And although we still had a vast amount to raise, it felt like the tide was beginning to turn.

Beyond the mountain of sponsorship that we needed to do the crossing, we had the other, even more daunting challenge of our own charitable fundraising target ahead of us. But how on earth do you go about raising £1 million for charity? We spent months studying people who had somehow managed it. Russ Cook was one. Another was Nedd Brockmann, the legendary Australian ultrarunner who had run the length of his country and, a few years later, attempted to break the 1,000 mile record. In the process, he'd raised the equivalent of around £4 million for a homelessness charity. The two of them were a huge source of inspiration to us. But what, exactly, had allowed them to reach those extraordinary totals?

At first glance, the answer seemed obvious: the scale of the physical challenge. Both had taken on feats so large that they were impossible to ignore. But that explanation only went so far. There were countless examples of people attempting expeditions that were just as ambitious, if not more so, but had raised far less for charity in the process.

In the case of Russ, one obvious difference was the scale of the media operation around him. As he ran the length of Africa, he'd released a fully produced 20-minute YouTube video every three or four days. By the end of the run, there were over 100 episodes in the series. The amount of filming and editing required to sustain something like that was staggering. From what we could gather, he had at least three people following him around at any one time: filming, producing, editing and posting across social media, with others rotating in or working behind the scenes. It was an operation of serious scale, and presumably serious cost too.

In any case, we couldn't have copied this strategy, even if we'd wanted to. This was supposed to be an unsupported row. We couldn't have a film crew following alongside us in the middle of the Pacific: quite apart from anything else, the cost would have been unfathomable.

But there was another issue. We found several examples of people who had taken a broadly similar approach: epic challenge, high-output video, strong storytelling, large online presence – and still they had only achieved a small fraction of that kind of money for charity, despite setting out with seven-figure ambitions of their own. Clearly, it wasn't just the scale of the challenge, or even the scale of the content. Something else made people care enough to give.

By this point, we knew we needed a team to help hit our fundraising goal. Once we were at sea, we would need to film and write about the experience, but we would be well and truly handing over the reins for everything else. An on-shore team was required to help share our story far and wide. Their goal was monumental but simple: try to raise £1 million for clean water projects. Each of the parties had their own responsibilities, and it was important that everyone knew what they were.

Jamie, Lachlan and I have many flaws, but between us we seem to be reasonably adept at surrounding ourselves with exceptional people; people who are experts in their field and who can actually make things happen. It is without a doubt our biggest strength.

Guy Maclean, our Australian first cousin, was stepping into the role of campaign manager once we were at sea. One of the unforeseen perks of the campaign had been becoming closer with our big cousin down under. As the campaign built momentum, Guy had originally volunteered himself to help to raise sponsorship over in Australia, and made strides in developing our fundraising approach. But it was clear that we needed a lynchpin once we cast off who could work full time on the project. Someone to keep the shore team aligned and maintain focus on the charitable target. Lachlan and I drafted up a job description, which we pinged over to Guy. It was done partly in jest – he had been excelling in a career as an offshore engineer for over a decade, so we were fairly certain he'd need to turn it down.

His WhatsApp reply was quick: 'Count me in. Let's have a chat tomorrow.'

Guy didn't have a background in fundraising, but he was used to managing big complex projects. What he lacked in direct experience, he made up for with terrifying competence and a can-do attitude. Being the oldest in the extended family, Guy's always been that cousin that the three of us have secretly looked up to. He's undoubtedly the reason that Jamie and Lachlan grew their hair out in the first place . . . which, when I think about it, correlates with Guy cutting his hair short again.

Aside from aligning the shore team, Guy would also be our primary contact. He would be our gatekeeper to the outside world, filtering the information that would reach us. Being family, that helped. All in all, it was a massive job, significantly underpaid for the time it would take, but we couldn't have had a better person doing it.

We would be in a vulnerable state, sleep-deprived, missing home, and often wet and fed up. We needed a team around Guy that would be sensitive to that, with the creative flair and ability to turn the repetitive grind into an exciting journey that was worthwhile following. Gregor and Scarlett and their incredible team at the Glasgow-based agency Story Shop – both friends from before our Atlantic row – took the lead on PR and managing our social media channels. The Atlantic had been a sort of pilot version that they had taken on and managed brilliantly. We knew there was no one else for the job but them. They understood what mattered and had the agility to move quickly when something landed. Half-captured moments from the boat would be built outwards, from a social clip to a PR angle, a conversation to a broader narrative. The immensely talented Jack, who came from a creative agency in Edinburgh called FKJK, joined them for producing some of the more polished short-form videos; the sheer volume and quality of content he can produce is simply astonishing to me. As if that wasn't enough, he turned around a complete redesign of the website and even began producing merchandise. Fuelled by white cans of Monster Energy drinks, he's an absolute machine.

Our close friends, Graham, Calum and Andrew from Glasgow video production house Lost Clock brought something slightly different but just as valuable. They had a rare feel for tone and had made a documentary about our Atlantic row called *Out of Our Depth*. The longer-form videos that they carefully created were beautiful and considered, without the edges being sanded off. They made things that felt recognisable to us and, I think, to the people who know us best. That mattered. We were asking people to come with us for months and observe our monotonous, strange and often uncomfortable existence. For that to work, the storytelling had to be honest and authentic. We trusted them for that, as we trusted the rest of the team.

The core shore team included several volunteers, all adding their own efforts and expertise. For sharing an email update from the boat each day, Jamie's girlfriend Em would have the line, sending on the words that we wrote in the log to friends, family and beyond. My partner, Fran, then helped to put a selection of these out on WeChat to capture a Chinese audience, alongside a family friend, Jane, who did the translations. From the charities, we had Jamie and Johanna representing Feedback Madagascar and Nick and Sarah, two of our trustees, representing The Maclean Foundation.

In many ways, the fundraising plan was not to have a rigid plan. We defined our resources carefully, ensuring we had broad capabilities – extra power, camera equipment, connectivity, workflows, contingencies – then assembled the best team we could, and aligned everyone under the clear goal: raise £1 million for clean water projects. But we were all entering completely new territory. None of us had experience in raising this much money. We had ideas of ways to share the story and engage a range of demographics, but there was no roadmap. The strategy was to try different things, double down on the ones that seemed to work, and remain agile and fluid throughout.

We wanted to tell the story to the best of our ability: targeted, local and international PR, cross-platform social media, live streaming and celebrity engagement; big cameras, small cameras, 360-degree cameras, drones; documentary-making, daily email logs, podcast-style conversations and interactive mapping. The Pacific (and not least a small rowing boat in the middle of it) is an extremely harsh environment in which to do pretty much any of these things, and requires some serious logistics and steadfast resolve to keep everything going. None of it would be remotely possible without the shore team driving it all forward.

The difficulty was that the machine kept on growing. What had started as an estimated £80,000 budget for the fundraising efforts didn't keep to that level for long. Bringing in Guy to manage the team once we were at sea added another layer to the operation. Our ambitions for video output also continued to grow, and so did the team around it. Before long, the projected cost for this side of the campaign had crept to over £120,000. That was a sobering amount of money to commit before we had rowed a single stroke. But if this was what it took to give ourselves half a chance of hitting the target, we felt we had to go for it.

There's one thing it's important to be absolutely clear about: the money required to build and run the campaign was funded entirely separately from the charitable fundraising. A handful of companies and private individuals helped make the project possible: backing the boat, the logistics, the media support and all the other moving parts. Every penny donated by the public on our charity fundraising page was ring-fenced for clean water projects in Madagascar. Not a penny of it was used to pay for the campaign itself.

That distinction mattered deeply to us. We were asking people to trust us, and we took that seriously. We never wanted money given for clean water to be swallowed up by the cost of telling the story.

The same principles ran through the entire campaign. We couldn't cut corners on the fundraising budget and expect to reach our goal, just as we couldn't cut corners in training and expect to row across the Pacific on good intentions and a few half-decent gym sessions. If we wanted backing, we had to earn it. If we wanted to get to Australia, we had to earn that too. Whether it was sponsorship or training, the answer was much the same: turn up, do the work, again and again. That was the deal. Long stretches of effort that often felt like they might lead nowhere or never end. A meeting that came to nothing. A pitch deck ignored. Another session in the gym. Another hour on the rowing machine. Another early start. You just kept going, trusting that enough honest work, accumulated over time, might eventually amount to something.

If Mark Slats was building the boat, Chloë Lanthier was building the crew. She is a Canadian sports scientist based in Chamonix in the French Alps who has spent decades at the sharp end of endurance sport and human performance. An expert on human physiology, biomechanics and sports-injury management, an accomplished endurance athlete in her own right, and a published author armed with the sort of experience that made our little operation seem endearingly amateur – Chloë continues to work with the NASA space programme and Paris Saint-Germain FC; she also worked with Rafael Nadal before his retirement – the fact that she agreed to take on three fairly ordinary brothers from Edinburgh felt like a sizeable act of charity in itself.

What quickly became clear, however, was that Chloë had no interest in treating us like amateurs. She approached our preparation with the same professionalism Mark brought to the boat. If he was thinking about hull shape, self-righting, structural weaknesses and how the boat would survive in a cyclone, she was thinking about the equivalent in us. That meant effective science-based methodologies to optimise our physical and mental performance at sea: how to keep us injury-free through a year of intensive training and also for months on the Pacific; how to improve our rowing mechanics and overall economy; how to keep us properly fuelled and hydrated for maximum energy and day-to-day recovery; how to prepare us not only physically but also emotionally, mentally and psychologically with ongoing training. She could translate the complexity of the human body into practical, progressive and highly effective training.

Chloë's role was multidimensional and far broader than that of a coach. She was, at various points through the campaign, a physiologist, biomechanist, strength and conditioning coach, nutritionist, physiotherapist, injury-prevention expert and occasional therapist, all rolled into one. She was thorough and holistic. Every session had purpose. Every block built on the previous one. At the start we went out to Chamonix to meet her on her own turf, where she carried out a full assessment of our physiology and musculoskeletal imbalances before issues accumulated. Then every few months she would come to Scotland to put us through our next programme in the gym, on the water and on the hills of Edinburgh. The rest had to be stitched around geography, with regular video calls and messages to adjust the programme, answer questions and review the data as we tracked our progress and reported back.

There's a particular kind of romance that people project onto endurance training. Dawn runs through misty countryside; a disciplined little exercise notebook; inspirational music booming from the heavens during slow-motion runs up sets of stone steps.

The reality, for me at least, was a little different. I was living in a shared flat in Bristol in a small double bedroom, and the only place I could fit a rowing machine was inside that bedroom, right beside my bed. It was so close, in fact, that with my head laid on the pillow, I could reach out and touch it. It felt like the rowing machine had moved in and started paying rent. The first thing I saw each morning when I opened my eyes was this unshapely metal intruder, patiently waiting for me to make good on whatever wild promises I'd made to myself the night before.

I woke up, simply got out of bed and immediately got onto the machine in my pants. No gentle transition or distracting myself with other tasks. It was as efficient as it was undignified. Just straight onto the machine before my brain had time to realise what was happening. Then, over the next hour or so, I would often become, without exaggeration, the sweatiest man alive. Not 'a bit damp'. Not 'good honest effort'. I mean full-body, industrial-scale perspiration. The kind of sweating that makes you wonder if the downstairs neighbours might complain about a leak. By minute 20 my bedroom had the atmosphere of a greenhouse. By minute 40 I'd be struggling to see due to the sweat pouring from my brow. By the end I'd be dripping onto the floor like a human showerhead, glaring at the numbers on the monitor, which remained completely unfazed by the fact that I'd just turned myself into soup.

For a little over a year, a standard week asked for around 25 hours of training, all of it threaded around work, travel and whatever annual leave I could spare. Most days meant time on the rowing machine and, more often than not, a gym session too. When we could, we added longer training blocks on the water to carry out drills and get used to extended periods aboard. You definitely start to question your hobbies, though, when you find yourself intentionally capsizing your boat in order to become comfortable with the possibility of it happening for real at sea.

Some of our training happened on Loch Lomond, where Cameron House Marina kindly gave us a berth for a spell over the winter months. Other sessions were rougher, such as training on the Minch – the water between the mainland of Scotland and the Outer Hebrides. We once tried to cross over to Stornoway and were turned back by foul weather shortly after halfway, which did little to reassure friends and family members who were already questioning our judgement. 'Are you sure you're ready for the Pacific if you can't even do the Minch?' we were asked, on more than one occasion. Chloë also incorporated other types of cardio, like uphill running, and a mix of training drills too: pool work was incorporated into the routine for confidence, abandon-ship practice in an inflatable life raft; and the occasional middle-of-the-night erg session to change our perception of effort and fatigue. At the absolute peak, the training load pushed closer to 40 hours a week.

And that was just the training. Around it sat everything else: sponsorship meetings, fundraising plans, boat decisions, logistics, calls, presentations, spreadsheets, and all the other obscure things that occupy you in a project like this. I was still trying to do my job as a design manager at Dyson to the standard I expected of myself. I'd been there for nearly a decade, and it had been a hugely rewarding job. A hugely rewarding career. But it was becoming impossible to ignore the fact that I was living two incompatible lives. Something had to give.

In the end, I handed in my notice and sold the small cottage I co-owned with a friend outside Bristol, which we'd spent many years renovating and were sad to see go. I moved back up to Scotland and into Dad's flat in Edinburgh. It felt like a strange step backwards, moving in with a parent, alongside my two brothers, in my early thirties. I believe Dad was genuinely quite happy about having his three boys home; he enjoyed the company but I suspect he could have done without the chaos. It felt like we had gone back in time, albeit bigger and with slightly more complicated toys: equipment storage and food testing in one room; a 3D printer in the other. We were on top of one another almost immediately. It was practical, necessary, but not exactly painless. Not only had I left behind the life I'd built down south, but my partner Fran and I would have to do a long-distance relationship at a time when most of our friends seemed to be moving towards something more settled. By then, the project had truly become all-consuming. If we were going to do it properly, we had to be all-in.

Chapter 4

The Currency of Morale

By Jamie

Saturday 30 March 2024; 368 days to go. Every so often you end up in a situation where you are forced to ask yourself, how on earth did I get here? For instance, on a rowing machine at 5 a.m. in a small gym on the west coast of the Netherlands. It's Easter Sunday and we're two-thirds of the way into a three-hour session from hell. I should've stayed in bed. Ewan and Lachlan are clinging on to my right, and the long limbs of Mark Slats are punishing the machine to my left. I feel for Ewan; he looks like he might cry. In fairness, we all do.

It was early spring, the second-to-last day of our time living in the one-person flat above Mark's gym. We'd been there for the past week, training in the mornings and helping with the construction of our ocean rowing boat throughout each day. Mark was midway through an intensive year of preparation for his third Atlantic crossing under oar, this time as part of a four-man Dutch crew. He already held the records for a solo and a pair and fancied a go at the fastest-known time to row from the Canaries to the Caribbean. Every so often, I could feel his eyes wander over to my output monitor, checking my power. I was sweating profusely and could barely see the monitor myself. I don't think the output was very impressive. With our egos firmly in check, we fell off the rowing machines at three hours and crawled over to get an espresso. I'm not even sure if Mark had broken a sweat.

We had learned a lot over the past few days. The hull of our boat hadn't long been out of the autoclave oven and freshly sanded; the anthracite grey of the carbon fibre was raw and dusty to the touch. Mark and his team had fixed the two halves of the hull together and were finishing the transverse bulkheads (vertical partitions) that segmented our boat from the bow (front) to the stern (back). These would provide rigidity, strength, and create numerous internal watertight compartments that we could access from the deck. They would store all our food, equipment, medicine and everything else we needed to survive alone on the Pacific Ocean for five months or more.

Within the first hour, Petre, a Ukrainian colleague of Mark's, handed me a drill with a large hole-saw attachment and pointed at the front cabin. 'You make hole here, yes?' he said, as he gestured towards a pencil cross.

I felt out of my depth. I tentatively pulled the trigger and the round saw whirled into motion. Pressing it against the hull, I could feel the teeth grind against the layers of carbon, which pushed back with resistance. *'Vazhche!'* Petre shouted, clearly forgetting I couldn't speak Ukrainian. 'Harder! You must press harder!'

Leaning in, I felt the first layer of carbon give way; the saw then accelerated through the foam core and hit the internal carbon layer, letting out a shriek before popping through the inside of the cabin. It didn't feel good, creating holes in something we fundamentally didn't want any holes in.

But it was the primary reason why we were here. To help and learn about a boat that would keep us alive as we traversed nearly halfway around the globe. We needed to understand her inside out; her construction, her material layering and how to perform essential repairs in the middle of a storm. Drilling holes, grinding carbon, installing instrument panels and fixing hatches were the best ways possible to learn all of this. As we lifted the row-deck into place and fixed it to the hull, things began to click into place. Having designed and built saunas for the past three years, I knew my way around most power tools and felt comfortable in a workshop setting – but there's a big difference to firing nails into timber joists compared to the millimetre precision required with carbon. Every sand, cut, hole and fixation is permanent. The more you botch it the more you might be affecting the boat's safety and overall performance.

We also sat down with Mark to hear his thoughts on the specific route for our crossing. Our own research had led us to believe that South America should be our starting point, with us ideally making landfall in Australia under the iconic Sydney Harbour Bridge. Having sailed around the world twice, Mark knew his way across the Pacific from east to west. Additionally, he had lived and worked in Cairns for several months, earning a living as diver for various fishing boats. He knew the waters well, and understood many factors we hadn't even considered. He suggested Lima in Peru as the starting point, due to its positioning just south of the favourable equatorial current. He didn't rule out Sydney as the place of arrival, but flagged that it would be very weather-dependent, especially in the final 2,000 miles. But aiming low down on Australia's eastern coastline was a good idea, just in case we had to change course and make landfall further north. We didn't know it then but this was sage advice.

We left the Netherlands with a deeper respect for Mark, his team and our boat. Seeing her in the flesh, understanding how she was constructed and leaving with carbon dust under our fingernails, it felt right. It felt important. And, crucially, it all felt very real.

Rushing for our flight from Amsterdam's Schiphol airport (we always seem to be running late for flights), I grabbed us three takeaway pastas. Scoffing them down at our gate as the final few passengers were called forward to board, Ewan remarked, 'That was surprisingly good. Pasta was a bit overdone, but tasty nonetheless.' Lachlan nodded as he scraped a bit of wayward sauce from his t-shirt; 'Last time I had those sorts of pasta bows was on our Atlantic row; I think I still have a bit of PTSD.'

I handed them both their boarding cards: 'You know we really need to start thinking about our food for the Pacific. Remember those conversations we had about homemade meals on the Atlantic? I can't do another month of those store-bought ones, let alone 150 days. I'm certain we could make something tastier – it will make such a difference to the crossing.' We boarded the plane, and as the KLM flight took off, I typed a reminder on my phone: 'Research freeze-dried food.'

On any multiday endurance challenge, food is of the utmost importance. It is the fuel that keeps us going, providing our bodies with the energy and nutrients that allow us to continue to function and perform. Without correct nutrition, our bodies turn on themselves, tapping into stored energy reserves – primarily fat – as a source of fuel. This is known as entering a calorie-deficient state. Once the fat is gone, muscle tissue is broken down, leading to the loss of lean muscle mass and, ultimately, the reduction of our physical performance. We become weak, fatigued and begin to lose power and weight. It can happen without you even noticing. You become more irritable and there's a fogginess to your thoughts. A feeling of emptiness, and a sluggish inability to make it go away.

Alongside the weight loss it would become a serious problem if we lacked certain micronutrients in our diet. For example, a deficiency in vitamin C could lead to a condition called scurvy. In extreme cases this results in weakened blood vessels, severe bleeding and eventual organ failure.

Over the past few years, I've become increasingly interested in food not just as fuel for our bodies but for our minds. The impact it has on our experiences and the psychological effects it can have on our state of being. It has the power to make or break an expedition and, for my two brothers and me, it is the currency of morale.

The idea of preparing our own freeze-dried food for our Pacific crossing came at the end of our Atlantic row when food became what we dreamed about. It was born from dissatisfaction with what is currently available on the market. There are a multitude of different freeze-dried food brands out there, ranging from organic, clean-label options to more processed, higher-energy meals. Some are nutritional, some are not. The calorie content varies a good deal. All options are expensive. And most don't taste very good.

The process of freeze-drying (or lyophilisation, to be technical) occurs when water is extracted from a product, resulting in a dehydrated food that is light and can last much longer than what you'd buy in your local supermarket. Through deep freezing, vacuums and a process called sublimation, you can preserve a food's structure, nutrients and flavour far better than through other more conventional heat-based dehydration methods. It is perhaps more commonly known as space food. Since the mid-1960s it is how NASA has been preserving the food to keep its astronauts alive. An astronaut needing a meal will simply add boiling water to the freeze-dried food, wait ten minutes, and then: *bon appetit.*

We all love food but I'm probably the fussiest out of the three of us. We spent a good deal of time testing different freeze-dried brands for our Atlantic campaign, assessing the ones that struck a good balance between taste, ingredients and calorific content. Despite all this, after 35 days at sea, there were very few meals left that were enjoyable to eat. If you eat the same average meal every day for over a month, you're bound to get sick of it. Worse yet, you tend not to finish your portion, or even skip a meal, edging into a calorie deficit without even knowing. As I forced down meal after meal, my mind wandered to homecooked stews and flavourful curries. I fantasised about food most days. Pies and pizzas appeared in my dreams. A crumbly shortcrust pastry, tender pieces of meat cooked for hours in a rich sauce, baked beans, buttery mashed potato . . . I promised myself I'd bring these homely comforts with us if we were to embark on something like this again.

Once we had committed to our Pacific endeavour, I knew I had to give it a go. I estimated that for five months at sea we'd consume approximately two thousand meals between the three of us. That is four main meals each per day, for up to 150 days, with a couple of hundred extra as backup. Alongside a large portion of porridge and a snack pack of nuts, dried fruit, chocolate and oatcakes, we'd have a personal daily allowance of six thousand calories.

It seemed like a lot but, based on our Atlantic experience, I knew it would be necessary. Having never cooked for more than a dozen people in one sitting, I struggled to get my head around two thousand meals. I envisaged the largest wedding I'd been to, perhaps two hundred people, and multiplied it by ten. That didn't help. I thought about what I ate each day. Porridge, two main meals and a handful of snacks. I'd be cooking enough food to last me the equivalent of one thousand days on land. I'm bad at meal planning at the best of times; prepping for close to three years didn't seem like a very good idea.

I learned the basics of how the process works, and the unfortunate cost of the equipment. Buying a freeze-dryer and doing it in-house was off the table, both from a financial perspective and a logistical one. I don't think Dad would have been very happy if I replaced his washing machine with a freeze-drying unit, no matter how many space meals I made him.

My search extended to anyone in Scotland who might be able to advise and assist. To no one's surprise, there didn't seem to be any Scottish companies that made freeze-dried meals – however, there did seem to be a couple of Perthshire-based farms that freeze-dried specific produce.

I contacted each of them and awaited a reply. A couple of weeks went by, things weren't looking too hopeful, and then a glimmer of optimism: a message from a man called Pawel appeared in my inbox: 'Jamie, I was away on my holidays – just saw your message. If you haven't sorted yet, get in touch – we might be able to help.'

Pawel, who was the manager at Arbuckle's Farm near Dundee, generously offered full use of their freeze-drying facilities and said he would happily advise wherever he could. But he flagged that his experience was almost entirely with soft fruit and berries, and so we would have to test all recipes thoroughly before attempting anything *en masse*.

Looking at calculations of the internal volume of our boat I didn't think two thousand meals would fit. Maybe with food strapped to the walls and ceilings of each cabin, but that would negatively impact the boat's ability to self-right. We hadn't capsized during our Atlantic crossing, but with so long at sea this time round it felt somewhat inevitable.

Then I thought about the repercussions of not taking enough food. I imagined getting so close to land and failing due to my miscalculations. Hungry and desperate, bobbing off the coast of Australia, fatigued, exhausted and unable to go on. Would two thousand meals even be enough? I would be compromising the whole project if we ran out too far from shore.

With a brief set of instructions from Pawel on the size and thickness of food, I set about my first round of freeze-drying tests using the equipment at his farm: veggie bean chilli, lamb stew and a mix of pastas. The chilli and stew were a resounding success, but I had mixed feelings about the pasta. It came out overcooked and watery. After a few further rounds of experiments, I concluded that most things in curry form worked well. The pasta worked best if the sauce was freeze-dried independently. If the two were then rehydrated separately and then combined it could create a meal that was almost unrecognisably freeze-dried food. Gnocchi was a disaster – I'm still not entirely sure why.

I spoke with Chloë, who not only knew a great deal about fueling and hydration for expeditions but had also developed a plant-based freeze-dried sport hydration formula in collaboration with one of Europe's major freeze-drying companies. Through this, and her wealth of knowledge of the human body, she understood which food would supply long-lasting energy, enhance fluid intake, optimise muscle repair and be easily digestible, keeping us healthy on the Pacific. Consulting her on what I had learned through my tests, she advised I keep recipes as simple as possible and highlighted the importance of packaging. We discussed nutritional qualities of various foods and the practicalities of preparing food in adverse environments. If the meals weren't packaged correctly, they would deteriorate within eight weeks or less. They would also be impossible to eat directly out of the bag, if the materials couldn't withstand boiling water. I took note and added packaging tests to the 'to-do' list.

Thursday 28 November 2024; 125 days to go. After six months of testing and a multitude of trips to Arbuckle's Farm, time was beginning to run out; departure for Peru was fast approaching – we had four months remaining in Scotland. I needed to commit to a short list of recipes: meat and veggie chilli, lamb saag, chilli chicken curry, Thai sweet potato curry, and a variety of pastas with the sauce separately prepared. Heavy on the spiced goods, but flavoursome, nutritional and calorie dense. Everything was punched into an Excel document, and with some spreadsheet wizardry from an ex-colleague of Ewan's, I could dial in quantities and create full nutritional breakdowns of each meal. Multiplying everything to create one thousand portions, the weights and quantities of ingredients began to grow: 18 kilos of lamb, 25 kilos of chicken, 200 onions, 75 kilograms of rice, 150 tins of chopped tomatoes. Looking down at the small selection of pots, pans and utensils in our dad's flat I soon realised this wasn't going to work. I needed a commercial kitchen: multiple ovens, hobs, trays, pots, blast chillers, etc. But, as usual, I'd almost certainly left it too late. It was a week before Christmas and most places were booked out or closed for the festive period. Lachlan suggested our old school, The Edinburgh Academy, and, after a few phone calls to the headmaster and the kitchen manager, we were down at the junior school getting a briefing on all the equipment.

They closed for the holidays later that same day and so timings worked out well. I had a couple of days to source the final ingredients, and with a bulk order of meat from an organic free-range farm near Perth, I thought we might just pull this off before the school reopened on 3 January 2025.

The following week was stressful and gruelling. As time ran out the days got longer and more frantic. Ewan and Lachlan joined for a good stint, but food was my responsibility, and they had other time-critical areas of the campaign to focus on, such as equipment checks and customs paperwork for Peru. Friends helped here and there, but my absolute crutch was my beloved partner Em. In five days we racked up 160 hours in that kitchen between us, chopping onions, roasting meat, stirring sauces, boiling pasta and rice. At times it felt never-ending.

Sleep deprived and somewhat traumatised, we loaded the pots and trays of food into a rented refrigerator van and drove north to Dundee. I had read a few advisory articles on commercial food preparation and had grown increasingly anxious about the 'danger zone': between the temperatures of 8 and 60 degrees Celsius any bacteria in food multiply rapidly. The longer the food remains in this range, the higher the chance of contamination. I couldn't help but spiral to worst-case scenarios of severe food poisoning and mouldy meals out on the Pacific Ocean. It would be a disaster, and it would be entirely my fault.

Pawel had been very strict on the thickness of food before it went into the freeze-dryer. Anything greater than two centimetres ran the risk of not fully dehydrating, leaving a moist layer of food at the centre of the batch. This would turn mouldy in a short period of time. As I watched the thick trays of food get loaded into the walk-in freezer my anxiety levels began to peak. I wasn't confident they were thin enough.

We drove home in silence; I was convinced we would have to start again. I looked at the date on my phone: 30 December 2024. There wasn't the time to do it again. We stopped at a supermarket on the way home to grab something for dinner. I sat quietly in the van outside Tesco, holding Em's hand, staring ahead, exhausted and anxious. What if this had been a terrible mistake? Thousands of pounds spent on ingredients, weeks of time, the faith that Ewan and Lachlan had put in me. All of it wasted. Why had I thought I was qualified to do this?

We returned ten days later, and, to my horror, my anxious thoughts became a gut-wrenching reality. Most of the trays had been too thick, and a layer of frozen food could be seen at the centre of the blocks of the now partially freeze-dried curries and stews. I felt a drop in my stomach. That nauseating feeling when you realise you've really, potentially fatally, fucked up.

Pawel was still away, and so his brother Mike, one of the directors of the farm, handed me an Opinel penknife and calmly instructed me to start chopping. We cut the larger blocks into thinner strips, exposing the frozen layers within. These would be passed through the machine once more to remove any remaining water. Mike was as cool as a cucumber; I think by this point I had developed a nervous twitch.

Returning home with a bag full of pasta sauce, the one meal that had dehydrated fully, I wasn't sure what to do. Could we start again? I doubted it. The junior school had returned, and their kitchen was now out of bounds. We could rent somewhere but the combined cost of new ingredients and renting a kitchen was one we couldn't afford. I phoned Pawel and he said all would be ok, but I wasn't convinced. I sat in Dad's kitchen, holding a cup of tea with both hands, and prayed. I'm not religious, but it seemed to help. The food was due to be sent to the shipping agents at the start of February, in less than two weeks' time. With the additional round of freeze-drying, we would have less than one week to package everything up before it was all loaded into a lorry and sent away to Peru.

With snow on the Perthshire hills, I made the final trip up to Arbuckle's. Pawel took me into their packaging room and pointed towards 12 large sacks on the floor. 'Are they for me or for the bin?' I asked.

He laughed and said, with a tap on my shoulder, 'Don't worry, the food looks good and is very dry. I think it will be ok.'

'I think' was as good as I could ask for. At the end of the day this was an experiment and a gamble. One that I wouldn't know the outcome of until land was a thousand miles away.

Driving south to Edinburgh, Dad called to say that a few packages had arrived for me earlier that day. Hoping that these were the mylar bags, label printer, oxygen absorbers and vacuum sealer, I went through the steps in my mind to transform the sacks of dehydrated food into our daily meals. My additional research and experiments on packaging and shelf life had drawn two major conclusions: vacuum sealing and the addition of oxygen absorbers would not only reduce the size of our provisions but help with longevity. Without the presence of oxygen, far fewer aerobic pathogens and fungi could grow. My internal anxieties were being manifested as anti-mould defences. The absorbers were probably unnecessary, but I was determined that a distant cousin of a mushroom must not be the thing that brought this whole project down.

We had recently received some quite concerning advice from our shipping agents that Peruvian customs may not look very fondly on twelve hundred vacuum-sealed opaque packages arriving at the national port. The unlabelled, unidentifiable packs may cause suspicion and result in delays or even disposal of the goods. It would be a complete disaster, second only to the looming 'mould-gate' awaiting us on the ocean. I needed to make sure each meal looked legitimate. Ensuring that font sizes, formatting, nutritional information and allergen markers were all correct, I established a formal-looking label that met international standards and codability. With the addition of our logo, the Arbuckle's emblem (with their permission), and a global standards barcode, I was happy that it should sway even the most discerning customs agent.

Looking down at the first finished meal, I felt a small surge of pride. 'Got there in the end,' I thought. But there wasn't time for a pat on the back. The pallet truck collection slot had been booked for the end of the week; we had three days and needed to average four hundred finished meals per day otherwise there was a risk of missing the shipping deadline. As so often is the case with my brothers and me, we frantically got to work.

The dining room became packaging HQ; vacuum sealer at one end, label printer at the other, sacks of food strewn across the floor. The quantity of freeze-dried food needed to be weighed for each meal – on average 175g resulted in a thousand-calorie meal. The labels were added, oxygen absorbers inserted, and the packs vacuumed and heat sealed.

Em joined the packing party, and with one final all-nighter, the boxes of finished meals were ready for collection. I met the lorry driver kerbside. He asked if everything was ok? I felt elated but also slightly nauseous. That strange sleep-deprived feeling when you know you've been running on black coffee and electro-bagpipe music for a little too long. The boxes fitted snugly onto the three pallets, and with a spin of the forklift they were loaded into the back of the truck and whisked away. It was over. Well, there was still the worry that the contents of those pallets wouldn't all cram into the watertight, sealed spaces in the hull – but at least it was now out of my hands.

Tuesday 11 March 2025; 22 days to go. The food was the beginning of a series of deadlines; our departure date for Lima being the most pressing – we were leaving the next morning. Packing had been going on for what felt like several weeks. It came to a head the day before our flight, as we filled Dad's flat with all manner of ocean-rowing-related paraphernalia: safety equipment, electronics, spares, repairs, cooking equipment, even a miniature accordion. I was not sure what customs would make of the guitar without a case that had solar panels and a fishing rod strapped to the side.

I was also a little concerned about our medical bag. Under the guidance of our team medic, Dr Calum Fraser – a university friend of Ewan's – we had amassed quite the array of medical supplies: antibiotics, EpiPens, tourniquets, Penthrox (the good stuff you get in hospital when you break a limb), alongside all the standard bandages, dressings and painkillers needed for an unsupported trip of this nature. With some last-minute additions from our surgeon uncle of some local anaesthetic and an Israeli bandage – a first-aid device used in war zones which is designed for rapid control of severe bleeding – I wondered where Peruvian customs would think we were headed.

The taxi arrived early. Lachlan and I carried the bags downstairs, but Ewan was nowhere to be seen. Despite nearly two years of preparation, he hadn't packed any of his personal items. The last few minutes in Dad's flat saw him desperately throwing clothes into a bag. Four odd socks, a few t-shirts, some shorts for training, and a warmer layer. Thankfully for him the clothes for the row had been shipped independently. Two fifty-seven a.m. depart; 17 minutes late. Not bad by our standards.

I held Em's hand as we sat in the taxi in silence. I don't think any of us could believe it was happening: we were leaving Scotland for Peru. As the airport came into view, I could feel her grip tighten. It had been an emotional year but, in general, we'd both managed to keep it together. This had always felt like a future problem, one that was too overwhelming to consider that it would actually happen one day. We dropped off the seven hold bags and made our way through to departures. As we approached the security gate, I turned to face Em, and her eyes began to well up. I began to well up. We hugged. I could feel her tears on the side of my neck. There wasn't really anything I could say. At that moment I hated myself a little bit. No one was forcing us to go; we had chosen this. And I was the one responsible for causing her this pain. With one last kiss I turned and let go of her hand. It would be the last time I would see her for almost half a year.

I wiped away the tears, took off my shoes and walked through the body scanner. I gave Lachlan an anxious glance. He'd drawn the short straw for the medical supplies, which had to travel with us as hand luggage due to the nature of the medications and prescriptions. The yellow drybag paused on the conveyor belt, stopped, and then popped through the other side. Miraculously nothing had been flagged. With enough drugs to suggest we were either very prepared – or very unwell – we hurried to our gate. We were on our way to Peru.

Chapter 5

New Beginnings

By Lachlan

Wednesday 12 March 2025; 21 days to go. I peered out of the window from 30,000 feet up, out over the big blue below. Though we hadn't slept at all the night before, my mind was busy. The electronic map told me that we were passing over the Caribbean before entering the South American continent. Cotton wool clouds were arranged in an ethereal formation, shimmering in the water below. I squinted at the tiny islands and thought of Mum in her Caribbean paradise. There had been many emotional goodbyes over the past few months, but the most was the first. In January, we'd made a week-long trip back to Antigua to see Mum. It was the first time we'd returned to the island since arriving there by rowing boat five years prior, an arrival that had changed all of our lives. It was a massive change, but a positive one. She hadn't been happy in Edinburgh and was in need of a new chapter.

Though we were racing against the clock to get everything ready for the crossing, making this visit to Mum was just too important. Seeing Mum in her new home and in a good place was important for all of us before pushing off – for us as much as her. We also needed Mum's approval for the name of our boat. It was a personal topic; a conversation that we didn't want to have on a screen.

A month before the trip to see Mum, we'd put out a request for boat name ideas on social media. We'd been lucky enough to be involved in every part of her journey thus far: from the build in the Netherlands to her first outings on the west coast of Scotland. Our affinity had deepened in those months as we'd got to know her inside out. We needed a name that was relevant to us and our family. Many suggestions were put forward by friends, family and strangers alike: *Usain Boat* and *Boaty Macboatface* were two of the forerunners. But there was one name, put forward by my godmother, Amanda, that stopped all of us in our tracks. It was a name that we wouldn't have thought of, but was also completely obvious.

In the spring of 1996 Mum and Dad were expecting a baby girl. Ewan was four, Jamie two, and I was not yet born. Six and a half months into the pregnancy, Mum's maternal instinct told her that something was wrong. She was admitted to hospital and tests were done. She heard words that no mother should have to hear: 'There have been complications. There is no longer a pulse.' I can't imagine how the doctor's words must have rung out in the moments, days and years that followed. Two sentences that changed her life for ever, leaving a mark that will never fully heal.

The name of the child was Rose Emily. Rose Emily had passed away in the womb. We wanted to name the boat after the sister we never had. It was a gesture to Mum and Dad – we were well aware of the stress that the trip would cause to those we loved most – and a testament to a life that was never lived.

Serendipity is a funny old thing. Shortly after this name was put forward, Jamie, Ewan and I were on a very chilly training row on Loch Lomond. Jamie and I were reflecting on our strange realisation that both of our partners had Rose in their names – either as part of a double-barrelled first name or as a middle name. Ewan, who had been quiet on the oars, chirped up: 'You're not going to believe what I'm about to say, but Fran is also Francesca Rose.' All three of our partners were Roses: Heide-Rose, Emily Rose and Francesca Rose. Call it what you like – chance, serendipity or fate – but we were reassured by the feeling that it was the right name. But we first needed to get Mum's blessing.

We stood outside Antigua's small airport, hands joined. Mum's voice was strong and clear: 'You'll look after each other out there. I'll see you on the other side. All three of you. I love you all.' A tear welled on the inside of my eye and rolled down my nose. The Atlantic had been challenging for Mum. All three of her eggs in one basket.

'We'll look after each other, Mum. We promise. And *Rose Emily* will look after us,' I replied, failing to match any resemblance of the strength in her voice. She loved the name. We hugged one final time then entered the sliding doors. All being well, the next time we would see her would be on the other side of the planet.

Those times were all behind us now, memories in the archive. What lay in front was a new chapter as our lives approached a precipice. Calendars that had been packed were left blank after March 2025. I'd been asked on a few occasions if I wanted to go to this or that event in the summer – gigs, festivals, weddings. My knee-jerk reaction was quickly brought into check by reality. 'Sorry, I'm away,' I'd reply, hoping that further questions wouldn't ensue.

I looked at the screen in front of me and began following our route from Schiphol. We were on our second leg of the journey, from Amsterdam to Peru. Reaching Lima, I continued spinning the electronic globe. The full Pacific seemed like double the distance we would travel in ten hours on a flight. A vast nothingness, over four times the diameter of the moon. My brain tried to digest the information but it didn't compute, like a CD that had been entered upside down. Tingles of nerves formed in my abdomen. Memories of the Atlantic felt like a world away. What if I simply couldn't do it? What if I let Jamie and Ewan down? I didn't feel like the same person as I was five years ago; or was I?

I thought of the monks who spend years up in mountain temples. One of my recent rowing-machine audiobooks had been *From a Mountain in Tibet*, the extraordinary true story of Lama Yeshe Losal Rinpoche's journey from a remote Tibetan village to the Samye Ling monastery in the Scottish Borders. Lama Yeshe had done a couple of five-year stints in solitary retreat. Over a decade, on your own, in silence. A life of dedication and sacrifice towards a spiritual practice, something that most people didn't understand. It was a strangely reassuring thought. It put time into perspective, making five months at sea not seem too long, after all.

The plane bumped on the asphalt runway, jolting me awake. It doesn't matter how many flights I take, landing always scares me. The small rubber wheels seem neither big nor sturdy enough to land a large flying object that weighs hundreds of tonnes. But, after a couple of bumps, we were safe and sound on the South American continent.

One major hurdle remained before we could relax with a metaphorical cold beer (much to Dad's dismay, we'd all stopped drinking alcohol six months prior): being reunited with all of the equipment that had been loaded onto the flight in Edinburgh. We weren't sure what customs would make of our hand luggage. Ewan was carrying the guitar with solar panels and the fishing rod strapped to it. He'd told Jamie and me that this was a 'mini' guitar, but it looked very normal-sized to us. 'It's called a Taylor GS Mini for a reason. It just looks normal-sized when I hold it because I'm small,' Ewan reassured us.

We'd take some more persuading. How all of this kit would fit on our boat, we didn't know. We'd made some basic estimations with CAD drawings by guessing the volume of our combined equipment and food, but they were guesses at best. It was one of the unknowns that we'd only uncover by seeing it in the flesh.

Miraculously, the KLM flight staff turned a blind eye to Ewan's gaslighting guitar experiment, and all eight of our hold bags had navigated their way from Edinburgh to Lima, via Amsterdam, in one piece. We were through. All that was left was a taxi ride to La Punta, a district to the west of Lima, where beds to collapse in were promised.

It was then that we saw the small Jack Russell in a black waistcoat. A sniffer dog was beelining straight towards us, a small Peruvian man in police uniform in tow. My heart sank. 'The medical kit,' I said to Ewan, with a sigh.

'What's in the bag?' barked the man in Spanish, pointing towards our medical kit that was full of drugs.

None of us spoke Spanish, so all we could do was produce the laminated prescription list, given to us by our doctor, Calum, and hope for the best. 'Sorry, I don't speak Spanish,' I replied, with the most harmless expression I could muster as I handed him the list. The man glanced at the pages, evidently not reading anything, then shrugged.

'I need to see what's in the bag,' he said again in Spanish, with an impatient tone, pointing at the bag.

Jamie placed it on the ground in front of him, unrolling the sealed top. The dog edged closer, wagging its tail. I winced as the man delved a hand in. 'Odds of our medical kit not getting confiscated?' I said to Ewan, turning my back to the officer.

'One in ten maybe?' Ewan replied with the raise of an eyebrow.

'Excuse me,' the man said. In his hand he held something that none of us expected. 'Is this your *plátano*?'

I looked at Jamie; he looked back blankly. 'Ah, yes . . . my bad. *Plátano.* Banana. That's mine from this morning,' I said apologetically. In my half-conscious state as we passed through Edinburgh airport duty free we'd made a customary stop at Pret a Manger. Food foresight is something I take very seriously – being stuck without snacks is my worst nightmare. Grabbing an extra banana for later on in the journey, I'd stuffed it into my hand luggage.

'I'll have to confiscate this,' the man said blankly, gesturing us towards the exit.

'Muchas gracias!' I said, with a grin, returning the bag to our mound. It's remarkable how your estimations of someone can transform so rapidly. I could have given him a hug, but deciding it would have been completely inappropriate, settled for an enthusiastic thumbs-up. Unbeknown to us, this wouldn't be our last run-in with the Peruvian authorities, but we were into the country and, by some miracle, none of our kit had been confiscated or damaged. We had our work cut out

– it was exactly three weeks until our intended departure date of 2 April – but we were here.

'La Punta here we come,' Jamie said as we left the bright airport lights into the humid Peruvian night.

The Yacht Club Peruano is situated in La Punta, a breezy seaside town of ice-lolly vendors, cafés and restaurants. The relaxed pace of this weekend destination stood in sharp contrast to the intensity of everything we were going to have to get ready while we were here. A narrow finger of land reaches southwestwards into the Pacific, with pebbly beaches on both shores. Tsunami warning signs are found throughout the town. It's a very long way before you'll reach your first islands if you cast off and head west – as we were about to find out – with French Polynesia sitting 3,700 nautical miles away.

Connecting with the yacht club had been one of our only successful cold calls in the entire campaign. Jamie pinged off an email to an anonymous address. Gonzalo, the club's secretary, came back within a few hours asking if we'd like to jump on a Zoom call. I remember waiting in the virtual meeting room, leaning against a silver birch. It was our last week with the boat in Edinburgh, so I was doing some final tinkering. A friendly bespectacled man popped onto the screen. He was tanned and wearing an open-collared shirt, and looked like someone out of *The Godfather* – friendly, but not the kind of person you would get on the wrong side of.

Gonzalo warned us of the corruption in customs and logistics. We needed to get all of the support we could to try to ensure the boat and food arrived without delays or bribes. He urged us to get letters of support from anyone in high-up places: ambassadors, politicians, sports people. Anyone with an official position – in the UK or in Peru – that might be able to move the dial in our favour. 'We must get all the support we can for the project so we can hit customs with one big punch,' he said as he made a punching gesture towards his camera.

By the end of the call, Gonzalo had offered to store and launch the boat, help with our shipping and sort our accommodation in Peru, all without charge. Wary of people overpromising and underdelivering, we took it with a pinch of Pacific salt, but welcomed any support he could give.

A few months later, we could now confirm that Gonzalo had delivered on everything that was promised, and some. He'd even sorted us out with free SPF 100 suncream from the company he worked for.

By coincidence, Yacht Club Peruano was the place that the Kon-Tiki expedition had departed from 78 years prior. The 101-day quest, led by Thor Heyerdahl, followed the 4,300-nautical-mile journey from Peru to the Tuamotu islands by balsa raft to prove that South Americans could have settled in Polynesia. We would be departing from the exact same place as this historic voyage.

But that wasn't the only serendipity at the start-line. Two women, Jess Rowe and Miriam Payne, otherwise known as Seas the Day, were also departing on a non-stop crossing of the full Pacific. We shared the same rulebook: get to Australia without stopping at islands or receiving help along the way. And their planned departure was only a couple of weeks before ours. Two teams attempting the same world first at the same time – it was uncanny. The girls were a few weeks ahead of us in the agonising process: their boat had arrived, but their food had been held up with customs. We'd all been scooped up by the yacht club, who were helping in any way they could.

For the first fortnight, we waited for *Rose Emily* and our food to arrive. The days ticked by, and soon we were only one week out from our planned departure date. It was obvious that we'd need to push back, but unclear by how much.

As we waited, we couldn't tackle the extensive list of boat and food jobs, but there was still plenty to do. We had to clear the decks for up to five months at sea. It was an eclectic to-do list: checking in with the shore team for the final time to make sure everyone knew who was doing what; cancelling phone contracts and gym memberships; drafting up personal wills; final tweaks to websites and tracking pages; checking in with sponsors for the final time; creating cheery documents like 'crisis comms plans' for if things went wrong; wiping phones of all apps and media.

Rose Emily was being shipped under a customs system that Peru had only recently joined. Mark, our boatbuilder, had gone to the effort of flying out to us – at his own expense – to help with final boat prep. The boat was due at the yacht club on the Monday, so Mark flew out on the Tuesday then had a three-day window before returning to the Netherlands.

Wednesday came about, and there was still no sign of the boat. We phoned and phoned, but the only word we could get out of the Peruvian logistics company was '*mañana*' – tomorrow. We'd had a UK logistics company that had been good for getting the boat onto the container ship. For the Peruvian side, we were dealing with their partner company, who had their own agent. We found ourselves in a sea of middle people. Nobody took responsibility or gave us any answers. It felt like we were banging our heads against a brick wall. The sad reality was that the only way of speeding up the process was likely slipping someone a brown paper envelope. But, given that we had neither the means nor any desire to fuel Peru's corruption, that wasn't an option.

Thursday came and went.

So did Friday.

There was still no boat. It was like rowing against the tide; there was little we could do to make forward traction. Mark's wealth of nautical experience included two crossings of the Pacific under sail. He knew the ocean we were about to set off into, and we made use of our time with him by studying the routing charts to form an idea of what to expect. Mark would be part of our core team of weather routers during the crossing, along with his colleague Tom, and a family friend, Sean, and his dad.

These paper charts detailing recommended routes, ocean currents, wind speeds and seasonal weather patterns for specific months had informed our decision to start from here. Although we would be covering more miles than if we'd set off north of the equator (for example, San Francisco to Taiwan), Mark believed that we'd benefit from more favourable currents and wind by setting off from Lima. We expected the Humboldt Current to carry us away from Peru for the first ten days, driving us north then northwest towards the equator. For the first 500 miles, we expected beamy weather (side-on wind and waves) and uncomfortable rowing as the wind blew across us from the south. About ten days to two weeks in, we anticipated the current to clock into the west and the wind to shift to an east/southeasterly – both aiding with western progress.

Two weeks of beamy seas was overwhelming. You'd never expect anything like that for an Atlantic crossing. But we hoped for several thousand miles of favourable rowing conditions on the other side of it. As we passed the halfway mark, we'd continue to ride the equatorial current west, connecting the constellations of Pacific islands, arcing our way southwest towards Sydney. We knew the final thousand miles would be the hardest part of the journey as the current died away and the prevailing winds became unpredictable, but the boat would be much lighter by that point in the journey. We'd estimated that we'd only be able to fit about 130 days' worth of food in the storage hatches, then would carry a further 20 days of emergency rations on deck. Hence, the ambition was to complete the crossing in 120 days. The safe-weather window for this crossing was April to October. Out of those months, you enter cyclone season in the west of the Pacific. It was essential that our crossing time didn't spill into October.

Friday afternoon came about, and we reluctantly said our farewells to Mark. We felt terrible about wasting his time. He'd flown halfway around the world to not see our boat arrive. Mark was remarkably understanding – I guess that's what you get when you've had as much life experience as him. But the knock-on effect of this was compounding. Mark would be much faster making any necessary repairs on the boat than us. We'd got stuck in with the build, but Mark knew her inside out. Our timelines were slipping, and we were all too aware that the runway ahead of us didn't go on for ever.

Infuriatingly, *Rose Emily* arrived the day after Mark left us, and, as we feared, the list of boat work that needed to be done only got longer. The antifoul – a special type of paint applied to the hull to prevent marine life sticking to it – had been rubbed away at the contact points with the trailer it had been sitting on during transit. More concerningly, neither of our two primary batteries were giving a battery reading, and one of our solar panels didn't seem to be supplying power. Although our propulsion on the boat was human-powered, we'd still be reliant on electricity for our satellite communications, producing water and our means to share the journey for fundraising. We had about 600 watts of solar power across the boat. The panels were positioned to maximise our charging capabilities: on the stern cabin for when the sun was coming up; on deck for during the day; and on the bow cabin for when the sun started to set. For additional power, we had a roving solar panel which we could move – depending on where was getting the most light. The solar panels were charging two 108 amp-hour batteries which powered all of our electronics, both fitted with monitors so that we could check their levels frequently. If you run battery levels too low, it can damage them irreparably (particular for older lead-acid batteries), and getting them back up to a healthy battery level can take a very long time. We weren't sure whether the fault was with the monitoring system or whether the cells had been damaged.

With help from one of the yacht club's marine electricians, we decided to install SmartShunts – a device for battery-level monitoring – onto both batteries and replace the solar panel. Ewan was confident that the batteries weren't compromised, but – to be safe – decided to install a spare battery as well. Diagnosing the problem took time, so did sourcing replacements. It would have been significantly faster had Mark still been with us.

None of this was in the plan. On top of the unexpected work, we already had our hands full: installing extra on-deck solar panels, applying all of our sponsor decals to the hull of the boat and sourcing an anchor, chain and new ropes. We also had an array of boat modifications that Ewan had 3D printed: seats for when we were off-shift, a carbon pole for the Insta360 camera, modifications to the water system, a Peli case for the laptop, and cameras for sending media.

Rose Emily is about 30 feet long and 6 feet wide and looks a bit like a traditional wooden clog. An exposed open row-deck, about the size of a large kitchen table, would be our home for 18 hours each day. At either end of the boat, we have two cabins for storage and sleeping, both about six and a half feet in length. The stern cabin houses everything we need to navigate – Garmin electronic chart-plotter, switchboard, autohelm VHF radio – whereas the bow cabin is purely for sleeping and storage. On deck, we have three rowing positions, two to be used day in, day out, and a third as a backup. We never used all three on the Atlantic, and were hoping this would be the case on the Pacific too. The seats roll forwards and backwards like on a river rowing boat to maximise the use of your most powerful muscle group, your legs, which would hold up far longer than our backs and arms. The hull was designed with safety and storage in mind, with the cavity broken up into sectional storage spaces, accessed through watertight hatches. Similar to the life rafts that you see on the sides of cruise ships, *Rose Emily* would still float even if the hull was pierced in multiple places, because of this sectional design. Two large hatches stretch down each side of the boat housing our watermaker and batteries, and a central wet-locker contains an inflatable life raft stored in a compact plastic shell. In the unfortunate case that we had to abandon ship, we would tug the rip cord, the CO_2 canisters would inflate, and we'd step down into the raft. Seven Henderson hatches, circular and screw-top, gave access to other storage compartments which, we hoped, would be filled to the brim with food. The idea was that as we ate through our food, the lockers would slowly transform into bins: every piece of packaging emptied, compressed and sealed into ziplock bags. Well, that was the plan, anyway. As things stood, we were beginning to wonder whether our food would ever turn up.

Though we had our work cut out on the boat, things were looking less positive on the food front. It was being air-freighted from the UK as a temporary import. To avoid hefty fines, we needed a green light from Peruvian customs. Only then could the food be sent from the UK. But the company handling the shipment on the Peruvian side had ghosted us. No matter how many times we called, they didn't pick up.

Our intended departure date came and went; still no green light. Our routine was the same each day. Each morning at the rowing club, we'd wake up at 5 a.m. to the swoosh of a rowing machine as someone started a morning session. I'd woken most mornings with a nauseous feeling in my stomach, anticipating the alarm that was about to go off. I'd lie there and flick through the things that most urgently needed to be done that day. We had lists of lists, and everything felt crucial. The stakes were heightened, knowing that if anything slipped through the cracks now we would suffer the consequences during our months at sea.

The importance of leaving Peru before the end of April was on all our minds. Because of the weather window for a Pacific crossing, if we got to May and still hadn't left we would need to consider postponing by a year. The campaign had already caused a considerable amount of disruption to our lives. We'd given up jobs, moved in with our dad and invested all of our spare time to train and work on the project. We had compromised time that we could have spent with our family, friends and girlfriends. Postponing would only draw this out. Pushing back a year wasn't really an option – it was now or never.

On hearing about our predicament with the food, more than one person urged us to talk to 'Willy'. Wilfredo was a man in his fifties. We'd often seen him in and around the yacht club doing errands. He had salt-and-pepper hair and bronzed skin. We explained our situation in the boatyard. Willy listened attentively, nodding. His response was simple: 'We can go to the office.'

He was evidently a man of action, and within an hour we were talking to a woman behind a Perspex screen at the customs office. Willy knew the process like the back of his hand, and spoke with a firm but soft tone. The woman explained that the application had only been made a week prior and it was typically a 30-day process. Our Peruvian logistics company had dropped the ball, which explained why they were ignoring our calls. The British ambassador to Peru, Gavin Cook, had given us a letter of support which had been printed out. We also had letters from the head of the navy, an Olympic sailor and Peru's motocross champion. It seemed ridiculous that we had to reach these high-up places to simply bring food into the country, especially since we'd be leaving with it a week later. We pleaded with the woman, and even offered her a box of chocolates that we had brought along, and eventually she agreed to see what she could do. She expedited our case and we had the green light from customs.

One hurdle was overcome. We now needed our Peruvian logistics company to give the go-ahead so that our food shipment could be sent from the UK. Today was a Thursday – if they didn't do this right now, we'd lose another three days. This was the final major hurdle in the way of our departure. Willy was unfazed: 'Tomorrow, we will go to their office. Round one: customs. Round two: logistics company.' It reminded me of Gonzalo's 'one big punch' on our first video call with him. How lucky we were to have met these people.

Google maps told us that the office was on the other side of Lima, a 40-minute drive from La Punta. As we entered the revolving doors of the towerblock, Willy ushered me away from the reception desk. 'If they know we're here, they might not open up.' Willy had done this before.

As we entered the fourth floor, I felt nervous. Our main correspondence had been with someone called 'JP'. He'd seemed irritable over the phone, as if we were inconveniencing him by getting in touch. I didn't know how they would react to us showing up unannounced. Willy knocked. A young woman, about 25, opened up. *'Hola?'* she said with a surprised expression on her face.

'Hello! We're here to see JP. Is he in?' Willy asked.

'Ehm, no, sorry. He's not at work yet. He should be here.' She glanced over her shoulder at a clock on the wall. The minute hand had a small cartoon plane on its end with the company's logo imprinted on the clock's face. 'He should be here in 15 minutes or so. Can I take a message?'

'Don't worry, we'll wait,' Willy said nonchalantly. 'We're not in a rush.' The woman gestured us towards a sofa on the other side of the office. As we took our seats, she picked up her phone. I don't speak Spanish, but it was obvious what she was doing. Willy raised an eyebrow.

'I'm sorry, but JP won't be coming in until after lunch. He has business elsewhere,' she announced, on putting the phone down.

It was 9.20 a.m. JP clearly didn't want to see us.

'Don't worry, we're not in a rush,' Willy replied to the woman without any hesitation, calling their bluff. 'We'll wait.' The woman didn't seem to know how to react and turned back to her computer screen.

Ten minutes later the office door swung open. JP was a man in his early forties. He looked better suited to working as an insurance broker, not logistics. Quite frankly, I was becoming sceptical about whether he even did work in logistics. He wore a pinstriped suit and sported a mop of combed-back charcoal hair. His beard and eyebrows were too perfectly formed for someone who didn't get manicured, and his beard came strangely far up his cheekbones. He didn't acknowledge us as he entered the office, but went straight to his desk and opened a briefcase.

'I've had 30 missed calls from you in the last three days. Thirty. Do you think that's acceptable?' JP said as he took a seat opposite us. He spoke as if he'd just done a run through of this interaction on his drive to work. There was no attempt to hide his irritation.

'Why have you not been accepting any of them?' Willy asked plainly. 'All we want is to speak to you.'

JP moved into Spanish. My head swung from left to right as the conversation pinballed back and forth. Willy's voice remained calm and collected, but JP appeared to be getting more and more agitated.

A moment later, Willy matched him. He stood up and took a step. The atmosphere was tense. Another man, Juanca, had entered the room. This was going to go in one of two ways: either we were about to have a fight – I could only hope that Willy knew more about that than I did – or we would find resolution.

JP's body language changed and his tone became softer. Willy took his seat again. I didn't know what he'd said, but it had worked. JP walked to his desk and rustled among some papers in his briefcase. He came back and handed me a pen and a sheet of paper. It was the paperwork for receiving the food. We were back on track, and it was all thanks to Willy.

Nine days after planned departure. Neon white lights drowned out any concept of time. Staring up at the tiered metal shelving units on every side, I scanned for anything resembling a nut. But not just any kind of nut, they had to be stainless steel – anything less would soon be eaten away by the soon to be ubiquitous salt. I'd been wandering these aisles for what felt like hours.

It was 11 April, almost exactly a month since we'd arrived in Peru. All being well we would leave Peruvian soil in under 24 hours. We were close now. I'd never experienced hospitality quite like Yacht Club Peruano's during this month. We hadn't paid a penny for accommodation, storing the boat or using their cranes. The food had finally arrived three days prior, so the yacht club had put out an announcement that we'd be departing tomorrow, Saturday 12 April. We couldn't let them down by pushing the date back. We had a deadline to hit. We were stripped of the luxury of doing it tomorrow. In only one day's time, we would wave farewell to life on land and bob over the horizon into the big blue. And then life would become a lot simpler as we pointed ourselves west.

I rested my head on the faux leather seat in my Uber back to La Punta, scrolling through my eclectic shopping list. Nuts, bolts and ziplock bags, epoxy resin, spare eating pots, 240-grit sandpaper for scrubbing the hull, more deck-scrubbing brushes, notebooks and pens. I paused at the pharmacy sub-list: multivitamins, face suncream. I was sure there was something else. Whatever it was, it was tough luck. We were out of time if we wanted to leave tomorrow.

Tomorrow . . .

Tomorrow?!

Over two years in the making and we were finally here.

I closed my eyes. I could make out the orange glow of streetlights passing the car window through my eyelids. It was 20 minutes of stillness. Twenty minutes of being seated and doing nothing before months of discomfort. 'If there's traffic, so be it,' I thought. 'I'm going to enjoy this.'

I worked my way along my lower row of teeth, pressing into the grooves. Ulcers lined the sides of my tongue. My immune system was down. The last month had been full-on. No matter how organised we'd tried to be – and we're far from the most organised people in the world – there was always going to be a lot to do. The boat and food delays had created a bottleneck for the last ten days. We were already sleep deprived, and we hadn't even begun.

The Uber came to a halt. 'La Punta,' came the voice of my friendly driver.

'Muchas gracias.' I reached for the door handle and tried my best to seem sprightly. I'd been dropped at the front entrance of the yacht club, a two-minute walk from where *Rose Emily* was being stored on the hard. I lugged my two duffle bags down the alleyway and pressed the gate buzzer. Manuel – one of the many friendly staff – buzzed me in with a thumbs-up and I shuffled over to the boat. Jamie and Ewan were both looking into one of the hatches with concerned expressions. The watermaker was in bits strewn across the row-deck. Jamie looked up as he saw me approaching: 'Do you want the good news or the bad news?'

'Let's start with the bad.'

'The watermaker isn't working. The pump is cooked. It must have been damaged in transit – corrosion, maybe.'

We hadn't thought to test the watermaker until now, largely because the water close to the marina wasn't clean, and we didn't want to damage the filter membrane.

'The good?'

'The good news is that the Italian is open for our final dinner. We're starving.'

The watermaker – our solar-powered desalinator – was one of the most essential bits of kit on the boat. It was completely useless without its pump. Though we had a spare, we couldn't leave Peru without either fixing the old pump or sourcing another in Lima. Ewan was sceptical about the latter. From what he could see, it was an unusual component, and probably not something we could pick up easily.

We did our best to forget about the situation we found ourselves in as we took our seats in the outdoor restaurant. Another friend from the club, Alec, joined us for dinner. He was about to set off to sail around the world. The sounds of Pacific waves breaking onto a pebbly beach punctuated the quiet evening, like lumbering giants collapsing onto a bed of marbles. The building Pacific swell was unlike anything I'd seen before. Though the waves were small, they were slower and more powerful than the waves found on the Atlantic or the Indian oceans.

'I wonder how Jess and Mims are doing,' Ewan said as we took our seats. We'd spent a lot of our evenings here with the Seas the Day rowing team before they'd left three days earlier.

'They're heading pretty far north, but I think they're both well. It's hot out there,' Alec replied.

There was a moment of silence as we all thought of these two remarkable women. Seeing their departure had been emotional. Jess's dad, Nick, who had served with the Gurkhas, had flown out to help with their final preparations. Just before they'd boarded their boat, he'd formed a small huddle: 'You're going to look after each other. You've got this.' Nick's voice wavered as emotion got the better of him. Two decades prior, he'd rowed across the Atlantic in 66 days. He knew what they were entering into.

The friendly waiter came over and took our order: burrata, leaf salad, focaccia, homemade pasta with ragu times two, Napolitano pizza, two big bottles of San Pellegrino. As we ate what could have been our final meal on land, there was a strange atmosphere around the table. It was an atmosphere that we'd become familiar with over our month in La Punta. A sense of foreboding niggled at our minds, taking us out of the present moment. I couldn't remember the last time I'd felt completely relaxed. We were so nearly there, it was truly the final straight, but it still didn't feel real. The weeks in Peru had felt like we'd been going nowhere, on a conveyor belt stuck in time. I'd snatched 15 minutes to talk to Heide every few days, making the most of being contactable, but it hadn't made me miss her any less. Jamie, Ewan and I weren't the only ones making a sacrifice for this project. Heide and I had only been going out for about six months by the time we left for Peru, and we were now facing the same amount of time apart. It wasn't exactly the conventional way to start a new relationship, but I felt hopeful that we'd grow together through the experience. 'It'll be easier when we set off, I promise,' I reassured her, pretending to know what we were heading into. But this was unknown territory for me as much as it was for her.

We walked three astride back to the boat, making a gameplan for the night ahead of us. Jamie and I continued packing. *Rose Emily* was filled to the gunwales, but there was more to go. Ewan dismantled the broken water pump, meticulously cleaned every component, then re-assembled it. He worked in silence, his headtorch illuminating the small pump as if he were performing surgery in an operating theatre.

Several hours passed with few words exchanged. This wasn't going to be the long last lie-in that we'd hoped for. This was it; the deadline that had been looming for so many months. The words had all been said. It was time to get it done.

Ewan was the first to speak, piercing the tense atmosphere. He looked up as if waking from a trance. 'This is the moment of truth. If this doesn't work, we need to postpone the trip.' His voice was monotone, a smudge of grease bordering his bloodshot eyes, like a mad scientist that hadn't slept in days.

We held our breath as Ewan brought the red wire towards the contact.

Deafening silence.

Then a gurgle; the pump spluttered, a mouthful of water came out of the small black tube as the pump was resuscitated. By some miracle, it had worked. The final barrier was overcome. The boat was ready to go: all that we needed to do now was sleep for three hours, finish our packing and we were ready to set off.

Day 000, Saturday 12 April 2025. We were up early. Jamie and Ewan headed for the boat as I went on a mission to collect our washing from the launderette and hunt for limes, mangoes and avocadoes. I explained to the teenager who served me: 'I'm about to row to Australia with my brothers, and this is the fresh fruit and veg we will take with us for the first few weeks.'

'Ah, ok . . . well, have fun. Have a good day,' he replied.

I chuckled to myself as I left the store. I suspect that my meaning had been lost in translation.

When I arrived back at the yacht club, it was time for the last bits of packing, final kit checks, a quick hull-clean with the power-wash; then we were ready to roll *Rose Emily* into position and clamber inside for the final time.

We peered up at a hundred faces that had gathered to see us off as the crane lowered us, foot by foot, down into the Pacific blue. 'Hector the Hero' echoed out on the bagpipes as Jamie regaled the crowd from the bow. No Scottish start-line would be complete without a set of Highland pipes. Though we hadn't known any of these people a month ago, we'd embraced many of them as old friends moments earlier – Gonzalo, Willy, Manuel, José Manuel – savouring every squeeze. They would be our final hugs from other human beings for many months. We would never forget the kindness shown to us by the people of La Punta, particularly our friends at Yacht Club Peruano. Their help had saved our expedition, and for that we were eternally grateful.

Life is full of new beginnings. New jobs, new neighbourhoods, new relationships, new states of mind. Without facing new challenges life can become rigid. You start to stagnate. Beginnings are one of the most exciting things we face in life, but they're also scary. It's as if you're stepping into the unknown with no thread connecting you to where you've been and where you will go. That's how we felt as the crane's slings passed astern.

My nerves and sleep deprivation were now being overridden by the adrenaline that was coursing through my veins. The local naval academy's brass band broke into song. The yacht club had arranged for them to come and see us off, immaculately dressed in their smart white naval uniforms.

It didn't feel real. Nothing did. We'd imagined this moment so many times in the months leading up to it. It felt like I was watching all three of us from above. But no, we were here. We were in the boat we'd helped to build, setting off from Peru.

I extended my arms and dropped the paddles into the water then pulled for the first time. My right blade clattered into Ewan's. We were clunky and out of sync. 'Plenty of time to practise that,' I thought to myself. We'd estimated about two million strokes each by the end of the crossing. This campaign had already been the hardest thing any of us had ever done – harder than rowing across the Atlantic – but the row hadn't even begun. The journey ahead was completely daunting and unmanageable when viewed in its entirety. But, as is often the case in life, the reality was that this beginning had been quietly forming under the surface of our lives for years. The row was the tip of an iceberg – starting was just another step.

We waved goodbye to Alec and Gonzalo aboard *Manu*, our final convoy boat, and pointed into an effervescent orange dusk. A cauldron of emotions bubbled within me. Excitement, fear, overwhelm. I couldn't believe we were here. It was really happening. We'd turned an idea into our reality. We didn't know what obstacles were ahead of us – if we did, we probably wouldn't have set off in the first place. Three brothers in a boat and the largest ocean on the planet to row across.

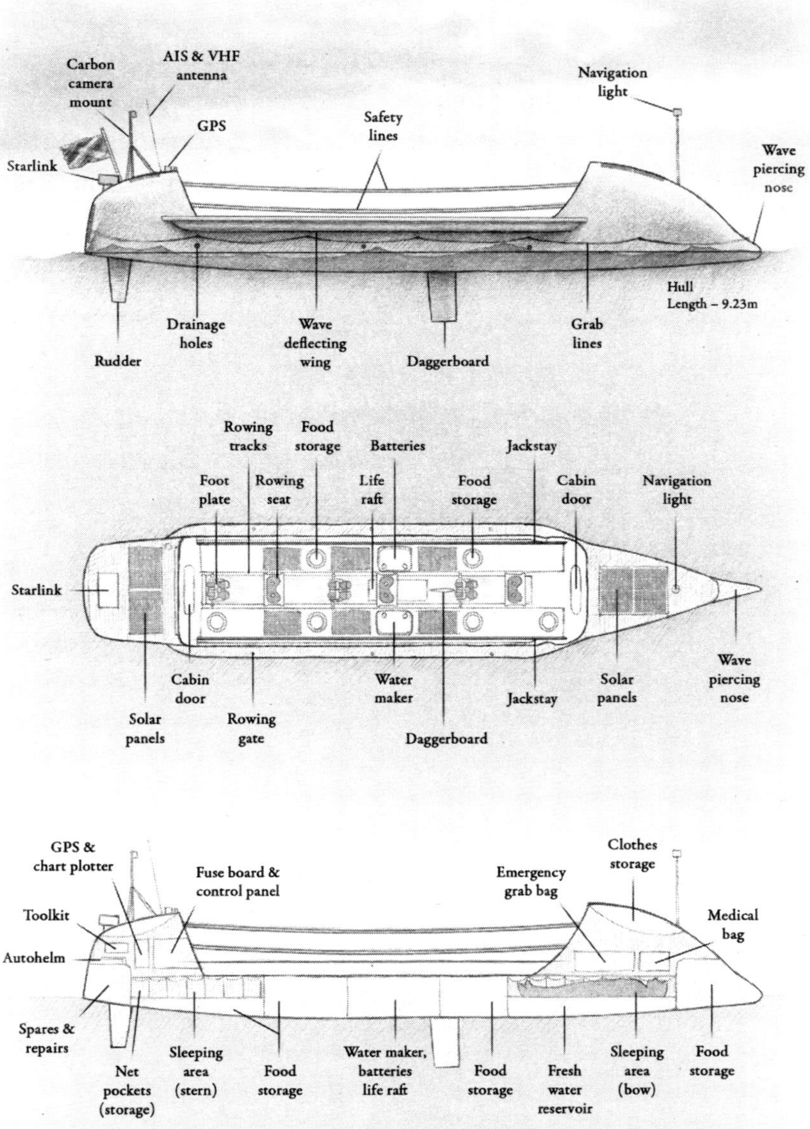
Carbon camera mount
AIS & VHF antenna
GPS
Starlink
Safety lines
Navigation light
Wave piercing nose
Hull Length – 9.23m
Rudder
Drainage holes
Wave deflecting wing
Daggerboard
Grab lines
Rowing tracks
Food storage
Batteries
Jackstay
Foot plate
Rowing seat
Life raft
Food storage
Cabin door
Navigation light
Starlink
Cabin door
Solar panels
Rowing gate
Water maker
Daggerboard
Jackstay
Solar panels
Wave piercing nose
GPS & chart plotter
Fuse board & control panel
Toolkit
Autohelm
Spares & repairs
Net pockets (storage)
Sleeping area (stern)
Food storage
Water maker, batteries life raft
Food storage
Fresh water reservoir
Sleeping area (bow)
Food storage
Emergency grab bag
Clothes storage
Medical bag

Rose Emily

Part II

Chapter 6

Baptism by Brine

By Ewan

For the first day or so we were protected by the coast. The invisible embrace of land held back the ocean and settled our nerves, like a calming hand on a restless dog. The humid haze and patchy sun glinted off the steady swell as the Pacific waves rolled past, like the waking breaths of a slumbering giant.

We'd done plenty of training, of course: countless hours in the boat on the west coast of Scotland to prepare; overnight expeditions on little sleep; and multiday trips through turbulent coastal passages. We'd performed man-overboard procedures using life rafts in wave pools. We'd even capsized the boat in controlled self-righting drills. Whatever the weather, be it wild, or calm, or freezing, we had been out in *Rose Emily*, putting down the miles.

But training has a comforting boundary built into it, whether you acknowledge it or not. There's the promise of a hot shower, or a good meal, or a lie-in with a cup of tea once you get home. The Pacific has none of those things. And nothing could have prepared us for the brutality of the real thing, of rowing perpetually through long days and dark nights. As the mountainous coastline of Peru dissolved into the ever-diminishing horizon, a clawing sense developed that those unfamiliar peaks would be the last we'd see for months. Yet there was, at the same time, a breathtakingly simple beauty to it: floating alone in the wide, wide sea.

One moment you're on land, living a carefree existence and taking life's daily luxuries for granted – the flat whites, the dry socks, the knives and forks. Next, you're out at sea and in the thick of it, and the transition is nothing if not jarring. An unforgiving world of waves and spray and shift patterns. Sink or swim. No margin for error.

The start of the voyage still resembled our training days in many ways, as if we were still waiting for our inner anchors to find ground – as if this was all just another dry run that we could eventually take a break from. We were still adjusting.

The boat felt heavy in the water, laden with supplies; but our course towards our first waypoint was true. A direct line west, to where far-off islands lay.

But then, after 24 hours or so, it was as if we had crossed over some ancient threshold. The rhythm of the ocean changed, winds from the south took hold and jostling waves rose up, pressing past and pushing us north. We rowed across surging gulleys of water, like peat hags in a sprawling Scottish moorland, cut deep and sharp by wind and time. The boat rose and fell as we urged her forward, but the Pacific was setting the terms as it slammed into the hull. It didn't take long before seasickness took hold.

As had been the case on the Atlantic, Jamie and I were most affected: an underlying feeling of nausea that worsened each time we lost sight of the horizon. Inside the cabins were the worst; hot and cloying. The gut-churning motion occasionally interrupted our off-shifts, as we lurched over the side to vomit. Our oar strokes carried on without remorse, but the westward bearing we had held slipped away. The excitement and adrenaline were slowly replaced with a queasy unease, as we left the dreamlike serenity of the shimmering Peruvian coastline behind. A northwesterly course was the best we could manage. At least Lachlan seemed unaffected by the sickness.

We knew mistakes were going to be inevitable and we expected early blunders, but still the first one shook us up. Lachlan's personal locator beacon, or PLB – the little device that was attached to each of our harnesses, which was a lifeline if you ended up in the water – somehow got set off. It's not the sort of button you press by accident. It's specifically designed not to be deployed by accident. And yet, in the way that all 'foolproof' systems are eventually defeated by fools, Lachlan successfully set it off anyway. I have little doubt that if it hadn't been him, it would have only been a matter of time before Jamie or I did the same. Somewhere back in La Punta alarms started sounding. A string of emergency contacts were alerted by the coastguard. People briefly became intensely concerned about whether Lachlan was still alive. Was it possible he'd been washed overboard, so soon after departing? We were indeed alive. And mostly just preoccupied with trying not to be sick anywhere that would prove tiresome to clean up.

This was the tone of those first days: a surreal reality, marked with anxiety, a little unease and, eventually, acceptance. Nothing catastrophic, but rough and clumsy, and without much of a routine. We needed to sharpen up, and settle into our new existence on the oars, before the mistakes began to count.

Eventually, a daily routine on *Rose Emily* began to take shape. By 6 a.m., or a little before, all three of us would be on deck, watching the first light return and yawning off the broken sleep as colour seeped back into our world. Lachlan, typically, had the final solo shift of the night and would start the day by making coffees on his break, boiling water on our small gas stove and pouring it into insulated beakers. A hot drink with the rising sun after emerging from a dark night was one of the few comforts that never lost its magic for us.

The night was split into thirds, meaning one of us was always on the oars, rowing alone through the darkness. We each had six hours set aside for sleep: Lachlan and I taking two three-hour blocks, while Jamie had it slightly rougher, with one three-hour block in the middle and two shorter 90-minute scraps either side. He was compensated with an extra 30 minutes in the morning if the weather allowed. We'd row for 90 minutes between each sleep, before handing on to the next person and climbing into one of the cramped damp cabins – one at the front of the boat, one aft. That was the theory. In practice, if squalls came through and wet layers had to be peeled off and dealt with, if the autopilot started misbehaving, if someone needed a hand in rough weather, or if your own mind jolted you awake in a panic before the alarm went off, those precious hours quickly became fewer. On particularly disrupted nights, if one of us had lost more than his fair share, he was allowed a shorter compensatory rest in the early morning, the other two picking up the strain while he slept.

Then the day shifts began. In the early days, we tried to be sensible, conserving our efforts for the long haul ahead. The typical rotation was to repeat shifts of 30 minutes on the oars, followed by a 30-minute break. This meant half the time there were two of us rowing, and half the time there would be only one. We called this shift pattern 'one on, one off', referring to the proportion of time spent on and off the oars. The ratio would always stay the same, but the length of the shift would vary – sometimes an hour on, followed by an hour off. Sometimes even longer if the oars felt good and the baking heat of the sun allowed.

In more demanding conditions, we moved to two on, one off; meaning there would always be two of us rowing at any one time. This was also known as a 'two-up' routine and would usually be one hour on, followed by 30 minutes off. Our rule was simple: if the boat was gaining enough from the extra effort and maintaining two on the oars increased our speed by more than 0.3 knots, we held it there.

If the conditions were really in our favour and one rower could keep the boat moving forward honestly enough, we'd have the luxury of one on, two off (or 30 minutes on, one hour off; also known as a 'one-up' routine) – although instances of this were sadly few and far between. We committed to keeping the boat moving above 2 knots, and if it ever dropped below that threshold, we'd change our shift pattern to have less rest and more rowing.

The worst shift of all, when the Pacific was properly against us, was the dreaded 'three-up' routine. For this, we prepared all the meals we needed for that day in the morning and then all of us would row without break, going for as long as we could with each of us snatching moments to eat, drink and use the toilet and nothing more. This wasn't particularly sustainable but could be maintained for most of a day in desperate situations. The plan for the crossing was to start with easier rowing shifts in the first few weeks and then build up to longer hours on the oars each day as we became conditioned to the effort. At sea, distance is measured in nautical miles. We needed to average about 65 nautical miles each day (roughly 75 ordinary miles), to get to Sydney in 120 days. This gave us a clear target to aim for. If we let our daily mileage slip down to below 52 nautical miles per day we'd simply run out of food and would need to and would need to re-provision, ruining our goal of completing the crossing non-stop and unsupported.

The seats themselves sat on four little wheels that ran up and down sliding tracks. Changeovers had to be quick and tightly choreographed: oars stowed, feet released from the Velcro straps, the rower then lifting themselves off the seat with the safety lines and stepping clear, while the next man clipped on and got straight to work. The aim was always the same: keep the handover tidy and stop the boat losing momentum.

Off-shift was never really off. You left the sliding seat, unclipping and re-clipping to the lines as necessary, checked battery levels, made water, filled bottles, slapped on suncream, used your pee bottle if you needed a piss, or the communal toilet bucket if it was more than that. Shitting in a bucket, half-filled with sea water, bracing yourself against the rocking of the boat was grim enough. Having your brothers less than a few feet away, claiming you're taking longer than they do, only made it worse. The Chuckle Brothers seemed to find this activity an amusing pastime. I'm fairly sure if I'd raised that sort of behaviour with HR back at Dyson, it would have been deemed inappropriate. Out on the Pacific, unfortunately, HR was in short supply.

Making meals was its own debacle. Pouches of freeze-dried rations would be dug from a locker, and water then heated on the gas burner (known as a Jetboil) before pouring it into the packets. We had to consume around 6,000 calories per day, meaning four main meals, plus breakfast porridge and snacks. Once finished, the packaging would be closed along the resealable edge, then folded and put away into a drybag that was allocated to rubbish. As the trip continued, we'd slowly eat through the bags filled with food, replacing them with empty packets and wrappers. By the end, a large amount of the weight we carried would simply be trash. Double-sealing everything was deemed critical – a hopeful bid to hold back the smell.

Brushing teeth was the first act of each morning and the last act of the rowing shifts, and felt like a revitalising experience. From day one, Lachlan was convinced we were going to run out of toothpaste. We frequently rinsed the salt from our skin with fresh water, where we could, especially in places that might begin to chafe. A proper wash was rare, and mostly we relied on baby wipes. They'd be folded up and stuffed in with the rest of the rubbish. Despite claims they were biodegradable, it didn't feel right chucking them into the ocean, so we added them to the pile of waste. The only thing that went over the side (intentionally) was used loo roll and the contents of 'the bucket', but hopefully you can forgive us for that.

Before departure, we'd committed to writing a daily log entry, taking turns to do so with each passing day. Partly it was for ourselves. On the Atlantic, we had noticed that memories had faded far faster than we had expected. Days blurred into one and details evaporated. Sleep deprivation does strange things to the brain. So this time we had pledged to keep a better record.

Mostly, however, it was for Mum and Dad. Neither of them is particularly savvy with technology, and they weren't about to set up social media accounts with much success. Switching their phones to silent, or operating the dreaded thermostat app, was quite enough of a challenge for them. So despite having the wonders of high-speed satellite internet on board, and a team of people back home to keep the rest of the world informed, we settled on a simple email update for our parents, and anyone else who wished to read about our experience first-hand. Not because of some old-fashioned romantic idea of letters home from sea or a yearning for simplicity. But because behind the reality of three brothers going alone into the world's largest ocean were two parents, happily separated (or 'happarated' as Mum calls it) who would be left stranded on an island of worry and uncertainty – with months to imagine the worst possible scenarios.

It was also a kind of social contract, creating accountability to our readers, much in the same way that publicly announcing our plans to row the Pacific had been. We had told people we were going to do it, and that had made all the difference. The only problem is that writing a daily log on your phone from a tiny boat in a churning sea is quite challenging. Let alone when you are rowing for over half the hours of each day. Producing something vaguely coherent – which wouldn't just add to the stress felt by Mum and Dad – while deliriously tired, frequently nauseous and perpetually wet, wasn't always easy. But we'd promised ourselves that we'd do it. And on day two, it was my turn.

DAY 002, Monday 14 April

EWAN: Song of the day – 'Sail Away' by David Gray

I awoke at 5 a.m., with the faint glow of first light starting to appear in the sky behind us, upon which we looked back. The night had been better than the previous, with less overwhelming tiredness and the body more accustomed to our new existence at sea.

Stronger weather pushes our course further north than would be ideal, making our journey to Australia less direct. It's a compromise between speed through the water and a fight with the side-on weather, which we have no choice but to accept.

Two casualties today, indicators that we are definitely not into the swing of things yet. The first was a wave coming through the stern cabin hatch while I tried to make water. We've been far too relaxed with the cabin door up to this point, with conditions on the first day and a half being more similar to coastal waters during training days. A wet bunk sharpens the habits, and the hatch has remained firmly closed for all but completely essential purposes since.

The second was Jamie's earbud, which he'd been listening to music on during the nightshift, and which fell from his pocket as he rowed and bounced off the deck for the fish to enjoy.

Clouds gather as the evening draws to a close. The nightshift looms. Much darker than the previous two, with their clear skies and bright moons.

One of the immediate new realities that made itself firmly known to us was space. Or rather, the complete lack of it. Our aim was to reach Australia without stopping for a resupply. And there was no support vessel following behind, carrying extra food. *Rose Emily* had been literally packed to the gunwales. She was piled high and crammed deep with provisions, and there wasn't an inch of extra space for a single thing more. Months of planning and procuring and sourcing had resulted in an incredibly cramped existence, with supplies squeezed on board in all sorts of awkward and creative ways. Everything had been put somewhere, and that somewhere was generally 'on top of something else'.

We had mountains of food. Freeze-dried meals, electrolyte sachets, teabags, tubs of peanut butter, packs of dried fruits and nuts, chocolate bars, oatcakes, sweets – everything that was going to keep us alive for the next few months – all packed into bags that were then packed into bigger bags that were then stuffed into every nook and cranny, like we were trying to smuggle a small supermarket across the Pacific.

We had spares and repairs: bits of rope, nuts and bolts, glues and sealants, various tools, replacements for everything that we thought might break, and several things that probably wouldn't. We had all manner of equipment: safety apparatus, comms kit, navigational tools, medical supplies, fishing gear. There was then an eclectic assortment of miscellaneous items, which had found their way aboard. Random things that I'd ended up buying during slightly panicked late-night shopping sprees after my browsing history had informed the internet gods that I was an 'ocean rower' and should therefore be aggressively targeted with ads for titanium carabiner clips, commercial-grade fish-descaling machines, and things that looked suspiciously like they belonged on an oil rig. We also had a guitar, an accordion and a set of bagpipes – a decision that raises more questions than it answers. Most precious of all were a handful of letters from loved ones, which were our only other personal possessions save a small pile of clothes, carefully tucked away in a safe place of our own. They would brighten up the darker days, when the time came. Mine were stored in the stern cabin on the port side of the boat, in a small net pocket that hung below the chart-plotter.

There were bags strapped everywhere. Some wedged into hatches, others tied to the roof of cabins, or fixed to the bulkheads with webbing straps. And, because we had simply run out of space, several bags were on deck – lashed to the safety lines and footplates at each rowing position. This was far from ideal.

We had tested the boat's ability to self-right when she was empty. But we hadn't tested her bursting at the seams and loaded with luggage. If we rolled, the extra weight and bags on deck would make it that much harder for us to come back up. But we had no choice. You can't row non-stop and unsupported across the entire Pacific Ocean without taking the things you need. And, unfortunately, you need quite a lot.

We begrudgingly conceded that the space allocated to the musical instruments may have been more sensibly used for something else. We had a romantic idea of reaching Australia having written an album underneath the vast expansive skies of the ocean that we'd just rowed across. The only reason we'd not been able to do this on the Atlantic was because we'd brought a ukulele and a mouth organ instead of instruments we could actually play. The reality soon sank in that a debut album probably wasn't likely, and an extra bag of freeze-dried rations may have been more appropriate.

At the best of times, I find it hard to pack for a long weekend away. Let alone six months at sea with no access to a shop or washing machine. Most of what had made it onto the boat was deemed absolutely essential and had been painstakingly considered; every gram of extra weight was additional weight we'd need to move from one side of the planet to the other by oar. Additional kilograms would equate to additional days on the water, amounting to weeks if we weren't careful.

Beneath the deck and inside the cabins, it felt like the inside of a tent. Except it was a one-man tent that had been filled with stuff for three. To get into the bunk required a sort of shimmying, sliding motion. You didn't step inside so much as insert yourself into it, like an oversized letter being thumbed into a postbox.

Sleeping was an interesting activity, if you can call it that. Jamie vividly described it as like 'sleeping in a sweaty crevice', which I thought was quite apt. The baking heat and high humidity are unavoidable, and once you slither into position you are effectively pinned onto your front or your back. So you just lie there, like a soggy corpse. It made me think back to Holland, and our time with Dick and Mark. It really did feel like the inside of a hot coffin.

DAY 005, Thursday 17 April

EWAN: Song of the day – 'Margo & Barry' by Beluga Lagoon

Shortly before lunchtime I made an attempt to clear the stern locker of all the spares and miscellaneous items we had brought for minor adjustments and repairs once underway. My intention was to locate the water-system spares, so we could adjust things slightly and make producing water on deck less precarious and frustrating. Our current situation requires the cabin hatch to be open and an awkward lean into the control panel to press the water-pump switch if we want water while on deck. We've already had a wave come through the hatch, and can't let this happen again.

After about 20 minutes, I had successfully filled the bunk with the entire contents of the stern locker and then, at the peak of the mess I had created, I became incapacitated with seasickness, my mouth filling with saliva as I tried to keep myself from vomiting, suddenly aware of how much I was sweating. Being inside the cabin with the horizon lost from view was a good way to bring this on. Several hours later I managed to muster up the energy to force myself back into the hot, cramped cabin to tidy away the bags of spares and loose equipment I had dispersed around the cabin. I found the bits that I needed and will do the fix in the coming days, but the stern locker has been essentially ransacked in the process.

Night fell and we were plunged into total darkness, without a moon to brighten our surroundings. During the final changeover, as Jamie and Lachlan were heading for their bunks, I jolted one of the safety lines (strong webbing straps that provide a barrier down each side of the boat, to which we can tether ourselves) while moving up the boat, somehow dislodging the carabiner holding the toilet bucket in place. It dropped off the side of the boat and into the water below. Diving to my knees, I tried my best to grab it, but the ends of my fingers merely brushed the hard plastic side, and I watched it swirl off into the darkness and disappear. In vain we tried to stop the boat, to turn back and rescue our bucket, but nowhere could it be seen. Dismayed, we bid each other goodnight and headed once more into the nightshifts. At least we have a spare bucket.

The lost earbud and the toilet bucket were a wakeup call. We had spares, but certainly not an infinite supply. And after a full week at sea, we hadn't even covered five percent of the distance to Australia. The message was stark: if we kept on this trajectory, sooner or later something disastrous would happen, and we'd end up in a desperate situation, calling a mayday and praying to be rescued. We needed to come to terms with our new existence quickly, however uncomfortable it may be.

And then, just as I was thinking that I didn't need to learn any more lessons from the ocean, I made the mistake of leaving the hatch slightly ajar as I operated the water pump from inside the stern cabin. A hose ran from the water tank, which was in a compartment under the mattress, out of the door and into a water bottle, which was on deck being filled. Jamie had sat watching me with a slightly disapproving look, observing the precarious situation from the oars. Seeing it coming, he yelled, '*Wave!*' as the boat surged up. I tried to pull back the hose, slamming the door shut as water washed through the opening. 'Fuck sake,' I spat through gritted teeth as salty water sloshed onto my lap, and as I twisted the handles to seal the flow. Jamie had seen the water go in, heard the expletives from inside the cabin, so thought better of following up on how I was doing. No doubt the fucking water bottle had been knocked over as well. I'd need to fill it again. Fucking thing.

This was not the sort of error you could afford to make, at any stage. The mattress in the stern cabin was now saturated, and there was an unknown amount of seawater sloshing around beneath it. To make matters worse, there really wasn't an easy way to dry it out. The whole thing was completely wedged beneath the mountains of snacks and freeze-dried pasta rations, which were sharing the bunk with us. We couldn't just unload things and move them elsewhere temporarily, there simply wasn't space. And you can't just stick them out on deck, or keep the hatch open to air things out. There are waves constantly washing over the boat from the side. And it means that trying to deal with anything while underway is invariably a complete nightmare.

There was no choice but to make peace with the grim situation in the cabin. A squelchy bunk with a constant stream of droplets condensing on the carbon-fibre shell, continuously seeping down the walls and into the sleeping space below. The inside of the boat appeared to be sweating even more than we were. But the wet sleeping pad wasn't the only casualty of the wave.

Back in La Punta, we had fully intended on getting the boat perfectly set up before pushing off for multiple months at sea. You don't send a rocket off into outer space without everything being ready to go first, right? The delays with customs, and the stream of technical issues had not been part of the plan, however. We had an entire month in the boatyard, but the time for finishing touches had disappeared into a frantic scramble of unexpected firefighting and getting the truly critical jobs done. Lots of things had been moved to the 'we'll-need-to-sort-that-once-underway' list. And one of the items on that list was an expensive pile of camera equipment, which we'd brought to document the journey.

This included about five or six different cameras of all shapes and sizes, a few microphones, various chargers and battery banks, an array of memory cards, and a laptop for sending all the footage back to our media team to edit. All of that had been sensibly housed inside a rugged waterproof hardcase, which was connected to the boat batteries via a waterproof cable. I then had a clever way of operating the laptop wirelessly using a phone, meaning it could be kept shut and everything would be out of harm's way. Or at least that was the idea.

Predictably, at the very moment the wave arrived through the hatch, the case was wide open. The computer was uploading files from a memory card, because I hadn't finished setting things up properly, and it was directly in the firing line.

I cursed my unbelievable stupidity and desperately switched everything off. I mopped up all the pools of water I could find and put all the kit back into the waterproof box with about a hundred silica sachets to soak up the moisture. All I could do was return to the oars, absolutely seething, and pray that things would dry out and spring back to life.

When I eventually tried to switch on the computer, some days later, a glimmer of hope briefly appeared in the form of a red battery symbol in the middle of the screen. But moments later, a small puff of smoke drifted out from the charging port. The laptop screen went blank. I sat there staring at the empty screen, holding the power down again and again, willing it to come back. Nothing. The air in the cabin felt claustrophobic. I just sat there with this horrible, hollow certainty spreading through me. This wasn't something I could just quietly fix later. We had lost our computer and the only means of sensibly uploading large video files to the team, and all we were left with was some utterly useless ballast. From here on, the only way to send things back was using a small memory card reader, which plugged into the charging port of our phones. For anyone who works in an industry where this sort of thing is required, it probably wouldn't even be considered a plausible backup option – more a cry for help. A carrier pigeon would have been a better option.

Suddenly, our ability to share the story had been hampered. Our strategy for raising money for clean water projects depended entirely on our ability to bring people on the journey with us – to share the story as it unfolded – and hopefully then the people following might reach into their pockets and donate to the cause we were supporting. I felt entirely to blame, and it made me feel sick. I could barely even talk about it with Jamie and Lachlan, or write about it in the log. More than anything, I felt I had let everyone down. I couldn't hold anyone's gaze for a while after that.

DAY 008, Sunday 20 April

EWAN: Song of the day – 'Hot Tears', live at KCRW by Leif Vollebekk

After several nights of being woken by the dreaded bleating of the alarm clock, only three hours after having gone to bed, things have certainly not become any easier. I fall asleep soon after my head hits the pillow due to sheer exhaustion, but it feels like only seconds later that I'm being summoned from my bunk again. I don't have any memory of my dreams in this state. Perhaps I'm too tired.

I've deliberately chosen a different alarm from my normal one, to avoid the likely PTSD from the sound of the thing in the future. What has had a marked improvement however, is how awake I have felt about ten minutes after mustering up every ounce of willpower to drag myself out of the cabin and get back onto the oars again.

I swung open the hatch at 05.55 hours, expecting to be greeted by the usual scene: a slightly relieved grimace from Lachlan, as he concluded his final strokes of the nightshift. Instead, however, I found something different. Lachlan was in hysterical fits of laughter, gasping for air and doubled over on the rolling seat. What had caused all the commotion?

Then I heard Jamie's alarmed voice calling out from the cabin opposite: 'Lala, Lala! All the electrics have gone off!'

Why was Lachlan cracking up in hysterics, you might ask?

Without the electrics, how would we navigate, make water, or communicate back to land? What you need to know, and what was making Lachlan double over with laughter, was that the bow cabin (from which Jamie had called) is essentially completely devoid of any electronic equipment, other than a light – which I could see was already switched on. Jamie had just woken up thinking he was in the other cabin and had thought disaster had struck. The chart-plotter, radio, illuminated fuseboard (and all the rest) are instead to be found in the stern cabin, which I was currently occupying. Sympathising with poor Jamie, we sent him back to his bunk for an extra 45 minutes of sleep: standard procedure if one of us had ever been in need of it on the Atlantic, usually following a broken night or tough day.

Additional note: a flying fish flew directly into my ear during the night. It might have been trying to tell me something, although I cannot be sure.

The imagined electrical apocalypse in the bow cabin had been a moment of hilarity – for Lachlan, at least. But it was a sign of things to come. When you're sleep deprived, your brain plays tricks on you, and we were far from accustomed to the relentless routine. You see things that aren't really there, when exhaustion compounds. And sometimes, it's hard to know what's real and what's not. On the Atlantic, Lachlan had emerged onto the deck for a solo nightshift, seemingly not fully conscious due to his exhaustion. He'd been found two hours later at the next changeover, asleep on the deck and without his harness on. Growing up, Lachlan had been known for sleepwalking every so often, but this was a sobering moment, which could have had grave consequences. Waking up for a nightshift in the middle of a storm to find your brother gone was a harrowing thought. This time we were making sure we had a thorough handover between shifts, always checking we were clipped on and awake.

The Pacific at night can be both beautiful and unnerving: stars like I've never seen them before. The dancing moonlight making the dark waves half known. The sound of blowing whales as they breach and sink back down. My consciousness reaching out into the darkness, past the boat's open sides, to where the horizon had gone.

We'd been warned about lone-wolf fishing boats that come from distant lands to catch giant squid from the deep. Nothing about that sounded fun. I always thought attacks on ancient sailing ships by tentacled monsters were the stuff of legend, rather than a genuine cause for concern for offshore mariners. That was until we learned that the eight-armed suckered creatures really do exist. Not only that, but they are found in these very waters, and can grow up to 13 metres long. That's about the size of a bus. A typical specimen is not some sleek, mythical beast either, but a pale, slimy, muscular thing with lidless eyes and a hidden beak at the centre of it all. The sort of creature that felt more real and less imaginary the longer you stared into the black water. It was a horrifying thought. The Kraken, it turned out, was indeed real.

It was hard sometimes, as my mind wandered through the night, not to imagine these otherworldly creatures taking hold of the boat and pulling us down into the abyss. I'd try to steady my oar strokes and breathe calmly. 'It's all in my imagination,' I'd say to myself, and yet the thumping of my heartbeat would continue drumming in my ears.

The warnings we had received, however, were not about the giant squid themselves, rather the solitary fishermen – rogue hunters of the squid and other creatures of the deep – who linger far offshore for many months at a time. They slip into Peruvian waters to make their catch under the cloak of darkness. It wasn't the illegal fishing that concerned us, however. It was the violence that sometimes follows in the wake of these shadow fleets: armed robberies at sea; unpleasant, opportunistic interactions that happen when desperate people, expensive equipment and a vulnerable target converge in the same remote patch of ocean.

One night, after crossing into international waters, I spotted a light on the deepening skyline. At first it was just a point, flickering as it rose and fell between the troughs in the distance. But as night closed in, rowing alone through my shift, there was something different about this light that didn't move against the stars. It remained defiantly in the south, becoming brighter and brighter. It was coming towards us, directly.

I checked our AIS map (a system used by vessels to indicate relative position and speed). It's how collisions are avoided between ships in the night. Most large, professional boats should be visible on this map; they are often required to be so under maritime law. But there was no signal. No friendly electronic handshake. Something didn't seem right.

I continued to row, considering my options. We would be an easy target. Unable to make a getaway. Straightforward to board. My imagination filled the empty space with worst-case narratives. And the light kept on coming.

Our own navigation light was off, as it normally was. Rowing at night with a light on isn't standard practice, unless land is nearby or we expected passing vessels. One of us was always on watch, rowing through the night, so it would be unnecessary to drain the batteries in this way. At that moment, we shouldn't have been particularly visible. But anyone determined enough could track our position via GPS, which was currently being broadcast for all to see.

It was less than half a mile off now, and I could see the white floodlights on the masthead were flanked by red and green sidelights, marking its port and starboard sides. If it was a legitimate fishing vessel, turning our lights on would help them see and avoid us. We could call on the radio, to warn them of our presence. But if it wasn't legitimate, that would just help them find us. There was something that didn't feel right about making ourselves known in the immediate darkness. Too exposed. Too vulnerable.

The boat sat low in the water, scarred with rust and old paint, windows dark and foreboding, with no figures visible within. Metal gantries and rigging were visible above the empty deck, along with a tangle of cables and winches for hauling great weights from the drawing depths. The sound of the diesel engines grumbled across the water as they bore down upon us.

I had to do something. Time had run out.

I dimmed what I could. The deck screens went black. And then I changed course. Not by a small amount. A proper turn. Upwind. Away.

Rose Emily went dark and angled off, now pointing into the oncoming southerly weather and aiming as far behind them as possible. I reckoned we should clear them undetected, unless they changed direction. The motion of the boat was suddenly different, which woke Jamie up. He was accustomed to the beam-on (side-to-side) roll. We all were – we'd been persevering with it since leaving Peru. We were intimate with the most subtle sounds and deviations. He stirred in the cabin, half aware of something happening. I rowed hard, adrenaline coursing.

I pictured the Peruvian flares that we'd bought, tucked away in the drybag. There was a bright orange flare pistol there, shaped like a toy gun. Only five rounds, each with deadly potential. The gun had been suggested by people who knew. I imagined how I'd use it. Squeezing the trigger.

But then the boat passed by, maybe 50 metres behind us, its hull piercing through the waves as it carried on into the night.

Maybe it had just been a lonesome fishing boat, after all.

Then slowly, unmistakably, the boat's position drifted to starboard. Had they spotted us? Were they coming back to get us? But it was us turning, not them. I couldn't understand it. I hadn't changed anything and the autopilot should have been keeping us on course, taking us off into safety. I dropped the oars and scrambled to the control panel as Jamie swung open the hatch. 'What's going on? Why aren't you rowing?' he said, urgency in his voice.

'There was a boat. They weren't on AIS, so I changed course to miss them. Something didn't feel right. Now the autopilot's gone haywire,' I replied.

Jamie climbed out of the cabin and took up the oars while I fumbled with the controls, stabbing at buttons, trying to blindly right our course. We had continued to waver and were pointing back towards Peru now, and then following the mysterious vessel, as the bow swung to and fro. I flicked a switch on the fuseboard: maybe a restart would work.

Nothing.

I tried again.

Still nothing.

By this point my shift was supposed to be finished and I was due to go to my bunk and rest. But the numbers on the screen were refusing to settle. The compass was still spinning, the boat still turning, uncontrollably. We would need to steer manually. But to make any forward progress, it meant I'd need to take over the helm, so Jamie could row.

There's little choice when a situation deteriorates like this. I was fully awake and still wired from the scare. But when you don't sleep on a schedule like ours, you don't just 'catch up later'. You accumulate a deficit. My concern wasn't that I'd be tired, however. It was that in all of our training, I'd never seen this problem before. We were less than two weeks in, and our autopilot was failing.

I'd brought a spare steering motor – three of them, in fact – because that's a common failure mode. They overheat and burn out. It was almost expected. But this wasn't the motor. It was the brain of the autopilot, the digital compass that guided us. We didn't have a spare brain. If the autopilot died, we'd have to hand-steer for the rest of the Pacific. Which would add months. Quite simply: if the autopilot failed for good, an unsupported row would be out of the question because we'd run out of food long before reaching Australia.

I switched on the Starlink and picked up a connection. A message went to Mark the boatbuilder, thousands of miles away in Holland, where the sun would just be rising. He replied almost immediately, so I called to explain. Within the hour, I was engaged in a back-and-forth with the manufacturer of the autopilot. A software update was sent.

I uploaded it to the system, hit the reset button, and waited. The little screen flickered, paused, and then settled. The compass was holding. We were back on course.

Relief washed over me, though a trace of unease lingered at the back of my mind. The problem felt like it had gone away too easily. And as the sky began to lighten, and the dawn finally arrived, one niggling question still remained: why had it failed in the first place?

DAY 011, Wednesday 23 April

EWAN: Song of the day – 'Bonny Light Horseman' by the Bonny Light Horseman

Trying to balance on only two feet is nearly impossible in most conditions. The churning water moves the boat around with oftentimes erratic, unexpected motion, so three points of contact are generally required. Imagine trying to move around a bus to get off while it weaves through traffic. Now imagine the bus has gone off road, down a ravine, and turned into a bucking bronco simulator. Oh, and the next stop is not for several months. The requirement for a steadying hand on a safety line or handrail means jobs must be completed either with only one hand, or by employing an awkward lean to try to compensate for the lurching motions.

The next issue is space. We are three relatively large men, living in a space the size of a large dining table. And because of the rolling seats, foot plates, hatches and solar panels, nothing is particularly flat. It's pretty slippery when wet, which is most of the time. And everything is made further challenging owing to the fact that you are always fastened to the safety lines, which run up and down the boat. This means lots of unclipping and reattaching if you need to move from one point to another, with the added annoyance of interrupting whoever you need to pass. There's no going for a casual walk just to stretch your legs or change the music.

Today was a frustrating day. A day when we felt these barriers more keenly as the hours wore on. Hard work on the oars with not many miles covered: only 36.5 nautical miles. Each of our backsides becoming raw and chafed with the salt and rubbing. Jamie scalded himself with boiling water, then we discovered many of the videos that we've been sharing from the boat haven't been received at all. Lastly, the autopilot failed again, requiring another reset. The same reboot got it working again, but there was no obvious cause in the first place, and that made me feel deeply uneasy.

Repairs at sea are slow. A ten-minute job will usually take 30, with breaks giving way to tedious workarounds, clenched teeth and grunting. Finding a replacement wheel for the sliding seats if a bearing went, for example, first required digging around inside the cramped cabin locker, where a hundred other things had inevitably been piled on top of one another. Tools for the repair couldn't just be taken out and placed on deck – you'd need to keep a hold of everything lest they roll away and disappear into the sea. Then you generally only had one hand to tackle things, as your other hand was preoccupied with holding you steady. The reward for your effort was often nothing more than an unsettled stomach, and before you knew it you'd be back on the oars with very little to show for it.

Technical issues were frustrating and draining, but the underlying fear was that something might break that I couldn't repair. I might not have had the spares, or the tools, or the know-how. And while a decade of experience as an engineer was helpful, it didn't make me a magician – you can't always bodge things with duct tape and optimism. I knew that Jamie and Lachlan had placed their faith in me to keep things running, and I felt the pressure of that. The laptop incident had been tough to stomach. But I dreaded a catastrophic failure that would bring our journey to an end. Something avoidable, if only I'd had better foresight.

Then one evening, a distressing message came through on the satellite phone. It was Seas the Day, the other rowing team, who were 20 miles north of our position. They had lost the ability to steer after their rudder had delaminated and snapped. The punishing side-on sea had been cruel and uncompromising and they were in the midst of trying to make urgent repairs.

Twenty miles was a manageable distance for us to cover, and it would be a direct run if we adjusted course right away. We were the nearest vessel to them, about eight hours' row; a short diversion north in the grand scheme of things. And by pooling resources we could possibly make the difference between Jess and Mims abandoning their mission or continuing onwards. The bottom line was that our friends were in need, and if another boat is in trouble, you do whatever you can to support and make sure that they're safe. It's a responsibility you accept the moment you go to sea. It's a maritime code of conduct that everyone follows.

But attempting to come alongside would almost certainly create complications, with both boats being relatively unmanoeuvrable in a big, rolling sea. So, with heavy hearts and deflated spirits, we were eventually told to stand down by their safety officer, who was guiding them from afar, and accept the limits of what was sensible.

The truth was, sadly, that we wouldn't have been much help. We may have had a few things they didn't, but the damage was too extensive and neither of our own spare rudders would have worked on their boat, as the design was too different. Even with the best will in the world it was unlikely we could assist in a meaningful way. Their trip was over. They needed to be rescued by a vessel capable of towing them back to safety, or taking them aboard after they'd abandoned their boat.

The journey to this moment had been plagued with setbacks and disappointment for Jess and Mims. It was heartbreaking that their attempt had ended so early – for we knew better than any how hard it was to get this far: years of preparation and sponsorship, grit and grind, all of it just to reach that hard-won start-line in Peru. To be towed back towards it only a few weeks later felt desperately unfair. But if I'd ever met two women resilient and determined enough to battle through, it's those two. I had every faith they'd find a way, to regroup, to recover, and come back stronger. A sailing boat eventually came to the rescue, and they were towed back to Peru to plan a second attempt.

It was a sobering reminder that the Pacific doesn't care how prepared you are, and it sharpened the fears that I already carried: that, without warning, things could come to a sudden, shuddering end.

DAY 012, Thursday 24 April

JAMIE : Song of the day – 'Can't Stop' by the Red Hot Chili Peppers

I really feel myself attracting what I am thinking.

After a very frustrating day, with a multitude of technical issues – a scald on my toes, terrible rowing conditions, and the news of Seas the Day – it's been easy to fall into a negative headspace. Quickly the whole experience becomes hard and over-whelming.

Unsurprisingly, the first nightshift is bleak, to say the least. The discomfort when you're rowing, resting, eating or sleeping is ever present. There's just no escape. We need to get used to this. As Nedd Brockmann (an inspiration to the three of us) says: we need to get comfortable being uncomfortable.

We start the day determined to turn a new leaf. We can't control the weather, technical issues are inevitable, we must eat well, keep on top of hydration, and, above all, stay positive. There is a shift. Ewan steps up to the oars after having psyched himself up at the bow, 'Can't Stop' by the Red Hot Chilis is playing on the speaker, he's ready to go the full 12 rounds and then some.

In the afternoon, we decide to clean the hull for the first time. I dive into the big blue, harnessed to the boat. This makes me feel uneasy – 700 miles from land, 3 miles deep, you just can't stop thinking about killer whales and sharks. We spotted a fin tracking the rudder only two days ago. 'SHARK!' Lachlan had yelled, as he pointed off the boat. I try to block it out and dive below. You'd need to be pretty unlucky to get bitten by a shark out here, but none of us had forgotten about John Fairfax, the ocean rower who'd been bitten by a shark while rowing the Pacific, and we'd been advised to be careful in the water, particularly as we approached Australia.

There is up to an inch of marine growth on the hull in places, a staggering amount for only two weeks at sea. We scrape away for an hour, rinse off with fresh water, pop on our evening playlist – the same one we always listen to – and glide through the water at what feels like double the speed.

Maybe we're just starting to get a bit more comfortable in the very uncomfortable environment, but something is changing.

DAY 014, Saturday 26 April

EWAN : Song of the day – 'Kinnoull', live at BBC Radio 2, by Barrule

We've not had any autopilot issues for a few days. A promising sign. Conditions have largely moderated, which has allowed us to forge a more westerly course with relative ease. We've lost much more ground north than we would have liked already, although with the Humboldt Current running up the coast of Peru and the southerly conditions, perhaps we should have expected this. Admittedly, the calmer spell has given the poor autopilot a bit of a break from the unrelenting beam-on weather conditions (the nautical term for lateral wind coming 90 degrees off the side, or 'abeam', of the boat) which has likely helped a little. The tonal groaning and whizzing of the actuation motor (which drives the rudder back and forth) has been a slightly less dominating amenity of the stern cabin for a few nights, at least.

After some head scratching, we've made a few changes. The interconnected nature of our electrical system means that the symptoms (i.e. intermittent loss of steering) may well be the result of problems elsewhere on the boat, not necessarily the place you'd think to look first.

I've identified grounding issues (where a system lacks a stable electrical path) as a potential cause for the autopilot going awry, and after an amount of probing around with a voltmeter, I discovered a loose connection on one of the solar panels. The location of this stray wire could certainly have given rise to circuit instability, thus causing electrical disturbances throughout the system and sending the autopilot into disarray. The loose cable has also likely been causing a reduction in solar capacity. So, in any case, our ability to charge the batteries and make water should be improved. For now, everything seems to be running as it should. However, I don't think I'll count my flying fish just yet.

I remember feeling a faint flicker of relief after finding that loose wire. Not because it was definitely the root cause of the problem, but because it was something. A tangible thing I could fix. A dislodged cable is a huge comfort when compared to an unknown gremlin living inside the circuit board.

Relief at sea, though, is light on the water. It dances for a moment before slipping into grey. And another problem was emerging, one that no amount of probing with a voltmeter would solve.

Our medical preparations had been extensive, even bordering on obsessive. We had been under the calm, considered guidance of my old friend Calum Fraser, a general practitioner specialising in sport and expedition medicine – a fitting combination. The team was then bolstered by our uncle, another Jamie Maclean, an orthopaedic surgeon with decades of experience fielding the medical mishaps of his three reckless nephews. Between them, we felt in the safest of hands.

They had put together presentations and spreadsheets, backed up with mountains of research – as if we were submitting a niche thesis for peer review. We'd done heart screening, suture training and full-body composition scans. We had antibiotics for ailments that none of us could pronounce, and carried enough drugs to open a medium-sized pharmacy. There were letters for customs in various languages, colour-coded checklists and evacuation plans. We had enough sterile equipment to reassemble ourselves, should there be a collision with a tanker, or a meteorite.

Calum had been meticulous. We'd even discussed a prophylactic appendectomy (where you pre-emptively have your appendix removed – thankfully deemed unnecessary). It was thorough. Just about enough to keep Mum happy. And we congratulated ourselves on listening carefully; quietly smug for being so well prepared.

But there's always something . . . It began as a mild discomfort. The sort of thing you dismiss in the early days, chalking it up to adjustment. A bit of friction here, a little rubbing there. Nothing alarming. But salt water, damp clothes and endless repetitions act with grim efficiency. Within days, the backsides that had confidently set off from Peru were actively protesting. And not long after that, they were red raw and refusing to co-operate.

Now, this wasn't a new problem, previously unencountered in ocean rowing. This was about as common as it gets. We had been warned, explicitly, to bring barrier creams. Sudocrem, and lots of it. Not a couple of tubes. Gallons of the stuff. Enough for industrial-scale application over multiple months.

'Get it in Peru,' Calum had said. 'It makes no sense to carry so much out on the flight.'

We nodded enthusiastically. Sensible advice. We were satisfied that everything else had been accounted for, and patted ourselves on the back triumphantly.

But we were men with many lists – too many, in fact. The kit list. The food list. The packing list. The contingency list. In La Punta, we even had a list of other lists, proudly displayed on a whiteboard at the yacht club. And when it finally came to ticking everything off during the inspection, we came to the medical list. With little hesitation, we ticked it all off. Calum had been rigorous, no need to check again.

Somewhere between the antibiotics for tropical diseases, the Israeli bandages, the vaccines for yellow fever, and the tourniquet for shark attacks, we had managed to forget the one thing designed to stop our arses disintegrating. It was there on the list, but it hadn't mattered.

So here we were, a few weeks into the Pacific, gingerly lowering ourselves onto the rowing seats like pensioners easing into a hot bath, wondering: what if it wasn't the boat that failed, but us? Calum's diligence had gone so far as to alert every last coastguard in the South Pacific Ocean of our expedition. And then we'd bottled the basics and were at risk of a slow, undignified undoing. It wasn't the ending we'd hoped for – or wanted to explain.

With my pride somewhat dented, I sent Calum several photos of my aggravated skin. From there we made a plan. We adjusted the seats to reduce friction by putting the pads inside lightweight drybags. The single tub of chamois cream was doled out like wartime butter. Even the lip balm was put into service. We began rinsing with fresh water after every rowing shift. And Jamie discovered a pair of Lachlan's boxer shorts, decorated with teddy bears in welly boots, which became the only thing he could tolerate wearing, should he wear anything at all. It wasn't particularly glamorous, or heroic, or comfortable. It turns out that not much in ocean rowing is.

DAY 017, Tuesday 29 April

EWAN: Song of the day – 'Sunset Boulevard Expedition' by Leif Vollebekk

On my second shift of the night, I counted a remarkable nine shooting stars. The Big Dipper is in the north, rotating anticlockwise before diving behind the horizon as the night drifts on by. The North Star must be just out of view, which gives a comforting sense of familiarity despite not being visible. To the south lie many stars that I don't recognise, and stretching across the entire night sky in a southeasterly direction is the Milky Way, shimmering like never before.

I listen to the entirety of Leif Vollebekk's album *Revelation*, and it feels as if it was written for the moment.

Sometimes I go down to the ocean
Sometimes it comes to me
Sometimes I cross the sea
I wind up in Sydney Harbour
And I gaze up yonder starboard
I pick out brand new constellations
The stars are out of whack
So I place them in alignment

– Leif Vollebekk, 'Sunset Boulevard Expedition'

Like a thread that runs beyond the horizon, connecting you to land, a song can pull you forward, help to lift the soul, carry you home to a familiar place of being. We deliberately rationed music, carefully withholding it. We drew sparingly from that well, and when we did, felt its resonance all the more. We made it matter.

One hour of music during the day, shared between the three of us, usually with an artist suited to the moment. It would get us through the heat, or the rough, or the rain. Or join us at dawn, when the light was just so. It was diverse. From the Prodigy to Dido. We'd then have a playlist at sunset, the same one each day. Fifty songs, played at random, for an hour at most. It was a small ritual, faithfully kept. Then an album for the nightshift, where I'd meet an old friend. A kind of reunion. A trip down memory lane. Often something from childhood. From home. Nothing more, often less. Often silence. And listening. And talking about dreams of building cabins in the woods.

This was what we'd settled on. A habit from the Atlantic, where corroded cables had restricted use of our phones. At the time, it was a crushing blow, rationing our music like that. But in the end, it was one of the best things that could have happened.

DAY 020, Friday 2 May

EWAN: Song of the day – 'Through the Echoes' by Paolo Nutini

Looming above the little multicoloured boat in the dead of night, a cloud gathers and grows. The dim light of guiding stars slowly fades, and my world is plunged into darkness. With shoulders heavy from toil, the rushing sounds of breaking waves fill my mind as they blindly burst through the swell, summoned by the murky depths below and shot skyward with unearthly power. A threatening, shapeless presence towers above, black against the dark sky. Alone, I pitch myself against the clamour, holding course against the odds.

Stars find gaps, and I'm joined by Jamie. 'Still here?' he says.

'Still here.'

The grip of night begins to lessen as we row together, exchanging few words. The brooding storm before us swells, yet with resolve we push forward, daring to steer up high against the wind.

And, as fate would have it, when we eventually emerge, a faint first light brings with it an altogether different view. Our unknown oppressor, that terrible mark against the sky, shows face. Not one great mass but many smaller wisps of cloud, now arranged before a fringe of gold. Tracing their edges as the colours change, we're filled with wonder, a magnificent white mountainous scene before us. Rays of light cast through the patchwork clouds shine down upon the sea, no longer seeming to fight our onward progress but urging us forward. I suppose that shining a light on fears can sometimes make them altogether disappear. Also, the cloud looked remarkably like a giant cauliflower.

One thing we had been so looking forward to was seeing wildlife up close, but much to our disappointment these encounters were few and fleeting. Not the bustling underwater wonderland we'd all been hoping for, while bobbing about in the world's largest ocean. On occasion a whale would pass, never staying long. Blowing in the night or flicking its tail above the water to make itself known before vanishing again. One had emerged recently, its flukes about half the width of our boat. Only Lachlan had spotted it, and thought it might have been a sperm whale, though he couldn't be sure. I wonder how often they passed beneath us unbeknownst. A rare sighting of a curious shark, tracking the boat in our wake, appearing in the wash, then slipping back below before we could get a proper look. Distant pods of dolphins, otherwise engaged. Perhaps we just weren't very good at looking – yet.

There must have been all sorts of activity beneath the surface. Sudden eruptions of flying fish suggested as much, bursting from the water and gliding a hundred feet or more, fleeing an unseen foe. They became our staple visitors. Skimming past the boat by day, evidently surprised to find something in their airspace and banking sharply to avoid us. At night we'd hear the fleshy thud of fishy missiles as they struck the cabins and skittered across the dark deck, often meeting their demise.

Pelagic seabirds – seabirds that spend most of their lives far out in the open ocean – were our other steadfast companions: inquisitive booby birds performing flyby inspections, tilting a dark eye towards us as if checking what sort of strange creatures we were; scattered flocks of terns swooping around unseen shoals of fish, wholly indifferent to our presence; joyful storm petrels skipping playfully across the surface, so light and cheerful. They never failed to lift our spirits.

And then there was Steve.

The only bird plucky enough to alight aboard *Rose Emily*, landing squarely on Lachlan's head. He was no tropical wonder of technicoloured plumage or melodious song. Steve was a seagull, plain and simple. Not being very imaginative chaps, we promptly named him Steve, although the gender remained unconfirmed. I'd love to blame our lack of creativity on sleep deprivation, but prior experience would suggest otherwise. After all, as boys we had shown great imagination in naming our pet hamster . . . Hammy.

The excitement on board, upon the arrival of our new guest, was wildly disproportionate to the reality of the situation. Could this be a solution to our hopeless method of sending back video files, having lost the laptop? Do you get carrier seagulls? Steve hopped onto the Starlink satellite dish and Lachlan tried to feed him a flying fish from the night before, presumably as a means of bargaining. Then Jamie ambled aft to say hello. Steve met him eye-to-eye, still perched on top of the satellite dish. Apparently not liking what he saw, he turned, evacuated his bowels all over the Starlink, and left.

DAY 026, Thursday 8 May

EWAN: Song of the day – 'Ruairidh's Revenge' by Beluga Lagoon

Weather is a fickle thing. If one aspect is off, it can completely negate the supporting effects of another that may be helping us along. Too much of a side wind and we slow down significantly, sometimes getting pinned. If this happens, the boat speed drops to almost nothing, and the waves arrive from the worst possible angle, usually crashing over the hull.

If the wind is in our favour but the waves are off then other issues ensue. There might be significant rocking, which makes rowing inefficient, frustrating and lopsided. Worse, beam-on waves usually mean lots of salt water coming aboard, washing over the deck. What follows are numerous physical discomforts, like salt sores, legs being smashed by oar handles, and plenty of effing and blinding.

Currents are somewhat mysterious and harder to predict. If they are working against the boat they can make it feel heavy and sluggish, reducing speed. Sometimes it can feel like rowing through cement, with vast amounts of effort required to move the boat along its course. Turbulent water swirling around the hull makes for irregular rowing strokes and further frustration.

The sun and rain have less of an effect on actual boat speed, however nobody wants to row in 30-degree-plus temperatures and baking sun, nor torrential rain and high humidity.

There was no let-up. Beam-on conditions had turned everything into a lopsided plod. The boat never seemed to settle into flow. One side of the body was always working harder than the other, until we felt bent out of shape, with blistered hands, scarred shins and sores in places that made every shift uncomfortable. The salt and rubbing from the seat pads had inflamed our backsides. Angry boils, deep in the skin, had emerged – the worst of them were right on the sitting bones. Discomfort never really left us. I'd sometimes see one of my brothers shifting his weight on the seat between strokes, and I'd know he was battling the same demons as I was. We'd all try to distract one another from the suffering. 'Look, that cloud looks like a surfing penguin,' I'd say, though it was tenuous at best.

At first we clung to the belief that it was nothing more than a phase, something to accept and push through before we finally reached the ocean proper. In the scale of it all, it was meant to be a short stretch. A few hundred miles, with the prevailing weather pushing us north and the cold flow of the Humboldt Current pulling us towards the equator. Then we'd be free of it. The routing charts agreed; centuries of knowledge of meteorological conditions were on our side. Once we cleared that invisible boundary and stepped out into the 'real Pacific', the trade winds would do as their name suggests. We'd soon be running with the weather and everything would be easier, and, to be honest, we simply couldn't bear the thought that it might be anything other than that. Superstition and the story we had told ourselves clouded our reality, as we plodded on with thinning hope.

At first it was 'once we clear the coast of South America'. Only a few hundred miles – less than a couple of weeks. And then it was three weeks. Then another. Five hundred miles became a thousand, then a thousand became two.

One afternoon I dared to check the chart-plotter, zooming out as far as I could go. I was wedged inside the stern cabin, hemmed in by bags of food and supplies, staring at the monitor on the port side by the hatch. I could feel the thin film of sweat and condensation that blurred the screen as I swiped my finger across hundreds of miles of ocean. I was trying to make sense of the tiny line we had drawn across that huge expanse of blue. The month we'd spent at sea had crawled by and we were only halfway between Peru and the first of the Pacific islands – about a fifth of the way to Australia. I tried not to think about it. Each day I'd been painfully aware that ground had been conceded. Ground that we would need to claw back in the weeks to come. But how far had we drifted? I moved around the map on the rugged, slightly unresponsive touchscreen. My stomach dropped as the numbers started to become clear.

The planned route was a straight line west, from La Punta to a waypoint off the southern end of Fatu-Hiva, a volcanic island of the Marquesas archipelago in French Polynesia, around 3,600 miles away. Sydney lay roughly 4,500 miles beyond that, in a southwesterly direction. The problem was, we'd been drifting north.

The difference was subtle. Instead of holding 270° on the compass (due west), we had averaged 277°, a handful of degrees off. Surely it didn't matter that much? Over a few hours, perhaps not. Over thousands of miles, it was another matter. It had been the only real strategic disagreement between us so far. Jamie and Lachlan preferred letting the boat run a little further downwind. Their justification had been reasonable: it would be easier rowing, less discomfort and better speed through the water. The thinking was that the weather would turn in a week or so, and we'd make up the lost ground when the conditions changed. But the weather hadn't changed.

I had felt we should accept a rougher row and a bit of discomfort in the short term to put us in a better position over the longer term. It also avoided adding extra miles to our journey, and I felt there was a risk that the forecast might be wrong. To me, it was the better trade-off. But the vote had always gone against me, each time I proposed a change. Whenever the weather had come a little in our favour, I'd nudge the boat south a few degrees, accepting I'd have a greater chance of getting wet and more of a beamy grind throughout my shift. Later, I'd find that Jamie or Lachlan had taken us back to the previous heading. We'd argue about it, then each time the decision would be two against one, and we'd slip a few more miles north.

How much did seven degrees on the compass cost? A day or two, perhaps? The sick feeling in my stomach gave way to a wave of frustration and anger as I realised we'd been pushed over 325 miles towards the equator. But it wasn't only those miles that we'd added to the journey. To get below Fatu-Hiva we would need to row back south again – another 325 miles. In other words, we had added 650 miles to the crossing. Weeks more rowing, maybe more. All I could do was shake my head and glare at the chart-plotter.

This was never going to be a heroic dash. It was a grinding never-ending endurance test with an infinite horizon and an indifferent sea. The Pacific covers more of the Earth's surface than all of the landmasses of every continent combined. The scale defies comprehension. And in that moment, I felt the weight of that more than ever.

But the lost ground wasn't the worst part of the reckoning. It was the news that had made me check the chart in the first place.

We had received a message from our router, which must have been as difficult to send as it was for us to read. The weather was no longer showing any sign of backing in our favour. The long-range forecast suggested that the beam-on conditions would remain entrenched. Not for the next week, but potentially until we reached the Marquesas – two thousand miles away. Another month at least.

I knew exactly what this meant. We had already spent a month living those conditions. A month of rowing crooked, sleeping damp and telling ourselves it would soon end. By giving those miles away, we had put ourselves in a worse position. A month to get here, carried by the hope of shifting winds. And now, no choice but to turn into the wind and slog through even worse conditions. The beam-on wind had blown that hope away. And the thought made me feel sick.

I was bitter for a while, and tried not to let it fester. There was no point directing any of it at Jamie or Lachlan. We had all made the best decision we could with what we knew, and, in truth, we were equally at the mercy of the weather. Dwelling on it wouldn't have helped. There was nothing to do but keep rowing. The horizon stretched out into eternity. A tiny boat in a huge, empty sea.

DAY 029, Sunday 11 May

EWAN: Song of the day – 'Lonely Island' by Amble

Northbound rain clouds drift, blurring the boundary between water and air before rising into the dawn sky above our transom. Dark grey and purple. Then juxtaposed with torn strips of orange light as the sun starts to ascend. Heavy squalls connect the sea and sky, mercifully missing our position by a few miles.

The water around the boat glistens with an oily appearance, soft and silvery, as it often does during these mysterious waking hours. The rest of the sky is placid: mostly clear with occasional billowing cumulus clouds, distributed with curious regularity and similarly sized, as far as the eye can see and eventually creating a distant wall of pink and grey on the surrounding horizon.

The heat of the sun and monotonous conditions make the day crawl by at a snail's pace. We cast a hopeful line and pray for change, both in our dinner plans and to the south by southeasterly weather.

Alas, we feel our morale slip as several tuna taunt us, skipping out of the surf a few metres behind the boat, jumping over the trawling line – not interested in our bait it would seem, and apparently mocking our attempts with frantic acrobatics. We resort to whispering sweet nothings to the sea.

Little changes and we catch no fish. Yet as the sun dips below the horizon, a full moon rises out of the sea, and it's another clear night, at least.

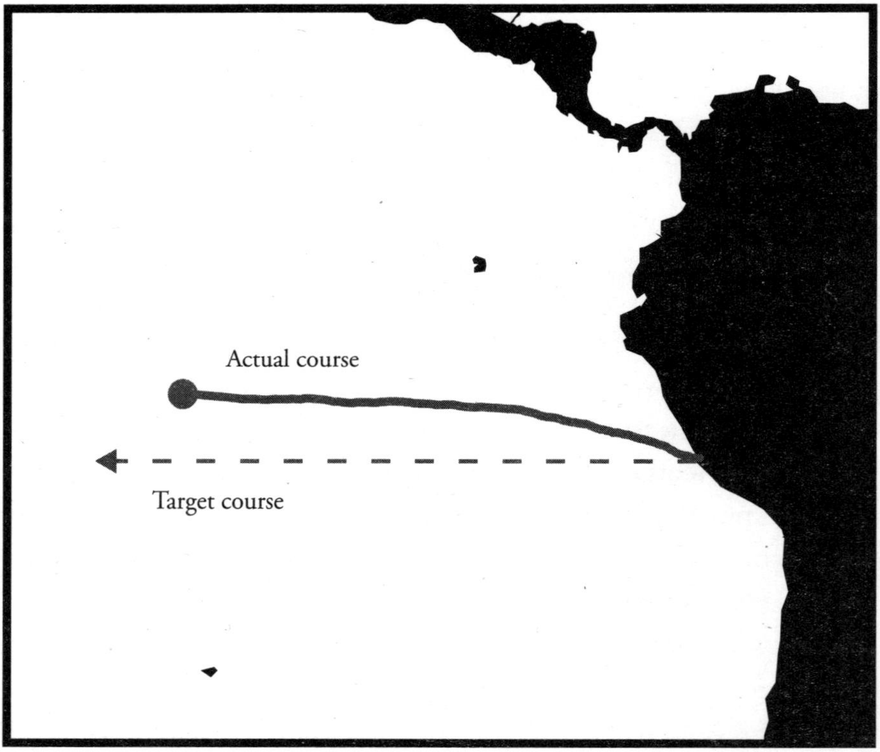

Day 30: The lost miles north

Chapter 7

Furthest from Help

By Jamie

There's a thread you follow. It goes among
things that change. But it doesn't change.
People wonder about what you are pursuing.
You have to explain about the thread.
But it is hard for others to see.
While you hold it you can't get lost.
Tragedies happen; people get hurt
or die; and you suffer and get old.
Nothing you do can stop time's unfolding.
You don't ever let go of the thread.

–William Stafford, 'The Way It Is'

After a month at sea, we entered the most isolated part of our crossing. We were the size of a midge floating on a huge loch. We'd been floating for 30 days and yet we still had over three-quarters of the loch to go until we reached the other shore. Specifically: 1,900 nautical miles rowed; over 5,800 still to go. An overwhelming prospect. Looking to the stars for perspective didn't necessarily help, it just amplified the magnitude of it all and highlighted the insignificance of us and our tiny boat. We all face existential questions throughout our lives, but they have never been more at the forefront of my mind than while floating in the middle of an ocean. My brain struggled to conceive the scale of where and what we were doing. There was a limitlessness, an unknown, a key missing piece of the puzzle that blocked my understanding. Like the feeling you get from a stirring line of poetry or a moving piece of music, there is an unmeasurable, uncommunicable wonder in these otherworldly places.

DAY 030, Monday 12 May

JAMIE: Song of the day – 'Isla' by Beluga Lagoon

The wind has picked up to around 18 to 20 knots, gusting at 25, and has moved a fraction to the east. That's the break we have all been praying for. A three-and-a-half to four-metre swell propels us forward as we attempt to surf the waves. These conditions raise our awareness; we are all slightly on edge. It's exciting but also quite tiring.

As we make our way westward into the heart of the southern Pacific Ocean we are entering a truly isolated part of our planet. Peru is now over 2,000 miles behind us, back to the east, and the Marquesas Islands are approximately the same distance west. A course directly north of around 1,800 miles would make landfall in western Mexico, and the nearest landmass to the south is Easter Island, 1,100 miles away.

A huge, vast nothingness in every direction. I've never been to a desert, but I imagine the feeling is similar. Exposed, raw and empty.

A good friend of mine, Alex Mackison, did his thesis on emptiness; conceptualising and studying the potential and beauty of the void. He recently told me, after he did a trip to Japan, of the application of emptiness in a Japanese tea ceremony. The teacup, once filled with tea, is simply a cup filled with tea. Or water, or milk, or apple juice, etc. Once filled, its possibilities become drastically limited. But the potential of an empty teacup, of a space that is yet to be filled, is endless.

Space gives way to possibility. The emptiness of the Pacific, much like a giant teacup that spans over halfway around the planet, has almost limitless potential. This nothingness allows our minds to truly wander. I don't think it will result in some sort of great epiphany – our cognitive abilities very much limit the potential of this. However, it does, at least for us, provide a rare opportunity to think in an unobscured way.

As my mind wanders, I spot a face forming in the clouds overhead. The profile appears as it extrudes out of the cumulus mass. Holy shit! It looks like Donald Trump. Hopefully something a little more profound will appear in the coming days.

Had we been on the Atlantic Ocean, we would be arriving into Antigua in a few days after 35 days at sea. I think back to that surreal moment: the flares, the foghorns, the familiar embrace of family and friends.

I remember our conversations just prior to arrival and the question being asked, 'How much would you have to be paid to wave to those on the shore, ready about and do it all again?' I recall the figure being high. And yet, we're staring down the barrel of just that; plus turning around and rowing back to the Caribbean again. Three times the distance of that monumental challenge six years ago.

Would I get off tomorrow if the option were there with no repercussions? Genuinely, I don't think I would. Even though it's been achingly hard at many points on this journey already, we knew what we were signing ourselves up for. And we were drawn to what lies in the uncharted waters beyond 35 days at sea.

Water stretched for thousands of miles in every direction. We realised that for many weeks the closest people to us were the astronauts on the international space station as it passed overhead. They would join us on our solo shifts, a twinkle of life amidst the dark night sky.

It is impossible to know exactly how you will react or feel in such a remote part of our planet until you are physically there. It's only by existing, unhurried, in a place so alien to the everyday that you're forced to address – and eventually embrace – the scale of it all. This acceptance was in many ways a coping mechanism. The barrelling waves and endless horizons hadn't changed for weeks, and they were inevitably going to last for several months more. We looked inwards to the boat and to ourselves, focusing on the smaller things, those within our control, like small acts of kindess between one another or a message of support from home. The gift of sharing out the sweets from one of our daily snack packs, or the act of preparing each other's meals. Small rays of positivity that would allow us to get through the next shift, or day, or week.

It had been incredibly hard and we still had so far to go. The news of the unchanging beam-on seas for the next 30 days had been a tough pill to swallow. Coupled with the realisation of the miles we had added due to our northern arc, our positive feelings towards this row balanced on a knife edge. To help prevent a negative spiral, we did what we could to distract ourselves from the ever-present discomfort and monotony.

Our daily distractions and companions existed as figures in the heavens. The clouds form all manner of shapes and sizes when land is no longer an obstacle. To help with the passing of time we started a new game of finding things – objects, people, animals – in those clouds. A never-ending source of amusement, it forced us to be ever present, scouring the vast sky for that unmistakable shape. And with presence there came a peace of mind. An acceptance. Suddenly the scale of the challenge didn't seem quite so overwhelming. Mice made a regular appearance, stooping into the wind as they marched towards the setting sun; their backs bent, noses crinkled, battered by the elements as they scurried beyond the horizon.

It was a matter of disassociation, both physically and mentally. In many ways we wanted to forget that we were rowing; becoming so in tune with the boat and our bodies that a type of flow state could take over. This alleviated the connection between the action of rowing and the negative thoughts that arose from doing this activity all day and night. Our thoughts and conversations steered us away from what was mundane and exhausting and towards what was hopeful and pleasant. We moved into a more positive headspace that allowed us to enjoy the experience. I suppose it was like meditating. Our oar strokes acted like the grounding of breath, a metronome to the day. We acknowledged thoughts, considered them for a short while before casting them off into the ocean breeze. I thought of home, of our croft in the northwest of Scotland. The old oak tree and the birch and hazel saplings that would now be wrapped in new leaves of tender green. I imagined firing up the pizza oven, enjoying a chewy and slightly charred base, with plum tomatoes and molten mozzarella. I savoured each slice, sitting under the shadow of the canopy and listening to the song of small birds. A feisty wee wren let out a series of tweets. I listened to the high-pitched chirps for an unknown amount of time. The scene began to fade. I was back on the boat with a faint smile upon my face.

This was by no means the case all the time. In fact, it was more of an ideal to strive towards. Good days would come and go without me even noticing the passing of time. But during more difficult moments, when conversation didn't appeal and my thoughts were confused and hazy, I would be left uncomfortable and frustrated on the oars. I tried to fixate on something, anything, that would remove my mind from the present moment. Mental arithmetic of how long the next tub of peanut butter might last: ½ kilogram, perhaps 60 teaspoons, 2 each per day meant 10 days total remained. That seemed a push. And that didn't account for Lachlan's newfound habit of dipping his oatcakes on nightshift. My distractions, when in this sort of negative headspace, only fed off one another to make my outlook even worse. I now additionally resented Lachlan, or Lala as we call him, for his unfair share of our communal goodies.

We were aware of these negative spirals, and did everything we could to avoid falling victim to self-pity and discontent. But sometimes the heat of the sun was simply too great and the discomfort of raw skin rubbing on salty shorts all too apparent. The anger brimmed and boiled and would be released in a flurry of curses flung towards the ocean. As if somehow the ocean itself was to blame.

DAY 033, Thursday 15 May

JAMIE: Song of the day – 'Of Land and Sea' by Amble

The waves can't make up their minds. Like the wind, they're coming from all directions; slip, slap, slopping on board. It's been cloudy, with patches of sun throughout the day. We're grateful for the shade but need to be mindful about energy usage and our ability to make water.

The idea and application of physical disassociation was introduced to us by Chloë Lanthier. Disassociating upper and lower body, left and right; power on one leg, less on the other. In theory it made total sense, but it's only really after a month at sea with beam-on conditions that we recognise how instrumental this part of our preparation has been.

It's fascinating reflecting on some of the exercises we've done over the past 12 months and how they apply in reality on board *Rose Emily*. During our training, if Chloë said jump, you jumped. Extend that arm and lift that leg, you did it. Reach for your toes and crunch side-on with a ball between your knees, no problem.

The first time doing many of these exercises we ended up sprawled across the gym floor like beetles on their backs. I would hate to give the impression that our training entailed some sort of militaristic dynamic between us and Chloë. Or that it was blind faith. On the contrary, it was founded in deep-rooted respect for her knowledge and understanding of how the human body works and how best to physically and mentally prepare for a challenge like this. How our bodies are feeling at this moment in time (considering the conditions we've had for the past 30 days) is only a testament to this. We haven't had a single serious physical issue between the three of us. Of course, there's been the unavoidable deterioration of our skin due to sun, sweat and salt, but our muscles, joints and tendons feel remarkably good (albeit slightly lopsided). With what seems like a never-ending side-on wind and waves, it's impossible to get a clean stroke in. One leg pushes harder than the other, one oar misses, the other catches a crab. Not literally, but in rowing terms this is when one of your oars catches the surface of the water as you recoil and return for your next stroke. It is jolting and disrupts the flow of movement. Like tripping over a tree root while on a run, or missing a step when descending some stairs. We all feel slightly side-on C-shaped; our right sides working considerably harder than our left. A few more weeks of this and it might seem like there's three lobsters on the oars, baked pink by the heat of the Pacific sun.

Last night was a pleasant surprise. Aside from a wave landing on my lap mid shift, and a subsequent strip-down to wash off the salt, naked, under the light of a full moon, I would say I had my best nightshift to date. The boat and my body did the rowing while my mind was set free to ponder fond memories of people and places, good times had and yet still to come. It was a pleasant way to spend my 90 minutes on the oars.

The somewhat serene night ended with me doing an interview on BBC Radio Scotland at 4.30 a.m. boat time. I fired up the Starlink and connected just in time. I did put on my shorts for the interview, although they wouldn't have known. Went well, I think – always hard to say, in this strange sleep-deprived state. I crawl back into the cabin for my last 90-minute kip and dream of Nesquik powdered chocolate milk.

I'll be bringing some of that if there's a next time.

Day 35, Saturday 17 May, was a pivotal moment. It was the first major milestone of the crossing, marking a significant step into the unknown. I was nervous. Not because of a fear of the unknown, but an apprehension towards my intrusive thoughts. Those notions that come to you when you are alone or feeling weak. During the fragile moments of a solo nightshift or the half-waking state at the sound of your alarm. It was never a question of why, but what if? What if we began to hate the experience? What if our limit was 35 days? What if the autopilot broke again or the food went off? What if we failed? The thoughts would soon pass; however, it wasn't until we passed that five-week mark that I could begin to put some of my concerns to rest.

We had expected this part of the row to be monotonous and hard. But there were certainly moments when it felt like a never-ending purgatory of beam-on conditions – all day, every day – with waves crashing over our bodies.

The only thing we could count on for some variety were the roving squalls. What began as a grey haze of rain up-wind quickly developed into a tropical squall. We would estimate the time of its arrival, toying with the decision to either layer up or strip off. The latter would at least allow you to have a shower, but if the tempest had plans to remain for a short while then a chill could set in, and drying off without the sun was almost impossible. When that happened you would pay any amount of money for the best foul-weather gear available to keep you dry and comfortable when the environment was at its most hostile. Luckily we had just that, in the custom made garments from Atacama Performance, designed specifically for our trip.

Before you knew it, the squall hit. The whole exercise was like a choreographed dance; the weather had its own rhythm and we would desperately try to keep in time. The safety lines running up the length of the boat shook violently, sounding like the beat of a drum. The wind screeched as the pounding rain thumped against the deck. White spumes and salt spray were thrown into the air. Pushing hard with both oars, there was no other option but to go with the weather. A well-placed stroke at the crest on an incoming breaker was the moment we were waiting for. A heartbeat of suspense as the bow of *Rose Emily* hinged forward, a pause, and then dived furiously down the face of the wave. We were surfing with over a tonne of momentum; her flat-bottomed hull skimming along the surface of the water as the ocean rushed past.

If we had the time we enjoyed music in these moments of chaos. As a gale shrieks past, there's nothing quite like some singing to help calm the nerves. A scramble for our waterproof speaker, and if we were lucky, a selection of songs to reflect the feeling on board. Often, we would go electro-trad – 'Marx Terrace (Valtos Remix)' by the Peatbog Faeries or 'Iain McGee's' by Niteworks – think house music with an infusion of bagpipes and violin. Occasionally, depending on the time of day, we might opt for something a little more reflective. I recall opening the cabin door one morning after a particularly heavy squall to find Lachlan, alone on the oars, singing at the top of his voice to Dido's 'White Flag' – one of our mum's favourite songs.

DAY 036, Sunday 18 May

JAMIE: Song of the day – 'Candy' by Paolo Nutini

The wind has, thankfully, moved slightly eastward in our favour. Accompanied by smaller waves and a decent current, we make good headway due west under relatively comfortable conditions: 70 miles rowed today; 2,438 rowed in total; 5,443 still to go. The sun still punishes us overhead, but we'd be fools to think that'll change anytime soon.

The next three weeks is now the focus: keep a positive outlook while pushing on through to halfway at the Marquesas. This small cluster of islands has been our aim since we set off from Lima. Australia is still overwhelmingly far away, but the Marquesas, positioned just under halfway across this vast ocean, mean we will be so close to the tipping point of our psychological battle with the scale of this challenge. A few days beyond the islands and we'll finally have less to row than what we have rowed to date.

We'll use treats as milestones to give us something to look forward to. A Tony's Chocolonely chocolate bar for every 1,000 nautical miles rowed (we only have ten bars left) accompanied by a fresh cup of Cairngorm Coffee's Guilty Pleasure, our cousin's speciality coffee beans, roasted in Edinburgh and packed on board for special occasions. An extra packet of jelly sweets will be handed out every 500 nautical miles, to help span the gaps in progress. Our rationed use of music is working well and provides a daily highlight through the communal listening of a shared playlist called Singalong PAC. Beluga Lagoon, Paolo Nutini, Leif Vollebekk and Amble have been our regular companions as the sun dips below the horizon and the moving landscape is shrouded in black.

We've set our expectations of reaching our first islands on 9 June. After this date we should have fewer miles to row than we have covered to date, which will be a psychological turning point. The discomfort will no doubt continue till the very end of this voyage, but breaking it down into these bite-sized chunks makes it seem a little more manageable.

While digging about in the starboard deck locker for a tube of toothpaste I find a Tupperware of mine deep down in the bilges. Prior to departure I got quite excited at the prospect of trying to grow something on board to augment our freeze-dried rations. I dig out some of the planting paraphernalia: clear Tupperware, dehydrated coconut husk pellets and a variety of seeds.

I spend the next few off-shifts preparing the pellets, rehydrating them with desalinated water and sowing a range of lettuce seeds. Strapped to the top of the rear cabin my mini-greenhouse seems quite happy; my old teachers from Rudolf Steiner's would be proud. I've always enjoyed the process of planting things. I remember being immensely proud of my carrot patch at Steiner's, the fantastic and somewhat alternative school I attended until the age of 15. I draw so much hope from planting seeds. The potential of what those little things can become never ceases to amaze me. Time will tell if we see any life from this odd-looking lunch-box, but it's been a welcome distraction from the afternoon slump. I daydream of tuna steaks and a crisp fresh side salad; unhelpful but enjoyable.

It's a dark night tonight, with the waning moon cloaked in shrouds of cloud. The first shift goes well; however, I've eaten through most of my snacks due to an unlucky snack-pack draw in the morning. Each ziplock bag contains approximately 2,000 calories of food, including our breakfast oats. For variation's sake each pack is slightly different. They are packed at random inside two giant drybags in either cabin, and so selection, like pulling a present out of Santa's sack, is also at random. Yesterday Ewan accused me of rigging the system, which I took a little personally. While I was responsible for the packing, I had little control over the fate of each bag. He's missed out on Dairy Milk bars now for five days running and has taken it to heart.

The second nightshift is long and tiring; I struggle through with teaspoons of peanut butter to assist.

We are beginning to see improvements in the cabins as we eat through the bags of provisions. A somewhat musky smell has settled into almost everything, including us. It's not unpleasant, just slightly odd. Perhaps an outsider would say otherwise.

As dawn breaks I toast goodbye to the moon with a baby beaker filled with freshly made coffee. The bag, in reaching the two-thousand nautical-mile mark, has lasted well and provided much joy these past few days. The only thing that could make this moment even better – a freshly baked croissant. I've been thinking about pastries quite a lot recently. Alongside fresh fruit and veg, baked goods are really something you begin to miss out here. A crusty, chewy sourdough, or a flaky, indulgent pain au chocolat. I wish we'd brought some Stroopwafels on this crossing like we did on our Atlantic row . . .

The milestone treats of Tony's Chocolonely, Cairngorm Coffee and jelly sweets gave us highlights to look forward to, weeks in advance. Each evening the sound of Singalong PAC was significant, too: a small victory, a ritual that marked the end of one more day.

The instruments had, in many ways, been a nuisance up until this point. Other than declaring our departure from Lima, they had been awkwardly wedged in the top/front of the bow cabin. In big seas the guitar and accordion often became dislodged, bouncing onto one of us as we slept below, declaring their arrival on our unconscious bodies with a squeal or a twang.

But once we began to settle into our new life at sea, and one of us felt particularly inspired, the sounds of live music echoed across the deck and provided a rare opportunity to physically do something other than rowing. On the evening of 19 May, our 37th day at sea, I sat leaning against the bow cabin, bagpipes under my arm. My fingers were rough and calloused but I could still just about squeeze out my favourite slow air, 'Hector the Hero'. A couple of tunes later and the muscles in my lips began to go. It was a sign that I needed to play them more often, otherwise it would be a very squeaky arrival if I planned to play them when we made it to Australia.

We seemed destined to replicate our luck with the fishing rod in Scotland but we persisted every couple of days. There's a keen excitement in casting out a carefully selected shiny lure, and the anticipation that follows of what it might bring. We each adopted different methods, whispering promises to the water to entice a fish. Ewan occasionally sang, Lachlan would hum, I tended to keep quiet, channelling my inner hopes and dreams for a fish supper. As the tuna flung themselves out of nearby waves, they taunted us with the occasional wink. (Apparently, this is not possible due to their lack of eyelids, but they somehow achieved the same sentiment.) I was determined to catch something soon. The rod had been rigged off the stern cabin for over three weeks now, a daily reminder of what could be. I dreamed of a fried tuna steak on a bed of fluffy freeze-dried rice, topped with chilli and soy sauce. We'll get there with time, I murmured to myself.

Despite our greatest efforts, nothing seemed to work. At least not for the catch we desired. Flying fish, however, came at us in droves, with a tendency to strike during the night. At first sight they are wondrous little creatures, defying the odds of who and what they are by taking to the heavens: a leap of faith. Evading the jaws of their pursuers they would glide between the thresholds of worlds. Some succeeded, others were less fortunate, meeting a swift end by colliding with us and our boat. It was all quite sad. The small ones seemed to have the least

Highway to the world: with our 16-foot fibreglass boat, next to our dad, Charlie, near our spiritual home in Assynt, Scotland. We got lost out on the water many times on ill-advised fishing expeditions.

Building the crew: with sports scientist Chloë Lanthier, who put us through our paces for months on end, to prepare us psychologically and physically for the duration of the Pacific row – and, importantly, to keep us injury-free.

The three of us helping construct the Pacific boat in Mark Slats' workshop in the Netherlands. We knew that the best way of us knowing how to fix the boat that was going to keep us alive across the Pacific was to help build it.

Practising capsizing in training. A capsize at sea was one of the things we most dreaded happening out on the Pacific. Doing it deliberately in training meant that we would at least have a chance of it feeling familiar if it happened.

A last lie-down, just before we did our final packing of the boat in Lima, Peru.

Lowering the boat into the water for departure at Yacht Club Peruano in Lima. Many friends, supporters and well-wishers came to send us off. You can just make out Jamie playing 'Hector the Hero' on the bagpipes.

Jamie being sick over the side of boat in our first days at sea. Seasickness was one of the first big challenges we faced, invariably made worse by losing sight of the horizon while we were in the cramped cabins. Lachlan, amazingly, was unaffected.

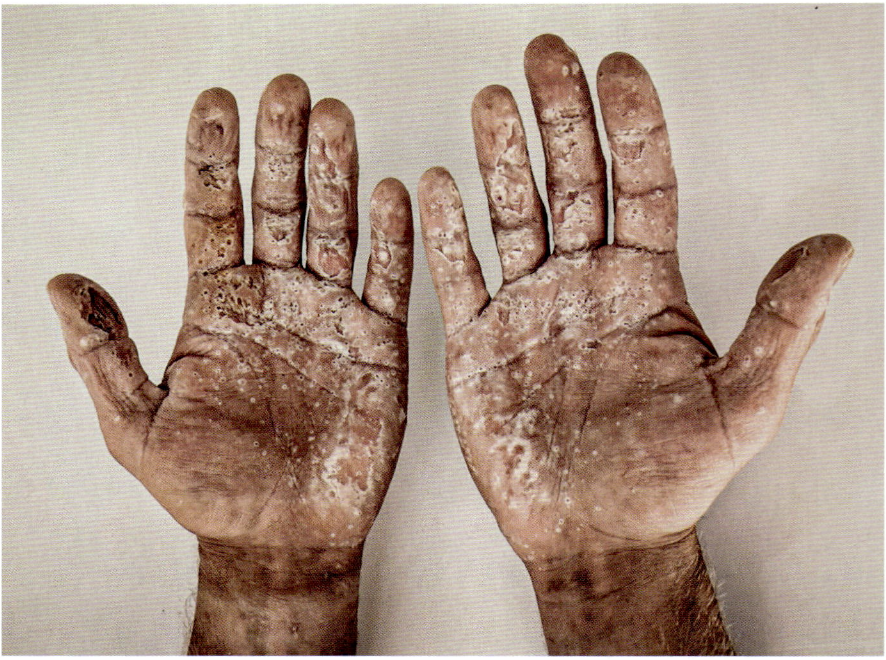

Ewan's hands after 35 days at sea. Spending so many hours at the oars each day, combined with the constant spray of salt water on our bodies, meant that our skin sorely paid the price.

Tropical storm on the Pacific. The threat of storms and squalls was constant. But when storms came, we were often torn between stripping off to enjoy the sheer relief of a rain shower, and the risk of becoming shiveringly cold.

Cleaning the hull of *Rose Emily*. Removing the layers of molluscs and gooey brown algae was essential for reducing the boat's drag in the water. Plunging into the depths was terrifying at first, but we soon learned that the routine lifted our spirits.

Lachlan playing the accordion. Music – whether played by us, or booming out from a playlist on our communal speaker – was essential in keeping our energy and positivity going through the relentlessness of the row.

Dropping anchor and chain at the Loyalty Islands, New Caledonia, while sheltering from a storm. Pausing in such a paradise should have felt like a heaven-sent rest. Instead, after rowing for so long, we found ourselves busying ourselves with jobs and itching to get going.

Australia ahoy. As we rowed into Cairns marina, after 139 days at sea on Saturday 30 August, 2025, we lit up our flares, and Jamie lit up his bagpipes – in his case, literally, as the flares set fire to his pipes.

Terra firma. Hand in hand, we stepped onto dry land together, brains wobbly, legs even wobblier, but overwhelmed with relief and a sense of achievement.

We'd rowed 9,753 miles, non-stop and unsupported. Our arrival felt dreamlike. This was actually the first time we had hugged each other – let alone any other person – since leaving Peru more than four and a half months earlier.

One of the cyanotype prints created by our mum, Sheila Maclean, that she made each week from the photos we sent her, to accompany our dad's weekly round-up of our daily ship's logs.

amount of control, perilously travelling at the mercy of the wind. Something that we seemingly had in common.

Every morning, we were met with a massacre on deck. Fledgling youngsters to foot-long monsters, their numbers mounting to dozens each day. Earlier on in the crossing I attempted to return them to their watery home, saddened by witnessing so much suffering and death. That quickly became quite tiresome. The ones that were missed during the morning clean-up rapidly began to rot under the scorching sun. Degrading bits of fish got stuck in every nook and cranny – drybags, hatches, shoes. It was extra admin we could do without. We had already fallen victim to several attacks from these wayward beasts, and as their size increased so did our concerns.

DAY 037, Monday 19 May

EWAN: Song of the day – 'Crescendo' by Niall McCabe

This new oversized variety of flying fish – at least the size of a large mackerel – has given rise to a certain amount of anxiety. Instead of just being a nuisance, with scales and chunks of rotting fish strewn across the deck, they have become something of a safety concern. How big should we expect these things to get? When we left Peru, they were no larger than the length of my forefinger. But if they continue to grow at this rate, they'll be the size of a small child by the time we reach Australia. 'That guy who was killed by a wee fish jumping out the water' would be how you'd be remembered, forever more. No one would believe, or care, it was some kind of giant mutant of the deep with flying superpowers. A terrible prospect.

It wasn't until day 37, a third of the way across, that our luck with the rod finally changed. Frustrating conditions in the morning had given way to a decent breeze and following seas. We rowed in silence, but for the sound of the waves and the oars. Then suddenly, something else. A new sound. The unmistakable high-pitched zip of the fishing reel. I didn't dare to believe it. A fish was on the line, which was spooling out fast. Very fast. We'd had a couple of nibbles like this over the past few weeks and all had gotten off. One even managed to bend the metal hooks on our lure; probably a blessing that it got away.

Lachlan, ready at stern position, unclipped the rod and ensured the line was kept taut. Winding up the tension on the reel, the fish continued to take yard after yard of line. It was clearly a whopper and it was very much in control. The boat slowed a little with the drag of this monster from the deep. Lala played it from port to starboard, and even up to the bow. Edging it in, we caught a glimpse of a long, silvery grey mass in the water. Mahi mahi, perhaps? It didn't have the right vibrant colours. Tuna? It didn't seem to be the correct shape. Shark? But there was no obvious fin.

I was on the oars keeping the boat on her course. Ewan stood ready, fish hook in one hand, action camera in the other. After 45 minutes of attempting to tire the fish, it was brought alongside and Ewan went in with the hook. The fish freaked; there was still life in it yet.

Diving below the boat, it wrapped the line around our daggerboard. 'Ya canny bugger,' I thought. Acting quickly, we shifted footplates to lift the daggerboard – a retractable board in the centre of the boat that helped to keep us on course in adverse conditions. The line was released, and the fish moved back alongside the port. Was that its final attempt at freedom? Who knows? It was now or never. Lala reeled in the final metre of line, Ewan swooped in with the hook and landed a successful blow, midfish. Heaving with all his might, he brought the catch on deck. Slight panic ensued; it was absolutely massive – somewhat similar to a gigantic mackerel, but one the length of Ewan. A quick message on the satellite phone to our cousin later helped to identify the beast. After a bit of back and forth it was confirmed as a wahoo. Aka, very good eating.

The fish was thrashing about on deck – this wasn't over yet. Ewan, performing an unconventional wrestling move, pinned it down. Knees pressing on its tail, both hands firmly grasped around its head, he looked slightly panicked. Amid shrieks and yelps he shouted, 'It's nearly the size of me, goddamn it, I can't hold it for long. Someone, in with the knife!' I grabbed the Leatherman from inside the cabin door and dispatched the fish as swiftly as possible. I figured a blade in between the eyes in the centre of the head should do the trick. The fish, thrashing with one last heave, freed its head and sheared off the blade of the knife. I stepped back. It was done. We took a moment to let it all sink it.

The fish was approximately 1.2 metres in length and weighed around 25 kilograms – the largest fish any of us had ever seen, let alone landed on a boat. After a quick bit of online research I got to work with the filleting knife; an hour and a half later and we had approximately 60 wahoo medallions about the size of a small fist.

The first were eaten lightly, fried with a pinch of salt. The second round with soy sauce, honey and chilli. Round three and four were poached in a tomato and chilli soup. We'd eaten about 3 kilograms each and we'd barely made a dent. The remaining fish was put into ziplock bags and stored in the bilges below the watermaker – the coolest area of the boat. We ate medallions for every meal that day, but sadly by breakfast the following morning it was no longer enjoyable. As the sun rose and the fish warmed, our lack of refrigeration had taken effect and the remaining couple of kilos of Wahoo developed the pungent fishy smell of something beginning to rot. We tossed the last fistfuls overboard and ushered our thanks to the sea.

As the sun hung low in the sky and golden rays of light shimmered across the waves, Ewan dug out his guitar and started up a tune at the bow. 'Candy' by Paolo Nutini. The high notes were a little off, and the guitar was definitely out of tune, but there was something truly magical about that moment. Lala and I hummed along, joining in at each chorus. As we floated along, the *'evening on my tail'*, it all just seemed to make sense.

Life aboard *Rose Emily* became an intensified and distilled version of life on land. Many things no longer mattered – emails, bin day, shopping lists, train schedules – but the simple things, like food, hydration and routine, had never been so important. My relationship with electrolytes had never been so profound. The days that we forgot to properly hydrate were unquestionably the hardest of the crossing.

The effects were both physical and psychological. Headaches, fatigue and muscle cramps might be obvious, but much worse was the overwhelming feeling of impending doom. My entire outlook on the day would shift, each task becoming ten times harder to complete. I was irritable, anxious and altogether difficult to be around. We all were. More often than not, when one of us fell out of sorts – the challenge too great and the ocean too vast – a litre of electrolyte would quietly settle things straight.

DAY 037, Monday 19 May (log entry continued)

EWAN

This morning, I awoke with a bit of a sore head, which progressed into a rather frustrating day of feeling pretty dire on the oars in the overwhelming equatorial sun: unable to focus on much, blinking back a sweaty headache, and wishing for even the smallest bit of comfort. Inspiration runs a little thin when things aren't going so well, and writing my log as the boat sloshed around required some extra effort.

Leftover electrolyte sachets in my snack pack from yesterday are a clear indication that I wasn't particularly strict with my hydration. I didn't drink enough and now I'm feeling the consequences. This is undoubtedly the root cause of my discomfort. Very little else has changed and it's something we experienced a few times on the Atlantic: poor hydration makes you feel terrible. I look out to sea and begin to feel quite overwhelmed. We're barely past mid-May, and with more than twice the same amount of time to go I honestly don't know how we are going to get through the next few weeks, let alone several months.

I'm off the oars and Jamie and Lachlan ask me to fill their water bottles. I feel a swell of frustration come over me, close my eyes and let out an audible, 'For fuck sake.' I'm tempted to say no, angry that they are robbing me of my precious few moments of rest. Why can't they fill their own fucking bottles during their off-breaks?

But then it dawns on me how unreasonable I'm being. Either one of them would do the same for me without question. I realise my annoyance is rooted in exactly what they are trying to avoid. And, swallowing my irritation, I ask them to pass their bottles back.

Prior to rowing an ocean, where life aboard is regimented and there are fewer variables, I didn't appreciate the extent to which hydration can affect your mood and wellbeing. I'm not just talking about having a bit of a headache. Your entire outlook on life shifts to become altogether more gloomy, long before you might feel thirsty. On land there are simply too many other things going on, which mask the experience and make it less obvious how much hydration can influence you.

Second only to hydration was our food. Thankfully, my fears and anxieties had not yet materialised; our supplies had not yet gone off.

We took it in turns to prepare the food for each day. Sitting at the stern position, one of us would dig out the Jetboil, freeze-dried meals and any special toppings required for that day's menu – limes, olive oil, mango chutney, chilli, etc. All eyes focused in. The Jetboil gimbal hadn't worked as planned, and so more often than not the stove and vessel of boiling water were precariously wedged in the corner of the deck. Once the water had been added to each mylar bag, like kids at Christmas we would wait for the food to rehydrate. Conversation often turned to the finer points of freeze-dried curry. Perhaps it was the case that our taste buds had changed, but the freeze-drying process had seemingly imbued a certain complexity to the meals we had on board – like the richness you find in a lasagne or stew the day after it has been made. The lamb saag was tender and rich, the chilli chicken punchy and full of flavour.

We knew coming into this challenge the importance of food on both our physical and mental wellbeing. It was why we invested so much time and effort in making the meals in the first place. It was the lynchpin in ensuring our emotional state remained positive. We had various methods for boosting morale on board: fishing, music, audiobooks, spotting clouds. But none were as effective as food.

DAY 39, Wednesday 21 May

JAMIE: Song of the day – 'The Load-Out' by Jackson Browne

We have hit one-third, both in terms of distance and time. At least we hope we have.

With 2,640 nautical miles under our belts we celebrate with a few treats: a new bottle of olive oil, instant hot chocolate and a packet of jelly sweets.

Frustrating conditions in the morning give way to a decent breeze and following seas. We expect it not to last but, as it stands, we're making good progress. This feels like the first proper milestone. However, there's at least x2 the same distance and time to go. It is all still quite daunting. We have provisions for 150 days, but due to the Fizzy Fangs fiasco (see below) we only have sweets for 60 days' worth of snack packs. That's a crushing thought.

We march on our stomachs. Big or small, when undertaking a physical challenge there's no escaping the importance of food. Safe to say, it's the one thing that's forever on our minds.

So what's on the menu?

We kick the day off with a lucky dip on the snack pack front. All contain the basics (oats or muesli, nuts, etc.), with the treats varying from pack to pack. The bag to hope for contains:

- Muesli – 150g
- Seeds and granola – 20g
- Dried cranberries and mango – 50g
- Salt and vinegar peanuts – 65g

- Kinder bars x2
- Nairn's savoury biscuits/oat cakes – 1 pack
- Nairn's sweet biscuits – 1 pack
- Drumstick Squashies sweets – 60g
- Mixed nuts (walnuts, Brazil, macadamia) – 70g
- Electrolyte mix x4
- Peanut butter x2 spoonfuls
- Freeze-dried berries – 10g
- Instant coffee sachets x2

The daily challenge faced by us all: what do you eat, and when? Break into the Squashies too early in the day and it's all downhill from there. This happened yesterday. I normally hold off on opening any sweets until after lunch, ensuring I have something sugary to help me through the heat of the afternoon. But for some reason I dug in at 10 a.m. By 2 p.m. I had three Squashies remaining. A pitiful amount. I didn't see the point in saving the final few so they were gone within the next hour. I knew I would regret it. I watched as Lachlan opened his at 4 p.m. He had a full packet for when he needed it most. He teed them up, three at a time, in a line beside his seat. Picking them off one by one in ten-minute increments. The packet lasted from late afternoon through to the twilight hours. I thought about grabbing one while his back was turned. Would he even notice? I'd need to unVelcro my feet, which would no doubt forewarn him of oncoming movement. Maybe I could just extend, a couple of inches more – like a dog trying to grab a treat that is just out of its grasp. Stretching, reaching, hoping that one might fall my way. Lachlan's head turned. 'What on earth are you doing?' he asked. 'Ahh, my lower back is feeling super tight, just trying to stretch it right out,' I answered. But I couldn't keep the smirk from my face. He knew exactly what was going on. He turned, popped the last one into his mouth and went back to rowing. The ruse was over. As I focused back on my oars I heard a little tap beside me: a Squashie had fallen from the heavens and landed on the deck right beside my foot. A small act of kindness. I looked up. Lachlan didn't turn, but I knew he'd thrown this desperate dog a bone.

Typically, 7 a.m. heralds coffee, occasionally made into a mocha if we feel we have deserved it.

Our biggest treat of the day comes at 10 a.m.: pasta (of which there are a few variants). We're obsessed with the pastas. Served with either tomato and garlic sauce, arrabbiata or ratatouille. A splash of olive oil and a sprinkle of Parmesan (supplies of which are rapidly dwindling), shut your eyes and you could be on a gondola in Venice.

Next up, at 1 p.m., either Thai red sweet potato curry or veggie bean chilli, both with a squeeze of fresh lime. The limes are stored in a small drybag on deck, but supplies are running low – we're down to the last half-dozen. They look a bit tired, with the occasional patch of mould, but any concerns regarding their appearance are ignored for the taste of something zingy and fresh. Three p.m. we line up a store-bought freeze-dried meal, either mac and cheese, another curry or perhaps some sort of risotto. All below average in taste, the flavours bland and lacking in texture. We've ruined ourselves with these homecooked meals. Five-thirty to six p.m. and it's time for something hefty: meat chilli, lamb saag or chilli chicken, a small ration of mango chutney on top; Pacific playlist in the background, we ready ourselves for the night.

That's 5,000 to 6,000 calories per day, depending on the meal combo and what extras can be scavenged from Ewan's leftover snack packs. Seems enough for now, but undoubtedly the hunger will only grow. We may be rowing 24/7, sleeping in hot/humid/cramped cabins and must share a bucket for a loo, but we shouldn't be starving anytime soon.

Little treats throughout each day were crucial. A small highlight to look forward to amid the grind of long hours on the oars. I love sweets. I always have. My multitude of fillings are testament to this. At five years old I discovered where the sugar bowl was kept and it was downhill from there. In the early hours of each morning I'd sneak downstairs, climb onto the kitchen counter and spoon granulated goodness into my mouth. It made me feel content, and a positive association was made. I got away with it until the next visit to the dentist, at which point six baby teeth were surgically removed. The sugar bowl was a little less appealing after that, but I still struggle to say no to a pick and mix.

Ewan and Lachlan make constant fun of me as I can never make my treats last. Once the snack pack is opened and I've delved into the sweet delights I don't see the point in holding off. I'm a scoffer not a saver. I reassure myself that I am making a conscious decision to eat my treats in a oner, embracing the full experience. Sadly, I think it is out of my control.

Sweet and sour are my real kryptonite. Unfortunately, the supermarket back home let us down and the 300 packs of Fizzy Fangs missed our boat shipment. I would see the occasional cloud that looked like a Fizzy Fang, taunting me of what could have been.

We searched for the positives within each day. Small acts of kindess, funny-shaped clouds, a Dairy Milk bar, or our favourite freeze-dried meal. Humour whenever we could muster a laugh. No matter how grim it gets it's amazing the power of a positive mindset to change your outlook on the world.

'It is easier to change your perception than it is to change the world' was a mantra of Chloë's that she had told us during our training.

The list of things you're not in control of in the middle of an ocean is long. But right at the top of that list is: the weather. Days of rain, weeks of beam-on conditions, the blistering sun, the crushing defeat of a heavy headwind. It is all too easy to become angry and frustrated and allow your thoughts to be engulfed by a cloud of negative emotion. Add in the salt sores, the terrible sleep, and the mundanity of it all and you quickly spiral into hating the experience. Ultimately, we had a choice to make: are we going to enjoy today or not? Changing your perception and looking for the positives in a situation can go a very long way.

We listened to Alfred Lansing's *Endurance* – about Shackleton's incredible and disastrous attempt to cross Antarctica in 1914. After their boat had been trapped and crushed by pack ice, Shackleton and his crew of

27 men survived for over 18 months in one of the harshest environments on earth. Living off dwindling rations, penguins and seals, they built makeshift structures to shelter from the freezing conditions. After a harrowing journey in an open-topped boat across the notorious Drake Passage, a small group of them trekked across South Georgia, securing a larger boat to return and rescue the other men. All 28 of them survived.

The discomfort and suffering on board *Rose Emily* was very quickly put into perspective. It was a good reminder not to feel too sorry for ourselves, even when times got achingly hard. It could be so much worse, and we ultimately had chosen to be here.

Despite my greatest efforts it was impossible to forget about my increasingly tender backside. The salt chafe had become almost unbearable. A lathering of cream helped, but the shorts eventually had to come off, and naked nighttime rowing became the new norm. I would have done so during the day as well were it not for the risk of full-frontal sunburn.

I thought to myself in these strange moments: 'What a peculiar sight for a passing ship: a multicoloured open-top boat, flying a small Scottish flag, with a completely naked man at the oars, wearing only his socks, shoes, harness and headtorch.' This would be a very odd sight at the best of times, let alone thousands of miles from land. I would row into the darkness, chuckling to myself at the bizarre scenarios we find ourselves in.

DAY 042, Saturday 24 May

JAMIE: Song of the day – 'Elijah Rose' by Leif Vollebekk

Today was just one of those days. It began so hopeful: fair winds and following seas. The fishing rod was out and the sun seemed bearable.

We started making fresh water at approximately 9.30 a.m., as we do every day. We had noticed a build-up of liquid at the bottom of the waterproof compartment that houses the desalinating system, and wrongly presumed it was general saltwater overspill that sometimes occurs with this unit.

Unfortunately, this was not the case. I tasted the water, which was unmistakably fresh; we've got a leak in our drinking-water system. The compartment had gained a fair few litres of fresh water by now as we used up precious energy from our batteries to try to fill the bladder in the bow.

Even on clear and sunny days, we have to get the timing right when producing water. We've learned this the hard way, producing water too late in the day, our batteries not recharging fully and being unable to run our navigation and autopilot at night.

Pipes are tracked for leaks, systems checked, cabin beds removed and hatches to the floor bladder lifted. The compartment is filled with water, nearly enough to have begun saturating the mattresses from below. It seems to be an issue with the bag. We drain all areas, remove the 75-litre tank and, upon closer inspection, identify a small hole in the top seam.

It must have occurred upon reinstallation in Lima, after our deep clean of the boat. We dry it, prepare it and plug it with rubber tape and epoxy. Carefully placed back in the floor compartment, reinstalled and checked. All seems good. This whole process, although relatively straightforward, takes approximately four hours. Everything takes longer at sea. We head into the afternoon exhausted and with our routine in tatters. Which doesn't bode well.

A hole in our water storage tank signified two major concerns. Firstly, it impacted our ability to make water at the optimum time of the day. Being the most power-hungry piece of equipment on board, our desalination system had to be run when the sun was at its highest in the sky. It was powered by lithium-ion batteries that were in turn charged by photovoltaic panels. Using the machine during overcast periods would drain the power from our battery cells, leaving us in a precarious situation as we entered the 13 hours of darkness every night. It was essential that we had enough power to use the autopilot until daybreak, keeping us on our planned course.

Without the ability to store water in the bag, and with a limited number of alternative containers, we would need to produce water at multiple times each day. We would be limping into each night unsure if the batteries would last until dawn.

The second concern was that of safety. Between the three of us we would need between 30 and 40 litres of water each day, depending on the heat. The primary storage tank, with its 75-litre capacity, allowed for extra water to be stored every 24 hours in case of an emergency. This would either be replaced the following day, or, if something drastic had gone wrong, such as the full loss of all electrical systems, we could live off this emergency ration while performing repairs. We had two other smaller emergency containers, but these were saved as an additional backup. If the system was unfixable, we would then need to weigh up hand-pumping water on every off-break – using a small manual hand pump we had in our emergency bag – or divert our route to seek assistance on a remote Pacific island, jeopardising our chance at the non-stop and unsupported attempt. Both would add weeks or even months on to the crossing, and with our limited food supplies, both would potentially endanger the entire trip. The more water we could store on board, the more time we bought ourselves if something went terribly wrong.

We limped through the next few days, unsure of how much liquid the bag could now hold. Reluctant to overfill and undo the repairs, we were forced to produce water at multiple moments each day. As expected, our battery levels took a hit. We entered each night with trepidation, unsure of what the night would bring.

The epoxy repair didn't stand the test of time. One of us regularly crawled down, flat on our stomach, to the bottom of the bow cabin to check if the leak had returned. After a couple of days we found an increasing amount of fresh water leaking into our storage compartment once again. Following a few frustrating off-shifts spent upside down in the cabin, I realised that it wasn't a single hole in the bag but a multitude of pin-sized punctures all along one seam. The system was disassembled and the bag brought out on deck. Most of our adhesives wouldn't stick to the PVC material, and considering the extent of the damage, we needed a radical solution. CT1, a building adhesive we'd packed at the last minute, seemed to be the only thing that would stick.

Sacrificing one of our roll-top drybags and slicing it up into strips, we glued what we could to the outside of the water tank. The repair was an ad hoc giant Elastoplast, held together with construction sealant and duct tape. After 24 hours of curing on deck, the now Frankenstein-esque bag was gingerly placed back into the storage locker. If it didn't stand the test of time, approximated to be another 80 days at sea, things would become quite challenging.

DAY 043, Sunday 25 May

LACHLAN: Song of the day – 'Letting Go' by Angie McMahon

Before leaving Peru, over six weeks ago now, we spent some time talking through the Maslow's triangle – a hierarchy of needs – for our power use on board *Rose Emily*. In the event of having issues, we wanted to have a clear idea of what we'd switch off or get rid of first. Crucially, we wanted to agree on this pyramid before becoming horribly sleep deprived, our ability to make good decisions impaired.

At the top of the triangle – the first to get the boot – are the luxury items that serve no purpose other than making our lives easier and more enjoyable out here: speakers, earpods, cabin fan, magnetic phone chargers on deck.

Further down, we have the story-sharing devices that drive fundraising efforts: our phones, cameras and the Starlink.

Next, there's the stuff that relates to our safety: navigational and communication equipment such as the autopilot, chart-plotter, Garmin inReach (similar to a satellite phone) and AIS (a tracking system that allows visibility between us and other vessels).

At the foundation of our triangle – the most essential item – we have our watermaker: our lifeline to be able to complete the trip. Producing water is of the highest importance. Without it, we can't hydrate or eat our freeze-dried meals.

Our water system works by drawing power from the three lithium-ion batteries we have on board. These are charged by solar panels on the deck and cabins. Their positioning on the boat (stern, middle and bow) means they capture sunlight throughout the daylight hours, from sunrise to sunset. At an optimal point each day, normally between 10 and 11.30 a.m., we run the watermaker. This ensures that as little energy as possible is used up from the batteries, as it is more efficient for us to draw power direct from the sun. This also reduces the chance of not having enough energy for the rest of the day to run all our other electrical systems, such as navigation and comms. But the watermaker is a hungry machine. The process of converting salt water to fresh is an energy--demanding one. Saline liquid is forced through a membrane at high pressure and a trickle of drinkable water comes out the other end. We can make approximately 30 litres of water an hour. It depends on the heat and how thirsty we are, but with rehydrating meals and an additional amount required each day for washing off salt and appeasing our tender areas, we communally require between 35 and 40 litres of fresh water each day. With one broken solar panel on deck, and a limited capacity to store water, our ability to produce this amount at the right time of day can be touch and go.

As we navigate between these water issues we're reminded of the why behind this campaign. We're often asked why we're passionate about clean water. Well, this pyramid answers that question. Water is the most basic necessity for people to live – something that is recognised as a basic human right. We all use it and need it every day. But it's difficult to truly see its value from a perspective that has never considered a life without it.

We find ourselves in the middle of the Pacific Ocean, closer to people in space than on dry land. Even in one of the most remote places on the planet, we're able to flick on a switch and produce water that's safe to drink, a luxury that many people on this planet do not share. These water bladder issues are figure-outable, but they have prompted us to pause and take stock. We're reminded of the ocean among the waves.

We've got a long way towards our £1 million target. It almost feels like a bigger challenge than the row itself, and we need all the help we can get to put the word out. But we're determined to get there.

With that amount of money, we could give 40,000 people in Madagascar clean water for life.

It was essential for us to keep the broader mission behind the row in view. Why we were here in the first place.

It was about living as rich and full a life as possible, about proving to ourselves what we were capable of, and about having a positive impact on other people's lives. If we ended it early we wouldn't have been realising the full potential of this row to achieve any of these.

When we first announced our ambitions of raising £1 million for clean water projects while rowing nearly halfway around the globe, I don't think very many people took us seriously. But now the hare-brained idea had resulted in over a month and a half at sea on the world's largest ocean. A big part of this, I think, could be put down to the belief of the amazing people we'd surrounded ourselves with. Friends, family and loved ones encouraged us and didn't dismiss our excitement.

But there were nae-sayers! We were indebted to them, too. 'You can't possibly do that . . .'; 'This is a terrible idea . . .'; 'What about your pensions?' Their concerns – undoubtedly voiced from the best possible places – spurred us on, giving us something to stubbornly prove wrong.

These trips are expensive, and without external support the campaign would have ended before it had even begun. There were a handful of sponsors that came on board at the earliest stages – Rare Whisky 101, M Yachts, Atacama, Norda – who shifted the dial of possibility.

The individual belief within each of us was coalescing into a shared belief. The idea of a whole being greater than the sum of its parts. Lachlan, Ewan and I are each fairly ordinary people with average abilities. Coming together, we can lean on each other's strengths, to gap-fill each other's weaknesses, creating a collective that's capable of doing bigger things. I guess this is one of the things we stand for: big things are possible when you work together towards a shared goal.

We could have woken up the next day and given up on the belief that we would make it to Australia. This would, I think, have been self-fulfilling. It would've instilled an unwillingness to commit to what was needed for completion. We didn't know our time-frame or the hurdles that were yet still to come our way. But we were committed to giving this our best bash, fuelled by the wave of support from around the world.

In many cases this wave of support came from places and people we could never have imagined. We had begun doing a series of conversations at sea to help spread the word and hopefully reach new audiences. Often, they took place first thing in the morning for us, but evening for anyone back home in the UK. We'd scoff down our oats while our guests enjoyed a freeze-dried meal – one of our homemade freeze-dried meals that had been sent to them by our shore team in advance. A name for these conversations, or podcasts, quickly took hold: *Dinner with the Macleans*. Which was odd in hindsight, considering it was never dinner for us.

Our first chat was with a legend of the endurance world, Mark Beaumont. Among many other accolades and records, Mark is the fastest human being to have cycled around the world, covering the 18,000 miles in a staggering 78 days. We talked endurance, motivation and the indomitable human spirit. Other than a brief test call with our cousin, this was the first proper video call with anyone since leaving Peru. It was bizzare but also uplifting, seeing Mark sitting in his office space, leaning back in a comfy chair with a gin and tonic in one hand and a veggie bean chilli in the other. I didn't care much for the gin, but I'd have taken that armchair in a heartbeat.

Our second call on the boat came as a major surprise. A chirp on the Garmin inReach was read out by Lala: 'Guy says we have a very exciting call tomorrow morning with another Mark.'

'Mark who?' Ewan asked from the bow rowing position.

'Not sure, waiting on the second message,' Lala replied.

Beep, beep went the Garmin. 'Right, ok, it's with Mark Whaleberg.'

'Mark Whaleberg?' I asked as I looked up.

'Yeah, Mark Whaleberg,' Lachlan replied.

To give a bit of context, Lachlan isn't the best at keeping up to date with the news, let alone popular culture or celebrities. He also isn't very good at names.

'You mean Mark Wahlberg?' Ewan interjected. 'That can't be right. He's a Hollywood superstar. Guy must be having us on.'

The next message came in: 'Just make sure you are online at 7 a.m. sharp, and join the link I send.'

Ewan continued: 'He's definitely having us on. I bet you the rest of my Snickers it isn't Mark Wahlberg. More likely to be Guy wearing a Mark Wahlberg mask.'

'You mean Guy wearing a whale outfit?' Lachlan chuckled to himself.

The evening was spent in anxious excitement. I don't think any of us actually believed it was going to be Mark Wahlberg, but the shore team further emphasised the importance of not being late. Whoever it was, they were worth cancelling everything in the calendar to make time for. Luckily, the calendar was looking pretty sparse, and little shuffling of schedules was required our end.

Ewan and Lala ate their porridge at the stern while I rowed solo for the call. The clock hit 7 a.m. The iPhone screen in front of them went dark, and then, lo and behold, Mark Wahlberg appeared. Right there, in front of us, in the middle of the Pacific Ocean. Holy shit. They weren't kidding. We were face to face with Mark fucking Wahlberg.

'What's up, guys?' he said. 'You guys just out for a little stroll? Absolutely incredible, man . . . talk about inspiring.'

We had 15 minutes of Mark's time. We talked about the physical and mental challenges of the crossing, about our charity and the cause, about some of his movies, and how he would like to host us at one of his restaurants in Sydney when we arrived. He said he wanted to touch base with us again later in the crossing, we said goodbye and the screen went off.

'What the hell just happened?' Ewan asked as he sat down on the oars. 'That was the most surreal conversation of my life.'

DAY 048, Friday 30 May

JAMIE: Song of the day – 'Bonny Light Horseman' by Siobhan Miller

Throughout this voyage we try to prevent a condition known as 'claw grip'. Our hands, through the repetitive nature and strain of rowing, have a tendency to want to clench and close up when relaxed.

I work through a variety of hand-mobility exercises after most shifts, but the tension still builds. This is of particular concern when sleeping . . . One night I fall asleep with my hands together on my chest with my fingers interlocked. In my dreaming state my left hand is no longer mine. Whoever it belongs to begins to squeeze, pressing down between each finger. In response I counter by applying pressure with my right hand. This goes on for a short while, the imposter's hand trying to crush mine and my right doing its best to counteract.

I wake to searing pain and cramp in both hands, unaware that I have, in fact, been crushing my fingers together. I gently prise them apart, and stretch out the individual fingers to relieve the pain. This is the worst I've had it. I take a mental note to increase hand mobility throughout the day and to not fall asleep with my hands together again.

I wake once more, this time to a gentle drip on my right leg. A second drip lands on my chest. In my half-sleeping state I presume it's condensation that has built up overnight – however, after several further drips, I pull myself up, pop on my headtorch and take a closer look. It's 5.30 a.m. and I'm due on the oars in 30 minutes. I can hear the heavy rain bouncing off the outside of the cabin. The carbon acts like a drum, reverberating and exaggerating the extent of the squall. Water appears to be gaining access around the satellite phone antennas, which we had suspected had been damaged a little during shipping. An easy fix with some silicone once the weather improves.

I peer through the small cabin window and see that both Ewan and Lala have their foul-weather gear on. I opt for shorts and my heavy weather Atacama smock and clamber on deck. Dense rain cloud surrounds us as far as the eye can see. With the sun nowhere to be seen we won't be able to run the watermaker anytime soon.

It's been five days since the last hull clean. With very little wind and a gentle swell it's a good time to plunge in once again. It's my turn to wear the goggles. Aside from shark watch, I do the final inspection for any missed bits of growth. I prefer it when someone else wears the goggles. There's a peaceful acceptance when you're oblivious to what might lurk in the surrounding waters.

A red sail is suddenly visible on the horizon. This is the third boat we've seen in the past 24 hours. Prior to this we had not seen another vessel for over 40 days. A hopeful sign of us nearing the idyllic South Pacific islands and their surrounding waters.

The red sail appears to be heading in our direction. Excitement builds on board *Rose Emily* – perhaps they'll sail nearby and we can exchange hellos and a tune on the bagpipes. It would be a memorable moment, however fleeting. Sadly not. Their course takes them a third of a mile to our stern and they fail to notice Lala's frantic waving. They cruise on, head sail up, oblivious to the strange encounter that could have been.

We had learned by this stage that cleaning the hull would often lift our spirits. Not only did it provide a brief moment off the oars but a much-needed bodily wash. We used baby wipes to help with daily cleanliness, but with a ration of four each per day, we were often desperate for a proper clean. Anything to appease the salt and sweat chafe that was developing in some sensitive areas. We also knew that after five days there would be a considerable amount of growth on the underside of the hull – half-inch molluscs and gooey brown algae – which created a huge amount of drag and resistance in the water. We would plunge in for both the boat's sake and our own.

I dived in head first and began sanding away at an area of molluscs near the bow. Lala shortly followed and addressed an area beside the daggerboard. Ewan remained on board to keep watch and tend to the boat. I felt a light sting across my shoulder blades, similar to that of a nettle. I didn't think much of it until I heard Lala yell that something was caught in his hair and was stinging his neck. I pulled myself over to him and untangled a long tentacle caught up in his curls. On the end of it there was a small, clear, jelly-like bubble with turquoise highlights and a central crest; blue tendrils clustered at its base.

Ewan, noticing the commotion in the water, leaned over the side of the boat. 'What is it? Are you ok? Is there something in the water?!'

Up until this point we'd been so focused on the threat of sharks that jellyfish had passed under our radar. The small creature was unfankled from Lachlan's hair, scooped into a cup and brought on deck. The Starlink powered up and after a quick search it was confirmed to be a baby Pacific man o' war (a close relative to the Portuguese man o' war found in the Atlantic). Thankfully, at that size, they are more of a nuisance than extremely painful, but unpleasant nonetheless. I quickly clambered on deck; that was enough hull cleaning for one day.

DAY 054, Thursday 5 June

JAMIE: Song of the day – 'Hebridean Breeze' by Beluga Lagoon

We row hard to keep our course. The Marquesas, our next major waypoint, lie 80 nautical miles to the southwest. As the wind and waves endeavour to push us too far west, we push south as much as we physically can to ensure we don't collide with the island's shores.

Waves crash over the deck as we steer closer into the wind and conditions. If we can hold out for one more day we should round the bottom of Fatu-Hiva, the southernmost island of this archipelago, and then we can turn due west. From that point onwards we've been promised more favourable conditions. We shall see. If we've learned anything from the past 54 days it's to expect the unexpected from this 'peaceful' ocean.

The wise words of Iain McGilchrist, Lachlan's favourite polymath and philosopher, sound on the speaker. McGilchrist introduces us to the idea that we exist in a state of becoming rather than being. This really strikes a chord with me. One of the most exciting aspects of a row like this – and, in many regards, of life in general – is not who we are but who we might become as a result of the experience. We are in a constant state of flux, of evolution.

Through new experiences and environments, we not only create memories, forge perspectives and sculpt who we fundamentally are, but we physically change as well. On a cellular level, our bodies are in a constant state of flow – cells forever being repaired, adapted and replaced. Every second that passes, we are physically not the same person we were moments ago. This blows my mind. After seven to ten years, every cell in our body will have been fully replaced. The saying 'You are what you eat' comes to mind. Fascinating to think that over time we quite literally become what we ingest. I wonder what percentage of me will be peanut butter by the end of this journey?

As my oars dip in and out of the ocean, I ponder the potential of becoming and not being. I'm certainly guilty, as I think many of us are, of falling into the trap of saying this is who I am and therefore this is how I should act and this is what I should do. But that just isn't the case. We are physically and mentally becoming something different every day, and therefore there is the potential to continually change and grow – like the water that flows down the hull of our boat, never static, forever moving; a turn-door continually opening to the possibilities of what we can achieve and who we might become.

I'm very aware that the three of us have been dealt a very lucky hand in life: loving and supportive parents; amazing friends, family and partners; an upbringing and education in a safe context that has nurtured growth and a curiosity for the world. But the fact is, no matter who you are, you are becoming someone different to the person you were yesterday. The change is there, context allowing, it just needs to be steered onto the right course.

In my current setting, stroke after stroke, these changes are no doubt accelerated. And yet, due to the mundane and introspective nature of our day-to-day, they are more difficult to identify. What I do know is that we will be different people at the end of this voyage to the boys that set off from the shores of Peru.

As we fast approached the Marquesas Islands, our advice to date had been to get well below the coast of the most southerly lying island, Fatu-Hiva. It was the target we had been consciously trying to hit for literally thousands of miles.

About a month ago, after being pushed north of our intended course, we became very aware of how challenging it was to remake ground in a southerly direction. Every degree off the compass we strayed added miles and days to our journey. With seasonally uncharacteristic weather pushing us forever north, we'd spent most days fighting the wind and waves.

We had been warned that failing to get far enough below the islands could lead to uncertain sea states, challenges around international waters and a real risk of being blown onto the windward side of Fatu-Hiva – a sailor's nightmare. Our first waypoint aimed to take us 12 nautical miles south of Fatu-Hiva, keeping us in international waters and a favourable current. In a rowing boat, there's only so much you can do to fight against the wind. To be pinned by a strong breeze and a big sea against a coastline is a nightmarish scenario: the dreaded lee shore, where you lose control and the wind drives you ashore.

The morning of 7 June arrived with a fork in the road: continue on the same course, attempting to get south of Fatu-Hiva? Or pass to the north? The latter would allow us to turn downwind, meaning much nicer rowing conditions. It would, however, require accurate navigation through a very narrow channel just north of Fatu-Hiva to remain in international waters. A Garmin inReach call back and forth with the weather gurus, and the decision was made: we would pass to the north of the island.

There is change in the air as dusk approaches. Dark squalls pass on either side as we skip over the messy waves. Deep below us, the seabed climbs and drops in a series of vast mountains and valleys that are hidden from the eyes of people. These culminate into the first landform we'll see in 56 days, sitting 36 miles due west over the horizon.

DAY 056, Saturday 7 June

EWAN: Song of the day – 'Peace of Iona' by The Waterboys

Three times the size of Ben Nevis, the underwater peak of Banc Meihano towers out of the depths, standing alone and exposed to thousands of miles of open water on its eastern sides. Yet, unlike Scotland's tallest peak, it's doubtful anyone would have ventured to its dark watery summit or come to know its form. A giant subsea pyramid, this protrusion comes short of the surface by 54 metres and marks the first outcrop of the Marquesas Islands.

Little evidence can be seen at the water's surface of the sleeping mountain below, other than the churning sea. We row directly above, bound for the narrow strait of international water between Fatu-Hiva and Mohotani. A huge underwater valley lies before us, over 20 miles wide and two miles deep.

Knowing how these underwater landscapes can influence the flow above, I stand at the stern with my eyes glued to the churning waters ahead of the boat. I can feel Lachlan watching me. 'Is everything ok?' he asks. 'You look concerned.'

I move my gaze away from the ocean and meet his eyes: 'All good. There's just a funny feeling in these waters, don't you think?'

'I've been feeling it all day,' he replies.

As day falls away into night, a sense of foreboding settles on the boat. Under the bright moon we make our way due west towards land, tentatively tracking *Rose Emily*'s course and searching for signs of changing conditions. Although at first glance it appeared to be nothing more than the darkening night, as Jamie turned in and left Lachlan and me on deck, a fast-approaching squall started to show face.

Black skies etched into the ocean below, a continuous wall of water, heralded by the rush of chilling winds. Judging by the distance from the boat, I guessed we had five minutes before it hit. Lachlan was shortly due to call it a night, so I suggested I might do the last ten minutes of the dayshift alone, saving him from being drenched unnecessarily before bed. He pulled in the oars and started to make his way down the deck.

Suddenly, as if we had been plunged sideways into a waterfall, the squall was upon us. In an instant, the boat was violently turned sideways to the oncoming wind, which had come round to the southwest, about 45 degrees, in a split second.

Blindly, I pulled hard with all my strength to try to turn the boat. She was rocking now, bearing the brunt of the weather as it tore past us, waves crashing into her side. The headtorches did nothing more than illuminate the thrashing conditions, like driving on a motorway in heavy rain at night. I tasted salt, which told me that it wasn't just fresh water; the wind must be whipping up spray from the sea as well.

Shouting for Lachlan, I could make out that he was setting up in front of me, but despite there being only a metre between us, neither could hear a word the other said. We hauled together, moving faster and with desperation. But the grasp of the wind was too strong and, try as we might, it held us there for a few more terrifying moments.

And then, as fast as it had appeared, the squall blew past and the wind dropped, swinging round to the east again, just as it had been only five minutes before. We brought *Rose Emily* back on course and Lachlan put down his oars with a bit of a thump – I could tell he wasn't happy. We were both soaked to the skin, but he had now also lost a precious ten minutes of sleep. He threw a couple of curses towards the now distant squall, stripped off and stepped inside the cabin. As the door swung closed, he bid me good luck and good night.

As dawn emerged, I opened the cabin to find a mixed sky. Patches of blue, dark rain clouds, grey mist and unsettled seas. But despite the rough night, Lachlan smiled: 'Look, Ewan!'

'Land.'

DAY 057, Sunday 8 June

JAMIE: Song of the day – 'Arrane Oie Vie' by Mec Lir

I'm woken by howling on deck. I glance at the egg timer; three minutes remain and so it must be around 6 a.m. There's an excitement to the shouts. As I pull on my shoes and shorts I can just about make out the reason for the stir: 'Land ahoy!'

I've anticipated this moment for the past week and feel slightly anxious about its potential effect on our psychological state, for good or for bad. Up until this point, the idea of land has been a figment of our imaginations. To see it for the first time in so many days of endless blue horizons might evoke happiness, but it could also stir up a deeply rooted missing of home and a strong desire to get off this boat as swiftly as possible.

I poke my head out of the cabin and cast my gaze out over the swell. To port, approximately 12 nautical miles to the south, the majestic green cliffs of Fatu-Hiva rise out of the ocean. We've reached the Marquesas Islands; the first major waypoint on our voyage to date. For the last 57 days we've regularly spoken about this moment, clinging to it with hope during some long and frustrating weeks on the oars. As we crossed the vast open expanse of ocean that now lies to the east of us, this small cluster of islands, like specks of sand adrift in an Olympic pool, have given us purpose and direction.

Fatu-Hiva reminds me of the scene from *Jurassic Park* when they first set sights on the mythical island where the dinosaurs live. Incredibly steep ridges are cloaked in a vale of mossy green, the jagged peaks silhouetted on the horizon like the spine of a sleeping prehistoric beast. Clouds gather at the highest points, occasionally concealing the gullies between each ridge.

It is truly magical. It's been a childhood dream of mine to visit the South Pacific islands, and yet this is as close as we'll come. The passage between these islands is 24.6 nautical miles wide; however, the channel of international water in the middle, which we must remain in, is only 0.6 nautical miles across. All we can do is gaze from afar. Stray a little off our course and we risk drawing unwanted attention from local authorities. An unlikely event, but one we'd rather avoid.

The islands to the north of us unveil themselves as the rain clouds pass: jagged cliffs with an abundance of yet more greenery. There's a richness to these islands that I've only ever felt on the west coast of Scotland. Rich, rugged and beautiful. Yet I'm surprised at how I feel. As wonderful as it would be to step on land, this isn't where our journey ends. It wouldn't feel right to stop today.

But I can't help my mind from wandering. The feeling of sand and then grass between my toes, the juicy bite from a fresh fruit. Inhaling the cool moist air of the dense undergrowth and holding it in my lungs. The atmosphere is palpable; I can taste life itself.

I open my eyes and I'm back on the boat. I'll come back to these shores one day, a promise I make to myself.

As the sun sets and the Marquesas Islands disappear beyond the horizon, 'Arrane Oie Vie' by Mec Lir plays on the speaker. I can't understand the Gaelic words. I wish I could. We couldn't be further from home and yet they somehow seem to fit: poetic and ethereal, like a prayer being uttered to a force that's greater than ourselves. The haunting fiddle complements each word, giving them an otherworldly resonance. The lyrics and the music dance with one another, rising and flowing off into the evening breeze.

I wonder what it is like to live in such a magical place. A thin place where thresholds are blurred. It no doubt has its challenges; those shared by islanders across the globe. And yet that must be a sacrifice worthwhile to be so close to the spirits of sky, land and sea.

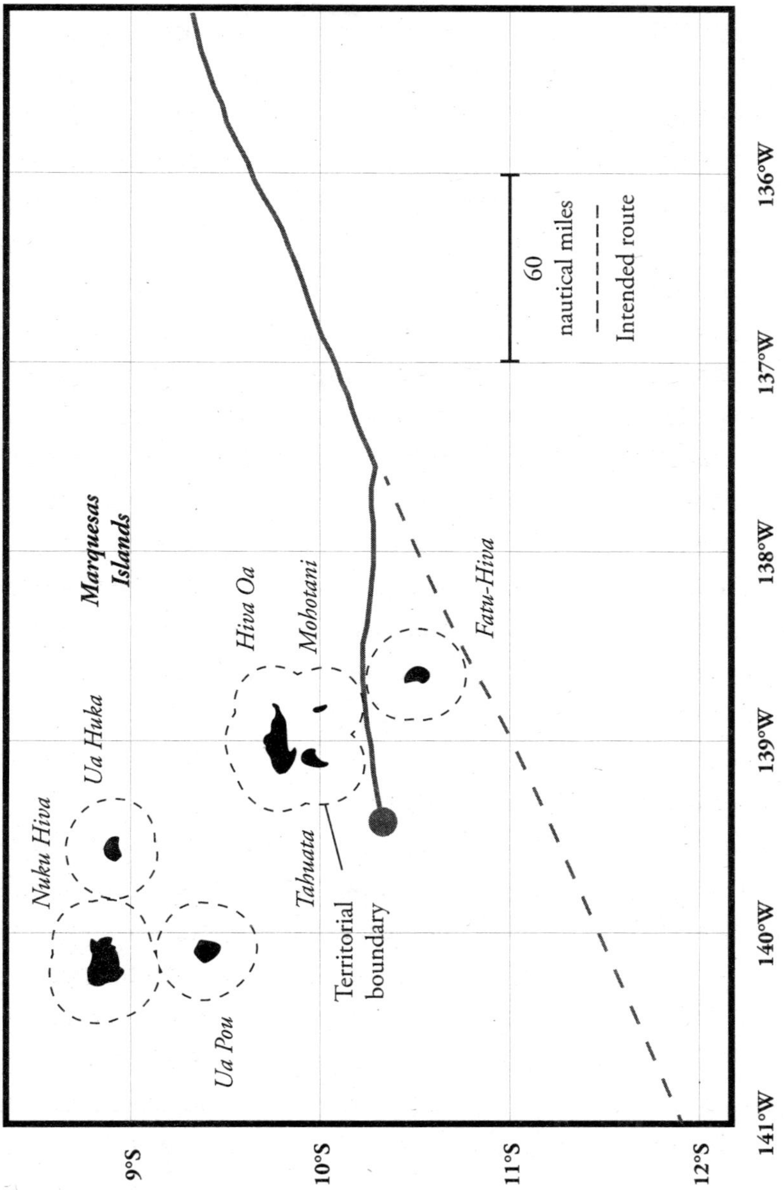

Route through the Marquesas Islands

Chapter 8

Reflections Between Waves

By Lachlan

What happens after darkness?
When resolve begins to waver,
And challenge is all you see;
Clarity is lost amongst surrounding waves,
And your mind obsesses over mounting days.
Remind yourself of these simple facts
That every ocean has another shoreline;
Every gale a final frontier;
Even the darkest Pacific night
Is followed by a morning light.

– Lachlan Maclean, 'After Darkness'

Day 058, Monday 9 June

LACHLAN: Song of the day – 'The Pilgrimage' by Duncan Chisholm

Calmer conditions and a favourable current have created a very different atmosphere to that of the crashing side-on wind and waves of the past two months. It may be very hot, but we distract ourselves with conversation.

'What would your perfect sauna look like?' Jamie broke the afternoon silence. We're all sauna fanatics and it isn't difficult to imagine ourselves in one in this hot environment.

I close my eyes and my imagination conjures up images of floating saunas anchored off our bothy in Assynt. 'It would have to be floating, surely.'

'Would you have a companionway to the shore? Or would you have a paddleboard or kayak?'

And we were away; an hour would pass with the click of a finger as we discussed the intricacies of floating sauna requirements and construction.

We take comfort in what we've endured so far on this journey and embrace a slower pace of life. I reflect upon my thoughts towards this body of water in the earlier days of the voyage: overwhelmingly vast and void of most life. I believe I was wrong. My appreciation for the subtle differences in the movement of the water makes me consider the life, or spirit, of the ocean. Although it continues to test us, slowly but surely it feels like she's conspiring in our favour.

We've developed a new highlight to each day: a flannel wash at sunset. We soak the microfibre towels in a Tupperware container filled with slightly chlorinated water to keep them clean. The nostalgic smell of chlorine tablets reminds me of my first swimming lessons. I don't think I actually enjoyed the lessons, but I did enjoy the tutti frutti chewing gum provided by Uncle Iain upon pick-up. I wish I had some tutti frutti now.

A full moon rises from the west, its pale golden light shimmering on the gentle swell, illuminating the deck. Cloud permitting, I watch the moon for hours each night. What a privilege; waxing or waning, she accompanies me through various highs and lows of this voyage. Four months of being held captive by the moon every night – that in itself is a remarkable experience.

The peaks of the Marquesas sank into a golden barley horizon. Music and audiobooks fell into silence as we relished the quietude of a moonlit night. It was a tranquil evening aboard *Rose Emily*. The Marquesas stood as pillars of a gateway to this new chapter, a jarring contrast to the miles leading up to our first sighting of land. There had been an air of excited anxiety on the boat. Islands meant hard objects to crash into – rocks, coastlines, other boats – as well as less predictable currents. As we threaded the islands of Fatu-Hiva and Mohatani, 12 miles offshore to remain in international waters, the wind died and shifted favourably into the northeast. Underwater mountain ranges were bending and forming the great ocean currents, conspiring with us to push us along at about a knot. No matter how hard we squinted, we saw no signs of human life on the islands, not even a sail. We agreed that it wouldn't have felt right to finish at that point – we were mentally prepared for more.

We thought of Thor Heyerdahl, the Norwegian explorer, as we passed the islands. Thor and his wife, Liv, had lived on Fatu-Hiva for 15 months between 1937 and 1938 in a bid to 'return to nature'. The purpose of their trip was to explore whether they could survive – or indeed thrive – on the island without modern technology or medicine. Their home was built from bamboo and woven palm leaves and they successfully lived off the land. The story has been lost in the tumultuous years that followed, but their time there inspired the Kon-Tiki expedition.

Reaching the Marquesas was a tangible indicator of forward progress. It was proof that the Pacific was not never-ending. At points in the first half, it felt like the ocean was debilitatingly vast. Though we'd been floating for weeks and weeks, we still had half of the journey to complete. We were moving so slowly across the chart-plotter that I'd questioned whether it had frozen on multiple occasions. 'What if we're not actually moving anywhere?' Though the sea-state and skies were constantly in motion, it felt at times like we were not. As a good friend, Kelvin, told me in a voice message, 'Your tracker might be the worst spectator sport in the world . . .' which he kindly followed with, 'but I still check it every day.' Seeing land was a much-needed indicator that we had made forward progress – albeit millimetre by millimetre – across our chart-plotter.

The 9th of June marked my 27th birthday. In many ways, it was a normal day in the office – which suited me. I'm not someone who enjoys a huge amount of fuss on birthdays. I prefer them to come and go unnoticed.

DAY 058, Monday 9 June (log entry continued)

LACHLAN : Song of the day – 'The Pilgrimage' by Duncan Chisholm

Orangey yellow gave way to blue as dawn's veil was stretched across the sky. The half-moon smiled above, its only companion Saturn to the east. There was warmth in the gentle morning breeze. A hot day loomed over the horizon.

We peacefully baked. Sadly, not the moreish, floury/sugar-based delights found on *The Great British Bake Off* which float around my thoughts so often these days – rather, we are physically melting under the baking heat of the sun, which glares down on us as we row 30 minutes on, 30 minutes off. I close my eyes and listen to the motion of the oars. The wheels of our seats swish with the pendulum motion of our strokes. Forwards and backwards. Pause. Forwards and backwards. Pause. This motion has been performed by each of us one million times already. Beads of sweat dislodge from the base of my neck and trickle down my spine, bound for the small pool in which I sit.

The afternoon concluded with an interview with Lorraine Kelly on ITV. Jamie and I squeezed into the stern cabin and waited on the Zoom for our five-minute slot.

Lorraine was a delight to chat to, and clearly has a lifetime of experience in putting people at ease. Our only regret was not asking her more questions – I hope we can speak to her again. Truly a national treasure.

It's not a birthday I'm likely to forget, that's for sure.

As we entered our final rotation of the day on the oars, Jamie gave me his Snickers bar from that morning's snack pack: 'Happy birthday, Lala.'

Jamie held the crumpled, deformed wrapper behind his back. The domino-sized parcel had been squished, melted, re-formed and was out of date, but I think it was the best birthday present he'd ever given me. And that's not to say his previous gifts weren't good. An amber glow formed on the horizon to the east. Half obstructed, half not, it lingered for a while, casting shapes in the dark clouds. There was a gentle luminosity to the moon's light. It gave a broad view of the ocean around us and clouds overhead, but without the glaring detail of the daytime sun. Jamie and I were due to head to bed in ten minutes to leave Ewan on his first nightshift. Another day was done.

'Ok, lads. I'm checking it.' Ewan's voice burst our silent bubble. His tone suggested that he'd been thinking about this announcement for some time. Reaching awkwardly over his left shoulder from the stern rest position, he twisted the phone out of the Quad Lock phone holder, swaying left to right as he held onto the lifeline. His phone illuminated his bearded face as he furrowed his brow earnestly, an expression he's had as long as I can remember. 'The distance we have rowed is 3,905 nautical miles.' He paused, then looked up. 'The distance that's left to row is . . . 3,904 miles. That's halfway in the bag. Happy belated birthday from the Pacific, Lachlan.'

We yipped and howled at the moon like a pack of feral dogs. We'd hit halfway as we entered day 60 – exactly half of our goal of completing the crossing in 120 days. To our astonishment, things seemed to be going to plan – for now. This marked the long-awaited point of being able to think: 'I just need to do the same again.' We had measured progress on our journey so far by balancing our miles rowed against the miles to go. It felt like the weighing scale was slowly tipping in our favour.

But marking an exact halfway point on an ocean voyage is a misnomer. We'd already gone off our intended course, adding over six hundred miles. We'd only truly know the halfway point on completion, especially given that what lay ahead was a more uncertain chapter, with challenging navigation and less favourable weather. But we had to celebrate halfway at some point.

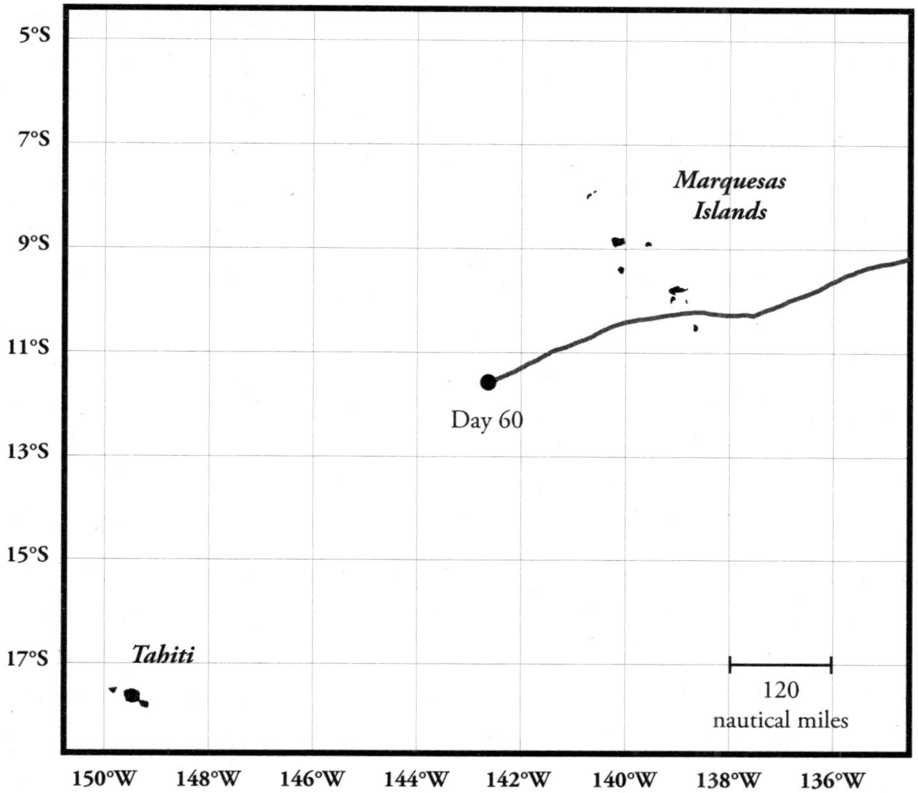

Halfway!

Only two days prior, we'd celebrated hitting £100,000 raised for clean water projects. Though it wasn't proportional to the distance we'd rowed, we anticipated that most of the funds would come in towards the last third of the journey. We'd need to show people we weren't all words before they'd part with their hard-earned cash. Celebrating the milestones – the small victories – had become one of our coping mechanisms for not becoming completely overwhelmed by the scale of what we were undertaking. It was no different to life on land, like waking up on one of those Mondays when you think: 'How am I going to make it through this?' Your list feels too long, the days too short. You look at other people and long for their composure. You just want to sink beneath the covers and pretend that you don't exist. How do we get through these weeks? We do the first thing. We focus on the first task, taking a step, and forget about the things that follow. The reality of anything is always completely different to how we think it will be, and there's no point in worrying about Wednesday when you're still on Monday.

Rowing the full Pacific was no different. As soon as we zoomed out too far and viewed the task in its entirety, it seemed debilitatingly vast. But breaking it down into chunks – just getting through that thousand miles or that day or that shift or that 15 minutes – was the only way we'd get to the end. As Chloë told us, it was important to not just focus on how far you have to go, but make sure you see how far you've come.

The following day, 10 June, we opened a small bundle of gifts from our friend, Duncan Roy, that were stowed away in the bow. Duncan is one of the top ocean rowing coaches and also one of the loveliest blokes you'll ever meet. Jelly Babies, freeze-dried ice cream sandwiches and Percy Pigs were wrapped individually with personal notes: 'To Lachlan. For halfway. Love, Dunc.' It was the perfect treat. Each Jelly Baby was a different fruit flavour. I closed my eyes and popped one onto my tongue, scanning through an imaginary fruit bowl to guess what it was. Duncan knew exactly what we were missing.

Jamie stood at the stern, a smile across his face, devouring his pot of Jelly Babies like he was swigging from a cup of tea. Ewan and I enjoyed a handful then squirrelled them away in the bow cabin, saving them for hard miles that lay ahead.

Ewan's alarm from the stern cabin marked the arrival of another dayshift. I flicked on the speaker. Our music listening was rationed at roughly two hours per day split between dawn and dusk. The less we listened, the more we enjoyed it. A few artists were on repeat throughout the journey. No matter how many plays, we never tired of their music – our enjoyment only deepened with familiarity. Leif Vollebekk's album *Twin Solitude* topped that list.

We'd been informed the day before of a 10.30 a.m. call with an anonymous guest. The primary purpose of these chats – other than to provide much-needed variety on *Rose Emily* – was, of course, to build our audience, which we hoped would aid us in fundraising. After the Marks – Wahlberg and Beaumont – and then rugby player Rob Wainwright, a surprise guest could have been just about anyone.

Ewan and I entered the stern video conference position: phone set to eye-height on a carbon pole, clipped onto the stern cabin, leaning back. Jamie plugged away on the oars in the background. A box with no camera popped up, the letters 'LV' in the bottom corner. We stood, swaying side to side, eagerly waiting.

The familiar face of Leif Vollebekk came into view with a friendly smile: 'Hey, guys! How's it going?'

Having any kind of call in the middle of the Pacific was surreal; having a 40-minute chat with one of your favourite artists of all time was next level. There was no awkwardness or apprehension – the chat flowed. They say you shouldn't meet your heroes. I'm happy to say this wasn't the case with Leif.

The days that followed my birthday had a tranquil feeling. There had been a profound shift in conditions after so many miles of the same. There was a change that couldn't be measured on a weather map or thermometer. A different aura. The light had a clean but gentle luminosity to it, like soft winter sun. We were in a state of awe as we watched the elemental dance around us. We were visitors in this wild landscape and, for a moment, could understand just how lucky we were. It was a welcome opportunity to reflect and turn our gaze inward.

DAY 060, Wednesday 11 June

LACHLAN: Song of the day – 'Morning Sun' by Melody Gardot

We find ourselves in a state of betweenness.

Between one ecosystem and another; between ocean and sky; between landmasses, countries and civilisations. Between the people who boarded this boat to leave South America and the people who will arrive in Australia. Our lives in Scotland are on pause – flat tenancies, magazine subscriptions and car insurances cancelled. Soon we will return to a new canvas, seen with a fresh gaze.

I've often thought of people in space during this voyage. Do they share this feeling of betweenness, or is theirs a feeling of disconnectedness? How does it feel to capture the whole of humanity in a single camera lens?

Three flashing lights – red, green and white – catch my attention overhead. It's our first plane in two months. I imagine the people sitting in this flying metal box. The seatbelt sign pings on as the plane starts its descent. Maybe someone looks out of the window at that very moment and imagines what it would be like down here on the ocean. They probably have better things to think about: onward travel, what they'll have for dinner, jobs tomorrow, the work assignment they haven't finished. I haven't missed thinking about those things.

There's something about being removed from civilisation that drives the mind elsewhere. A profound feeling of connection is met with an equally strong feeling of disconnection. Though we were physically isolated, we felt connected to ourselves and each other. The fluff had been burned away; the proximity between who we thought we were, who we wanted to be, and who we truly were, was smaller.

I looked at Jamie and Ewan's faces. Their beards were tinged with gold, their skin bronzed. There was a twinkle in their eyes that hadn't been there before.

DAY 061, Thursday 12 June

JAMIE: Song of the day – 'Into the Ether' by Leif Vollebekk

A pod of dolphins joined us in the late afternoon, bounding over the gentle waves, playful and curious. The ocean sends us these little reminders of the depth of life that exists below our small vessel. It's so easy for us to lose sight of the bigger picture as we bob along in our introspective bubble. I ponder what the dolphins must think of us as they plunge between the thresholds of our world and theirs. As they breach and exhale it feels like they are communicating with us. There's a wisdom to the creatures found in these wild places, as if they truly understand what it is to be alive.

I wouldn't describe myself as a religious person, but I do have a fascination – an openness – to the supernatural; experiences and events that simply cannot be explained at a materialistic level. In Celtic wisdom there's a phenomenon called 'thin places', where the veil between the seen and unseen becomes thinner, where the distance between our earthly world and the heavens above is said to be at its shortest, the known and the unknown converging. As the poet Sharlande Sledge describes it:

> . . . Where the door between this world
> And the next is cracked open for a moment
> And the light is not all on the other side.

I wouldn't say I'd ever visited somewhere that fitted this description before the window after the Marquesas. There was a cleanness to the light that spoke of something else. It's difficult to describe something so limitless within the confines of words.

LACHLAN

We're currently privileged to spend about 18 hours each day under an open sky. We see the thresholds of each day: day turning to dusk, night turning to dawn. One of my favourite philosophers, John O'Donohue, wrote about these thresholds of night and day.

He spoke of the nights being a time for calm; a time for the soul to restore itself. At night, we return to our true selves, unburdened by the weight of exposure.

Before the first vespers of light arrive, the night sky deepens. Then, as if by miracle, a glimmer of light appears on the horizon and the clouds above us come alive. The fingers of dawn pull the veil of night from the sky. The weights are lifted from our eyelids with a new restored energy. This energy hasn't come from sleep but a deeper well.

The new day is here, and with it comes an ocean of possibility. We know that this tranquil window will not last for ever. Things change in a moment at sea. But, until it does, we bask in a feeling of proximity – a feeling of closeness – to ourselves and the natural world around us.

The window wasn't to last for long, I was right. We'd learned to enjoy these moments the hard way. The tranquil net was to be lifted only hours after I sent this log. We were on a rollercoaster – and we had no choice other than to buckle in.

DAY 062, Friday 13 June

EWAN: Song of the day – 'False-Hearted Lover' by Leif Vollebekk

As darkness fell, we watched two of our batteries drain from being around half full down to dangerously low levels within an hour.

These batteries had issues with the monitoring system in the past. However, thanks to some lengthy delays with UK customs, our two replacements ended up taking nearly two months to arrive at Dad's flat. They missed the boat being shipped, and had to be left in the UK.

The sudden drop in voltage is bad news, a sign that it perhaps wasn't just the monitoring systems at fault. If the cells themselves are compromised, there's not much we can do to rectify them out here.

Limping through the night on the emergency battery, we managed to make it to dawn and were blessed with clear skies as the sun rose.

Though our propulsion was human-powered, we were reliant on electricity from the sun for all of our electronics. If we lost all power, we'd be looking at a 200-day-plus crossing and would definitely have to stop and reprovision along the way, taking a non-stop and unsupported crossing off the table.

Rose Emily fell into silence. Though we didn't talk about it, I knew that each of our minds were noisy. We'd need to prioritise our power for the most essential equipment on the boat: the watermaker and autohelm. Our 'luxury' items would be sacrificed: Garmin inReach, speakers, earpods, cabin fan, magnetic on-deck phone-charging points. We'd also need to switch off our tools for sharing the story for fundraising: phones, cameras, Starlink. We'd have to activate our Maslow's triangle procedure. As I wrestled with my inner voice, a quote that I'd noted down a few nightshifts prior sprung to mind: 'Acknowledge the wave, but stay with the ocean' – Yongey Mingyur Rinpoche.

I'd been listening to *In Love with the World: What a Monk Can Teach You About Living from Nearly Dying*, the autobiographical account of a Tibetan teacher hanging up his robes and taking to the streets. These eight words had so much wisdom. It was easy to lose all perspective in this environment. One thing doesn't go to plan and, before you know it, you've amplified the scale of the issue into being disaster.

But that wasn't unique to our situation out here. It was just as true in day-to-day life on land. So often do I become consumed by things that haven't yet happened. One thing dominoes into another. I have a bad day – or maybe a bad week – and suddenly my broader picture goes out of the window. I'm lost among the waves of my own misery, unable to see that things are, generally speaking, pretty good. Instead of catastrophising and tearing our hair out over all of the terrible things that could happen, our energy is better spent focusing on actions to improve our situation. Controlling the controllables is the best we can do, and, for things that are out of our control: hope for the best. Out on the ocean we certainly didn't have the bandwidth to get caught up in the 'coulds' and 'woulds'.

'Eating frogs' had become a mantra on board *Rose Emily*: doing the jobs you least wanted to do. Instead of wallowing, it was much better to focus on what we could do in the here and now to improve the situation. I reached into the bow cabin to dig out our hand-held desalinator. This device was stored in our grab-bag, the drybag that we'd take with us if we were abandoning ship. Other essential equipment inside the bag included flares, a spare personal locator beacon, emergency water rations, some high-calorie nut-butters and rescue blankets.

In the case of a dire emergency – losing all power or bundling ourselves into a life raft – the hand-operated water pump would be our lifeline. The process was the same as our watermaker, but slower and more labour intensive. An inlet would suck up salt water. The pressure built up from hand-pumping would drive the salt water through a membrane which would purify it through reverse osmosis. I sat in the lee of the cabin and began the repetitive motion. It was like having an arm-wrestle with myself, pushing the long lever down and up, as fresh water dribbled out of another smaller tube half the diameter of my pinky. It was an arduous job, and we could only produce about 4.5 litres per hour of pumping. But it was drinkable water, all the same. We would need to produce at least 20 litres, ideally 25, so half of our off-breaks would need to become hand-pumping sessions.

'It's time to deploy the Swiss army knife . . . In you go, Ewan,' Jamie said in jest. Ewan was small enough that he could bundle himself into a cabin or locker and would usually locate and fix whatever problem we were having. His skills as an engineer had saved our bacon before we'd even left.

He re-emerged 30 minutes later, his neck gleaming with freshly formed sweat: 'I reconnected the solar panels. One of them was a bit loose. I don't know why that would result in a drop in battery levels . . . all we can do is hope.'

For the time being we were thankful for the gentle squeak of the autohelm as it continued to run. There was little to be done but good management. The battery levels seemed to be holding again, and all that we could do was keep our fingers crossed. There wasn't time to dwell on anything out here. The next challenge was a 'when' not an 'if'; all we could do was hope that we'd be able to overcome whatever was thrown at us next.

And whatever that was didn't seem to be that far over the horizon. The conditions had built to 20 knots. An ocean swell was building from the south, perpendicular to the wind-driven waves from the east. We found ourselves amid a grid-like maze of converging sea-states. As the light was sucked from the sky, the inReach made its two-note chirping sound: a message from Sean: 'Expect a messy sea-state as you enter the Convergence Zone. Easterly wind at 20 knots, gusting 25. Be vigilant . . .'

Our weather routers had told us about the South Pacific Convergence Zone: unpredictable and powerful weather systems travelling from the southern ocean are funnelled between Australia and New Zealand. As they travel north, they collide with the mid-Pacific trade systems that we'd been riding west. Aside from being one of the wettest parts of the Pacific, it's the engine room for tropical cyclones.

DAY 065, Monday 16 June

JAMIE: Song of the day – 'Neverland' by Beluga Lagoon

The ocean retches and writhes as these two forces of nature collide. Boiling and breaking over our deck. It's been a wet and uncomfortable day. All shoes are sodden through; salt crystallises on my skin. Lachlan and Ewan opt for foul-weather gear; I opt for just shorts, accepting the ocean as it comes then washing down with fresh water before crawling into bed. We cling to the silver lining: we're moving fast.

It was going to be a wild night. We left Ewan to a half-moon rising, a strip of light shimmering as it reflected off the confused sea around us. *Rose Emily* was tossed like a rubber duck, rising high into the sky one moment, suspended on the crest of an oncoming wave, only to plunge down deep into the trough the next. The small boat sat low in the water, feeling every surge. Our bodies were connected to the flow through each oar. An elemental anticipation of motion had entered our subconsciousness after 65 days and nights of this relentless dance. There was no thought to our doing; we were completely in tune with *Rose Emily*'s movement.

By midnight we had changed the rowing position to the forward seat nearest the bow, hoping to dodge some of the sea spray and breaching waves in the middle position. It was unlikely that water would come over the bow. The bearings on the rolling seat groaned with every stroke. They wouldn't be changed until we could no longer bear it – we had to conserve our stock of spares. Riding out the final nightshift rotation, I took over from Jamie to take us back into daylight hours. These were the biggest waves we'd experienced up until this point, some of them soaring over 16 feet tall. Fortunately, the weather was aligned to our course in a southwesterly direction, bound for a waypoint 100 nautical miles clear of the Society Islands.

Rose Emily is, in essence, a 30-foot-long surfboard. Her flat hull and removable daggerboard allows you to dance on the surface of the water when wind and waves align. I watched the lines of waves behind us as they passed through us. One broke in a mass of spuming whitewash, careering into our stern and bumping us forward. Too early. We rose up with the second, a larger wave of about 12 feet. My stomach turned in excitement as if on a fairground ride. I took in the view as we climbed, noticing the silhouettes of waves all around like soldiers marching to some faraway battle.

It wasn't to be. The wave passed through us before it broke and we sank back into the next trough.

Big waves often come in threes. I increased my cadence, climbing the steep face of the next wave as it approached. Our momentum built as our speed matched one another. I gave one final stroke, pushing through my heels, just as the lip started to curl. The wooden handles pressed into my thumbs as I clenched with white knuckles. *Rose Emily* hung like a clothes hanger, her bow poking awkwardly over a precipice.

Time slowed in a brief moment of suspended silence.

The stern bucked upwards and we were catapulted forwards and down, down into the trough. I flicked my paddles up to stabilise us as she swayed from right to left. The boat felt lighter as we planed. For a moment, all friction was lost. We were one with the wave, gliding. I howled as we accelerated: 'One, two . . .'

It was then that I realised that this wasn't like other waves. Usually, surfs would end before you could count to three, but *Rose Emily* showed no sign of slowing. 'W-o-w . . .' opened into an 'a-a-a-h', as control slipped through my fingertips. This wave was considerably larger than any others. We'd been warned about double dippers: two separate waves, moving at different speeds, converging into a single, monster wave.

'Four, five, six . . .' As the sloping water began to curve up again, *Rose Emily* showed no sign of slowing, over a thousand kilos of momentum carrying her on. One of our greatest fears out here, aside from a man overboard, was a pitch-pole. If the boat's momentum was too great and a wave too big, the nose of *Rose Emily* could be consumed by water as we accelerated into the trough of the next wave, causing us to somersault stern-over-bow. Many sailors share fears of boats going down in this way. And, sure enough, as we reached the bottom, the sharp nose of the bow stabbed into the water and down she went.

A torrent of water burst over the bow cabin, thrusting me from the rowing seat. The oars were wrenched from my fists as their blades were submerged. There was no hope that I could restore any kind of control, anyway. There was little that I could do other than cling on and wait for our buoyancy to bring us back up. Jets of water sprayed through Jamie's cracked cabin door. He'd left it slightly ajar to encourage a little airflow as respite from the sauna-like conditions inside. The deluge of water found the gap and within seconds the bed was drenched.

There was a feeling of acceptance in my situation. I was soaked from the waist down, my hands clasped onto the lifelines on both sides of the boat. 'It was unlikely that water would come over the bow.' I'd had too much confidence in this dry haven.

And then, as quickly as it started, it was over. We burst out of the water. I peered through the slit in my hood, not knowing what I would find. A snack pack and a tub of peanut butter bobbed in the gallons of water that had filled the row-deck, draining out of the three holes on either side of the hull. The seats were still clinging onto the lifeline, three water bottles were still tucked beside the footplates. Within a minute, there was no sign that anything had happened. By some miracle, we hadn't lost a thing.

The cabin door handle creaked and Jamie poked his head out: 'What the hell happened there?'

'*Rose Emily* went for a swim.'

Chapter 9

Silence

By Ewan

Not all the words we wrote on the Pacific were shared. Some were sent ashore, but others we kept aboard.

The daily ship's logs were open to anyone who wanted them; a simple email sign-up that grew and grew with time. Every Sunday morning, Dad would curate a short summary, pulling out the best entries and anecdotes of the week gone by. He'd add a few thoughts of his own, if the moment was right. For some, that distilled version, arriving less often, felt more appropriate.

More importantly, it involved Dad in a way we hoped might keep his worries from gathering. He's a writer, after all, and understands the world through words. Mum, the artist, would create images to go alongside Dad's summaries: cyanotypes (photographic blueprints) of her boys in a faraway sea, which she made from the photos we sent.

On Sundays, for fear of sending too much, we held back the words we wrote over that 24-hour period. We would skip the day in favour of the weekly summary. And although we still wrote a log, only a handful of our dearest received our entries those days. They became more personal, more direct, less polished. Some of the extracts you have already read came from those withheld entries, though you would not have known it at the time.

And then there was the writing that didn't make the logs at all. Half-finished ideas for future entries, lines written in snatched moments, thoughts that drifted by with the changing skies. There were things we simply couldn't write, because we didn't yet know how. We didn't have the words. These were the lost logs of *Rose Emily*.

DAY 066, Tuesday 17 June – LOST LOG

JAMIE: Song of the day – 'Scapa Flow 1919' by Kris Drever

Even out here, adrift in the largest body of water on our planet, silence is rare. In between conversations, music and audiobooks, there are periods of quiet, but the soundscape of the ocean is always here. The rush of wind, the crashing of waves, the rhythmic splash of our oars as the blades dip in and out of the water for the millionth time or more.

With my other senses deprived, the sounds of this world are emphasised. The occasional screech of a tern pierces through the backdrop of sound. I wonder why they are here? It must be food that brings them so far from land, so far from anything. I'm surprised that more haven't attempted to land on *Rose Emily*, if not for a brief moment to rest their weary wings.

I rarely pay so much attention to the sounds that surround me. The last time was over a year ago as winter turned to spring on our croft. I remember sitting under a birch tree listening to a choir of small birds welcoming the new season, looking out to sea, to where white horses broke upon the shore, and thinking about the contrast in the rhythms of land and sea.

I listen to the constant trickle of water as it runs along our hull. You can make a good guess at our speed through the water by the rate at which this trickle flows. It's even more extreme when inside the cabin; the roar of breaking waves, the rush of water only inches from my face. Some nights it lulls me to sleep, others it awakens me in moments of thundering chaos.

As I row, the sound of the spinning wheels is almost indiscernible. A good sign: the bearings in the sliding seats are holding on. We're on our last set of new wheels and we're doing everything to promote their longevity. It'll be a noisy ordeal when they finally give up the fight.

A new sound drifts towards me, carried by the wind and waves. An ancient and primal sound. The exhale of a breath held for an unimaginable length of time, thrust into the air as the giant creature prepares to dive once more. Majestic, ancient and wise: the brief whale sighting, albeit distant, fills my heart with wonder. We're not alone out here; we never were.

DAY 069, Friday 20 June – LOST LOG

JAMIE: Song of the day – 'Imagine a World' by Ímar

Moonlight floods into the bow cabin as I lie for a moment prior to resting my head. An unfamiliar feeling takes hold: for the first time in 70 days and nights my body is totally relaxed. For five precious minutes I lie here and soak it in. I close the cabin door, set the alarm and slide down among the bags of food and kit. As I close my eyes I cling to that moment, to those fleeting seconds of comfort and peace.

The morning starts as any other: instant black coffee, oats and freeze-dried berries. It's too early to allow ourselves to dream about our arrival, but the occasional thought flits across my mind. A few close friends recently sent messages of encouragement. Some even suggested they will be there on the docks to welcome us in. What a thought. A slap on the shoulder, a hug, a pint or two sitting across from a familiar face. Faces that have borne witness to many pivotal moments in my life. Fellow confidants, mischief-makers, travel companions, teammates and kindred spirits. Only a fraction of them will be able to make it out in the end, I'm sure. It would be an ask that's far too great for me to ever make. But I know they'll be there in spirit if they aren't there in person.

The threads of our lives have woven across and away from each other over the years. At times together, but at many moments apart. Regardless of distance, they've helped to forge the person I am today. Regrettably, of late, I haven't given them the time they deserve. It's a topic of conversation the three of us keep returning to on this row. It usually comes up in passing, in the half-hour fragments between shifts: a friend's wedding that we've missed, a message from home. The remarks follow naturally – 'When we get home, I can't wait to see so-and-so.' 'We need to make time.' 'It's been far too long.' Out here, it's hard sometimes to think about all the people who make our lives so rich and enjoyable, and how much better we ought to be at showing them what they mean to us.

I think of Mum and Dad. Imagining them there on the dock when we arrive. Dad wasn't able to make it in time to see us arrive after the row across the Atlantic; the weather had changed and it wasn't meant to be. But not this time.

I struggle through the heat during some long afternoon shifts. I think of all these people; the friends and family that I'm determined to do proud. Whether it's in Sydney or over a beer back home, I look forward to letting you know how grateful I am to you.

UNDATED – LOST LOG

LACHLAN: Song of the day – 'Beauty in These Streets' by Cammy Barnes

When I was young, I was scared of silence. I remember lying alone in my bunkbed, in the room beside my parents', staring at the glow-in-the-dark stars Blu-Tacked to my ceiling. A high-pitched sound would fill my eardrums, as if I'd been stunned. It was like

I could hear the silence, a visceral gateway to my imagination being cracked open.

Now that I'm older, my relationship with silence has changed. It's not something I avoid, but a rare commodity that I seek out in my days. I'm lucky to spend a lot of time at the croft. The nearest road is a single track about 100 metres from the bothy. On winter days, only a handful of cars will pass.

We're surrounded by natural sounds up there, not the din made by man. The trickle of a burn as it longs to reach the sea. The rasping screech of a heron's call. The sound of air bubbling through seaweed, pushed through mud and rock with the incoming tide. The efforts of a seal, finding its favourite perch. The siren calls of a seagull gliding over the loch.

I was determined that we should spend an extended period of time in silence aboard *Rose Emily*, something I'd stated from the outset. It struck me that we had a unique opportunity in front of us. We were in one of the most isolated places on the planet, free of the sounds of other humans, and it would have been a shame not to take advantage of that. It felt important.

Uncle Jamie sat forward on the edge of his seat, spectacles balanced on the end of his nose as he peered through the screen to the other side of the world, brow furrowed with the patient concentration that a fiddly crossword might demand. As the connection finally settled, a smile softened his features and he visibly eased his posture. Beside him was Dad, slightly more reclined in the matching wingback chair.

I knew the embrace of those armchairs all too well. Their comfort was a fond memory of childhood. Long before I can remember, they'd been Grandpa's old resting place on his 'on-call' days. A place to be summoned from if the operating theatre called – a snug, low-slung cradle, deep and difficult to escape should you sink too far down. Somewhere to rest without turning in for the night. Close enough to the phone to catch the first ring, and kinder than bed sheets if he needed to rise again.

We fell into easy conversation as if we'd simply meandered through from the dining room, choosing to sit soft after a slow Christmas meal, the rest of the family murmuring somewhere close by. Although it was mid-summer, I sensed that the fire was lit – that steady warmth in the background from a familiar hearth. Even through the screen, I felt the give of those old chairs.

About a year ago, maybe more, Dad had lost his voice. It started one day without much of a fanfare, then slowly became worse as the weeks passed by. Eventually he agreed to see a doctor, and laryngitis was diagnosed. Nothing serious. Just frustrating. An ordinary nuisance. No prescription, just rest. But then it didn't clear up. Weeks became months, and months became a year.

On the video call, Dad sat smiling, listening, his eyes bright with pride and worry and whatever else was moving behind them. Uncle Jamie did the talking. Dad would try his best to respond, but the sound wasn't there, not enough to carry what he wanted to say. You could feel the frustration gathering, so we'd hurry to fill the space, as if our own voices might spare him the effort, spare him the indignity. It was out of character in a way that made my heart sink. He looked older – not in a grey-haired way, or the way that faces change with time, but in the way an old man can sit at the edge of a conversation and knowingly watch it pass. It felt cruel.

I'm certain, if I close my eyes, Dad's voice will always fill my thoughts. The voice of many characters from the bedtime stories he read me. Not just the sound of it, though rich and warm and unmistakably his, but what it did in a room. He could lift a moment and, without trying, everyone would lean in. His stories carried a magnetism, and so did he. That rare ability to meet people as they are, without fear or fuss, no matter who they might be – a stranger, or friend, or someone life had left behind. He was always entirely himself, unapologetically. Everyone was drawn to that.

But he wasn't himself just then. Seeing Dad beside his brother, quietened, wasn't right. It's not how my childhood memories were cast, the room loud and alive as crosstalk flowed back and forth. Even louder still if the third brother, Uncle David, was there. Three of them, bouncing off one another, as they must have done as brothers growing up.

We'd tried, in the months before we left, to coax him into a proper stretch of silence, to see if it would help. But it had been brushed off like dull medical advice, the kind he never quite believed in. It was hard sometimes to encourage Dad to listen to the doctor. Maybe it was his upbringing: his relationship with Grandpa, a wartime surgeon with a stiff upper lip. Or maybe it was simply Dad: stoic and stubborn and rebellious at heart. Unconcerned by his mortality and determined to live life full.

But we were willing to try anything that might give back even a fraction of what he'd lost, and knew we'd have more luck if it didn't feel like a directive. So we softened it to something else. We told him about our plans to do three days of silence on the boat, and asked him if he'd like to join. Not as a treatment, but a shared experience, despite the miles between us. He liked the idea of that, it appealed to his spiritual sensibilities; a kind of transcendence from his forced whispers. And so we chose a day. A small pact, held across distance. No fixing, or forcing – just a few days of space for us all, where silence would do what it could.

DAY 075, Thursday 26 June

JAMIE: A day of silence

A Haiku on silence:

Silence creates space.
Hidden truths behind each wave;
Quiet reflection.

We've begun our first day of silence on board *Rose Emily*. No talking, no music, no internet, no messages. Only the sounds of the oars and the ocean. Our ambition is to try to keep silent for three days and nights. There will, of course, be moments, most likely safety related, that will require the occasional word. But, in general, we're curious to see how a period of silent reflection will affect our experience at sea. Unsurprisingly, this was Lachlan's idea.

I do wonder how this will unfold – what is already quite a bizarre experience made even more extreme by the removal of the one thing we rely on most days to help pass the time: conversation. Will the days pass painfully slowly? What will be the effects on morale? What, if anything, will we discover?

There is undoubtedly something to be said about silence and its positive effects on our appreciation of our surroundings and our place within the world. When I think about it, I'm not sure I've ever spent more than a couple of hours in silence, especially on land. The humdrum of life, for good or for bad, is constantly grasping for our attention: phones, computers, cars, radios, colleagues, children, friends, family and so on. There is a cacophony of noise at every waking moment. We've grown so used to it that I think most of us feel uncomfortable in silence, uneasy with just ourselves and our thoughts.

I'm not sure these three days will result in any spiritual revelations, but if nothing else I hope it will add to the richness of our experience. With the wind howling at about 18 knots, it isn't really silent. But with its continuous presence over the last 75 days we've grown accustomed to its sound. We've allowed tapping and the occasional whistle to get one another's attention – for passing items up and down the boat, shift changes, or checking battery levels.

Today brought the most continuous cloud cover we've had all crossing, not a glimpse of sun from dawn till dusk. A nice break from the heat, but it comes with its own complications. Battery levels take a while to reach a point where water can be made, and only allow the bare minimum to be produced. Wet rations are issued for our mid-morning meal, and washing salt off after shifts is kept to a minimum. We scrape through, but the batteries do not get above 12.9V by the evening – far from ideal.

I put on a long-sleeve top after my rowing shift as a somewhat alien feeling of goosebumps and a chill hits my skin. Precipitation in the convergence zone is the highest in the whole of the South Pacific Ocean; I can feel the moisture forming on my hands and face.

Like on a wet walk on the west coast of Scotland where the air is damp and heavy: it doesn't rain, yet you are still soaked through.

As the nightshifts descend I realise that I already spend over half my nights in silence anyhow. But it's in the latter part of the second half that I usually rely on a little boost in the form of an audiobook or music.

My eyes feel heavy as I pull on the oars. I try some breathing exercises to sharpen my senses, and nibble on my last bit of dried mango. Although there's a strong wind and large waves, the ocean has been kind to us these past 24 hours, with only a handful of waves over the deck. Without the usual sound of voices, I notice the emptiness of it again: the hiss of water, the knock of oarlocks, the wind in the dark. Not silence, exactly. Just the sounds of the boat and whatever lies beyond the beam of my headtorch.

DAY 076, Friday 27 June – LOST LOG

LACHLAN: A day of silence

As night on *Rose Emily* descended, thick cloud cover spanned the sky as far as the eye could see. Ewan slogged on as we entered the final rotation before nightshift. Heavy drizzle started in the early evening – not the explosive downpour we've become familiar with, but far more Scottish. That relentless type that soaks you.

I sat in the stern position, contemplating the silent night ahead. The red light from my headtorch lit up the reflective strips on Ewan's hood, showing the vague outline of his face. In every other direction, we were in complete darkness.

Until we were not.

To the northwest, an explosion lit up the horizon, giving us a glimpse of the surrounding ocean. I looked at Ewan; he looked at me. No words were shared, but I knew he was thinking the same: 'Lightning storm. Exactly what we need in a full-carbon boat.'

The rain persisted for 12 hours. From the cabin it sounded like being inside an automated car wash. I cracked the door to peer out. The water sprayed in through the tiny crack. I lay back down to wait for it to ease off. At about 3.50 a.m., shortly before relieving Jamie for my final nightshift, I stirred several minutes before my alarm with a sinking realisation. I was damp. There's something particularly unpleasant about being woken up by the feeling of wetness on a boat.

'Probably just condensation,' I thought to myself, wishfully. But there it was again. A cold trickle on my mid-thigh. I slumped back, defeated. There were two suspects: the seals around the inversion pump, or the port-side aerial. This was one to tackle in the daylight hours.

Dawn is truly appreciated after nights like these. The rain eased and a slug of light could be made out on the horizon in front of me. I looked up at a handful of friends peeping down at me. Stars had never been so welcome.

We danced between active patches of high pressure through the morning of the 27th, hatches battened and ready for the inevitable onslaught. *Rose Emily* dodged and dived through the following sea as we rose and fell with each wave. The foam that had been whipped up on the surface of the churning water looked like an invisible army of mice scuttling down the faces of each wave, giving warning to the next gust. We heaved on the oars, eager to catch a wave as they began to break.

The silence was filled by the sound of the ocean, broken only by the swish of our oars. Every now and then, we caught eye contact and giggles ensued. The worst had passed by the evening, and rays of pinky red formed on the horizon to the west.

We were grateful for a clear sky going into our third night of silence.

DAY 077, Saturday 28 June

EWAN: A day of silence

Time has moved differently during the silent period: an ebb and flow with some moments passing quicker, others crawling past.

Navigating through the South Pacific Convergence Zone on our third and final day of silence, we've been met with hours of heavy rain, high winds, big conditions and a lightning storm – appropriately streaking across the sky without the faintest sound of thunder. An eerie sight. Apparently, lightning can be seen for up to 200 nautical miles at sea, and the sound may never reach you.

With the stormy weather came a drop in temperature. Woolly hats were fished out of the storage nets for the first time overnight. The lightweight sleeping bags also made their debut, which I had prospectively packed into each cabin in Lima. After the first few weeks at sea, I had concluded that they were a likely dead weight, so I was glad to see them used, even if only for a night. After escaping the driving rain and drying myself as best I could, I crawled inside the sleeping bag. The slippery synthetic material stuck to my skin, making it hard to move around, trapping my legs awkwardly until I eventually wriggled into position. The problem then presented itself in that, as the boat rocked from side to side, the layers of fabric between me and the mattress were able to glide extremely smoothly over one another. This lack of friction meant that my entire body slid back and forth, from port to starboard, with each passing wave.

Having consumed much of our food stores lining the berths, unfortunately this meant a reasonable distance. Wedging my arms either side helped to limit the movement of my upper body enough to find some comfort, and I eventually drifted off to sleep.

Having hung my foul-weather smock and sodden clothes on the stern cabin handrail after the last shift, I had expected to wake a few hours later to more driving rain and soaking-wet garments to pull over my head. But, instead, the storm had passed, and a bright sky with a fresh breeze greeted me. The static energy of the downpour still filled the air. Light streamed between clouds, and droplets of water sparkled on the boat's glistening surfaces. What a relief to have the wet night behind us.

Our next waypoint was Palmerston Island, a small atoll with around 30 inhabitants. Over the last few days we have been flirting with a more southerly course, which would have allowed us to pass below it – a more favourable route. However, unable to hold our line against the weather, we eventually opted to avoid the lee shore and take the northern course.

Carefully navigating clear with the chart-plotter, we passed by with no more than 15 miles clearance to our port side, yet no sign could be seen of the low-lying atoll. Like many islands in French Polynesia and the South Pacific, it sits only a few metres above sea level; an incredible ring of reef and sand, with a crystal-clear sea lagoon at its centre.

In silence we watched the horizon as the day passed, searching for the smallest indication of a beach or civilisation. Our progress was slow, with counter-currents working against us. But nothing became apparent, despite rowing within a few miles; not the smallest sign of difference among the surrounding blue expanse.

My thoughts turn to rising sea levels and the remaining years the island will still be habitable for. How might I feel if the waters were to rise above the place I call my home?

And then, almost without ceremony, it was over. Three days of holding back, of letting the sea be the only sound. By then, I knew its register better than ever. The amplified trickle of water running down the hull from inside the cabins, the low thud of carbon meeting waves as the boat lifted and fell, the knock of the oar cuffs, everything relentlessly in motion. The first words felt strange and heavy, and we returned to our voices more gently than we'd left them. I was glad we did it. Glad, too, that we could speak again. Yet as conversation began to re-enter the boat, I found myself listening for a voice that wasn't there at all. I thought of Dad, and the pact we'd made, and wondered how he'd managed it alone – whether it had given him anything back. I hoped it had.

Chapter 10

The Calm Before the Storm

By Jamie

You develop an interesting relationship with the weather when you spend every waking moment trying to anticipate its next move. In our stripped-back existence, it was the one thing that was always on our minds. It would make or break our experience. And it was the one thing that was completely out of our control.

There's a foreboding feeling on board a boat when a flare of lightning is first seen. I tend to question it initially, presuming that perhaps someone has taken a photograph and mistakenly used their flash. The second strike removes all doubt and secures a somewhat fearful state of mind. How far off do we predict it to be? Is it coming our way? Shall we change course? What will happen if we get struck?

One thing that was for certain, we were the highest, most prominent point for hundreds of miles around – a sitting target. Our slightly raised navigation light provided the shortest air gap for the electrical charge to travel to the ocean below. What the hell should we do? Removing the nav pole would reduce our height by half a metre, but the cabins still stood 1.5 metres proud of the surface of the sea. Being struck would spell disaster. If the three of us somehow survived, the millions of volts of power surging through our boat would fry all of our electrical systems. Any wires on board would literally explode. No batteries, no watermaker, no autohelm, no ongoing means of communication. Other than sinking us, it would be the ultimate top trump that Mother Nature could play.

We quickly messaged our shore team and got Sean the line. He rather calmly explained that he had been in a similar situation before, but in a steel-hulled yacht. We needed to preserve the electrical equipment we had on board by disconnecting whatever we could from the main circuit, so that if the system was overloaded we wouldn't lose everything. Ewan disconnected one of the batteries and some non-essential instruments. If we were struck, losing the autohelm would be inevitable, but we could try to save the watermaker at least.

The next instruction came as a bit of shock. Should the lightning storm pass directly over us, the conductive nature of the carbon-fibre hull would potentially attract the electrical surge. We needed to manage its destruction by rerouting it. The satellite message outlined how: 'Take your steel land-anchor chain, remove the rope and anchor, then fix one end of the chain to the highest point on board *Rose Emily*. Drape the rest of the chain down the side of the boat and ensure the other end is submerged in the water. If you're hit, this should conduct the electrical current and provide a path of least resistance down into the water, where the voltage will be diffused.'

Was that it? It felt too simple. Like being told the best way to deter a wild animal is to shout and act like you aren't scared. Invite the lightning in and attempt to control it. If it worked, we might avoid devastation. And if it didn't . . . well, at least it would all be over in the blink of an eye.

Ominous clouds loomed on the horizon. A grey mass marched towards us, illuminated by the occasional flash from within. As it stretched across the skyline, the wind had picked up and so we had no option but to stay true to our course, heading directly into the belly of the beast.

The anchor chain had been brought out on deck as a precaution, but the storm appeared to be travelling with us. Flanked on three sides, the wide horseshoe shape had miraculously kept its distance. Its wide embrace remained present but unfamiliar. As the flashes became fainter and less regular, all of us on deck started to feel relief. We were thankful to stow away the chain. Little did we know, this was only a taste of the weather challenges to come.

DAY 078, Sunday 29 June

JAMIE: Song of the day – 'Now Westlin Winds' by Dick Gaughan

The wind from the southeast dropped by the evening, but a counter-current of around 0.5 to 0.7 knots heralds dark, ominous clouds on the horizon, flashing bright with lightning as the light fades.

The past 24 hours have seen some of the most challenging times of our crossing to date. At least we've managed 28 miles. As the wind died down on Sunday afternoon, we knew we were in for some heavy rowing. What unfolded has made me very thankful for the long and hard hours of training we did in preparation for this row. Chloë did everything possible to ensure our bodies and minds were up for this test, and today I am particularly grateful to her for this.

As we reach the edge of the South Pacific Convergence Zone, we receive an update on the predicted weather forecast for the next few days. After a brief spell of favourable conditions, we anticipate some flat calm seas as we dance between two large active low-pressure systems (two large storms) that are rubbing shoulders in this part of the ocean.

Moreover, after 24 to 48 hours, the wind will move down to the south and southeast, build in strength and attempt to push us back north. Therefore, in the spell of high pressure (calm seas), we attempt to push as far south as physically possible to put us in a good position for the inevitable drift north towards the middle and end of this week.

The ambition: try to make it round the southern tip of the Tongan archipelago. If we can't make it far enough south, there is a viable gap between two of the islands. However, as with any landmass, our proximity to the islands could cause complications with both weather and routing.

As dusk approaches and we enter the first round of nightshifts, the wind has died down to nearly nothing. Although this allows us to point further south, it's heavy going on the oars. Each stroke is felt hard, from the calves to the glutes and up through the back and arms.

I feel the energy sapping from my body and have to constantly rely on snacks and electrolyte mix to ensure I can keep up the pace. The first nightshift slowly passes and I'm thankful for a break after an hour and 40 minutes of pulling through the treacle-like conditions.

My sleep is still sub-par; I wake every 60 or 90 minutes without fail. My body seems to have set an internal alarm clock and there's simply no sleeping through for a longer spell. Either that or my arms have gone numb and a repositioning is necessary.

I head out onto the oars, bid Ewan a good night, and settle down to what seem like similar conditions to before. Large clouds of rain and lightning loom on the horizon. They are very distant, though, so I don't give them much thought. The occasional flash illuminates the sky and boat, as if someone were taking the occasional photograph from above.

What I hadn't considered is that this thunderstorm is moving in a completely different direction to us and our boat. I feel the murmurs of a headwind tickle the back of my neck, and within ten minutes the breeze has wheeled around and built to 10 knots from the southwest, dead against the direction in which I struggle. With added counter-current the oars are incredibly heavy. My back quickly begins to ache and my hands throb. Each stroke I heave with all my might in an attempt to build a pathetic amount of momentum. I have to pause briefly to put on my foul-weather jacket as the rain begins to lash down upon the deck. Twenty seconds off and I feel the boat lose all forward momentum. I quickly get back on the oars and heave again.

It's impossible to know exactly what direction the boat is pointed, but I'm hopeful that I must be making a small amount of headway. I continue this struggle for an hour and a half then decide to check the tracker on my phone.

I've essentially gone backwards.

I can't believe it. Over the last 90 minutes I've covered 0.7 nautical miles in the desired direction. I've done a zigzag for a while, gone backwards for a bit, forwards a little, round, down and back again. My tracking route looks like a child's attempt at drawing a pony. Crushed, demoralised and aching all over, I finish my shift, failing to muster a smile when Lachlan climbs out onto the oars. 'I really hope your shift goes better than mine,' I say as I crawl into the cabin.

'How bad we talking?' he asks, a little hesitantly.

'My worst to date,' I reply as I swing shut the door.

I'll laugh about it one day.

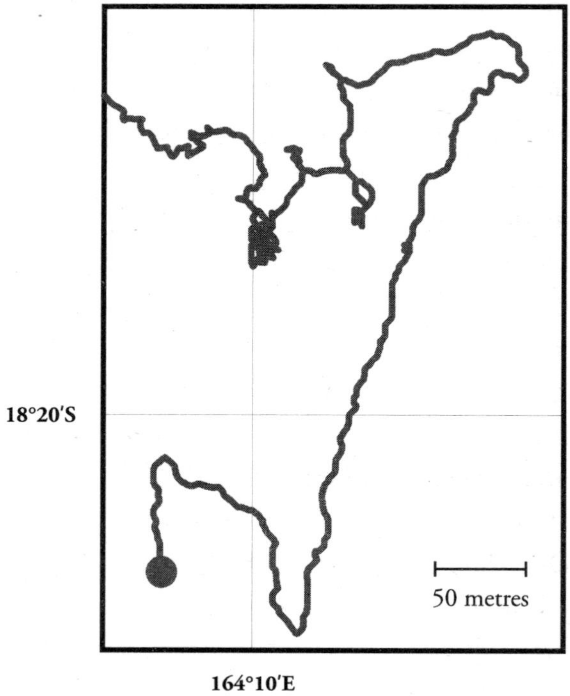

Going backwards

The 30th of June broke into a blistering hot day with light wind from the southwest. We slogged away, one hour on, 30 minutes off, with painfully slow progress as we fought 1.2 knots of counter-current and 6 knots of headwind. My head was foggy with the heat. Sweat dripped down my forehead; mixing with suncream, it stung my eyes.

Around mid-morning, the autohelm deck repeater turned off. Some investigation revealed that most of the electrics had short-circuited and we were getting no charge from any of the solar panels. It was the last thing we needed.

My mind turned once again to catastrophe mode, stacking up all of the challenges that will ensue if we can't resolve the problem. No water. No autohelm. No navigation instruments. Weeks or even months longer at sea.

Ewan put down his oars and prepared himself for a stint in the stern cabin. At this time of day it would be swelteringly hot and uncomfortable in there. Dismantling the electrical board he found that the main boat fuse had gone, suspected to be caused by the roving solar panel and a faulty plug.

Two hours later he reappeared, dripping with sweat as if he'd been locked in a sauna. We were back in business and the watermaker could go on.

We turned our attention to the next challenge. We had been warned of a big weather system which had been growing for the last few days. We were told it had changed course and was headed straight for us, due to hit in a couple of days' time.

We toiled on, determinedly positive, at a pitifully slow pace of 1.5 knots. Forty minutes on, 20 minutes off, repeated hour after hour.

'At least we aren't rowing with three on the oars,' Lachlan chirped up.

'Ha, you're not wrong there,' I replied. 'Although my back feels like I've been doing deadlifts for days.'

'Twenty minutes off "rest" passes pretty quickly, doesn't it?' interjected Ewan, as he glanced at his watch and readied himself for his next stint on the oars.

'Three days and we get another packet of jelly sweets,' I announced as I shared my inner calculations. 'I think we should up the Tony's ration. I found a couple of extra bars in the bow locker and I reckon we could have them every 500 nautical miles now instead of every thousand.'

'No way,' Lachlan replied. 'How long have you known this?'

'I've been keeping it for when the moment seemed right. Imagine, a Tony's nearly every week!' I let out excitedly.

Silence fell over the boat as we all reflected on the possibility of a double ration of chocolate.

The clock turned 16.00 and we stowed the oars to prepare for the weather to come. Rowing tracks were cleaned, wheels greased, all loose equipment stowed and some snack packs and camera kit moved between the cabins. Just as the sun started to drop in the sky, we got in the water to clean the hull. It felt good to be weightless, even only for a few minutes. The cool water lapped around me as I looked down for a second into the shimmering blue. The colours were mesmerising to my tired eyes, and a welcome break from the constant view of the horizon line. There was little growth but it was an excuse for a wash – especially as it was unclear how long it would be until it was safe to do this again.

I imagined how different the ocean would look in 48 hours' time. The gentle lapping waves rising to towering walls of water. The invisible power of the wind churning the sea all around. We anticipated the next few days to be the biggest conditions the three of us had ever experienced: 35-knot winds and swell nearing 8 metres in height. If the two aligned with our desired direction we'd be in for a fast couple of days as *Rose Emily* surfed from one surge to the next. We'd need to be extra vigilant with the cabin doors, and, of course, be tethered to the boat at all times, as was normal practice on even the calmest of days.

As the sun slowly fell from the sky, we sat on deck and watched its last streams of light punch out across the clouds. The deep rubies, maroons and coppers reflected off the waves and danced across our boat. We watched in silence, soaking it up, knowing that this was one of those tranquil moments that comes before a storm. Red sky at night, shepherd's delight. Turns out shepherds and sailors don't have as much in common as we hoped.

DAY 081, Wednesday 2 July

JAMIE: Song of the day – 'The Sailor's Bonnet' by The Gloaming

As the wind gets stronger the waves increase in size. A swell from the south clashes with the windswept waves and causes disturbance to what is otherwise a following sea. The lack of sunshine has limited water production and has meant all electrics have been off except the autopilot. There's a storm a'coming. There's a shared feeling of excited anticipation on board *Rose Emily* as the wind and waves build. We are forecast 25 to 30 knots of wind over the next 24 hours, gusting up to 35. Everything on deck has been lashed down or, if possible, stowed into lockers. External calls for the next 48 to 72 hours have had to be postponed; we need to keep focused and alert as the big weather rumbles in. It's at moments like these that you really begin to feel alive. The hope is that the wind moves from the south/southeast into the east, providing some promising surfable conditions.

With the frustration and exhaustion of the last few days we can't wait to hopefully make some good progress. We'll be endeavouring to move in the same direction as the big swell – anything else would be hard going and dangerous. But there are always rogue waves. Ones that defy all rhyme or reason, travelling perpendicular to both the prevailing wind and the oncoming waves. These black sheep of the surf are outliers, but they do have impeccable timing. You've either just changed into dry(ish) socks and shoes, or you're nearing the end of your stint on the oars. Things are looking up, you've made it through unscathed and are about to tuck into your chicken tikka masala. But then, as if sensing this slight feeling of warmth and security, the rogue wave strikes. Barrelling over the port side, it knocks you off your seat, salt water saturating every last inch of dry on your being. You're left there stunned and strewn across the deck. You were so close and yet so naïve. We are in an open boat that sits approximately 20cm from the surface of the sea, and we're rocking and rolling in 30 knots of wind with a 4-metre swell. If you expect to stay dry for longer than 15 minutes you need a bit of a reality check.

The wind and waves gradually pick up throughout the day and, as predicted, they move a little to the east. It's a powerful sea-state and we're moving fast as a result of it. Our Atacama foul-weather smocks have been on all day, we accept that our lower halves will routinely be drenched, and so shorts and wet shoes are all that are needed. At night, as darkness prevails, I might treat myself to some naked rowing to help appease the chafe. The air temperature has definitely dropped a little, helped by partial cloud cover for most of today.

It begins to get dark and the surf continues to build. We're in for a wild night indeed. Lachlan, sitting against the stern cabin and preparing our final meal of the day, has just about packed away the Jetboil when a large rolling wave catches up with the back of the boat. Its speed is far greater than ours and it crashes over the stern cabin. A deluge of water comes down, Lala's hood isn't up, and the sea floods down the back of his head and neck. His head slumps, hair sodden. Robbed of his last dry sanctuary.

I held on tightly to the handle above the cabin door. The boat careered down one wave and climbed up the next, jolting under the power of the ocean. We were balancing on a fine line of barely feeling in control. Using our body weight alongside the oars helped to keep *Rose Emily* on an even keel as she bounced along the surface of each wave.

We'd had two knockdowns over the past 24 hours, where a rogue wave had attempted to flip the boat. They barrelled in from the port side, perpendicular to the prevailing wind and waves. As they collided side-on, *Rose Emily* violently rolled 90 degrees to starboard as we clung to whatever we could find. We were certain everything had been stowed or secured, but still we lost vital items. One wave claimed two of our rowing cushions, the precious padding desperately needed to keep our backsides from becoming red raw. We were now down to the last three.

The second had taken a water bottle and a tub of peanut butter. I'd often been the most emotional on this crossing to date, but for a brief moment Lachlan was inconsolable. He raged and threw insults at the ocean, verbalising his anger in a foray of foul language. 'We'd only just opened that fucking tub, goddamn you!' he shouted as he threw a punch and a kick to the next oncoming wave.

'You'll only make her angry,' I called out from my rowing position.

'Angry! I'll give you angry!' He gestured rudely to the sea.

'Just let him vent,' Ewan murmured. 'I'd rather him punch the air than you or me.'

Lachlan slumped down at the stern position, and no words were exchanged for a short while.

As the sun set, I stowed my oars and warily made my way to the bow. Being in a storm in daylight is one thing, but the darkness of night makes everything more intense. I brushed my teeth, stripped down, and waited for a lull in the waves. No matter how brief a manoeuvre, unclipping to enter the cabin was always unnerving in big conditions like these. I shifted my weight and unlocked the door. As we entered the trough between two moving mountains of water, I flung aside the door and stepped inside. A wave crashed against the hull sending white wash over the deck. I yanked the cabin door shut as some wayward spray landed on my bed. It was a small price to pay for safety.

Shorts off, baby-wiped down, I fell into darkness as my head hit the makeshift pillow. In those brief moments of suspended consciousness, when the world already feels upside down, *Rose Emily* was hit. Thrown against the side of the cabin by the force of the wave, bags and belongings cascaded down, burying me in chaos. I felt water gushing in through the ventilation gap surrounding the cabin door. Why had I not fully locked it this evening? I was certain this was it, the capsize in the night that we had all been dreading. Dazed and confused, I reached for the handles. They weren't where they should be. I realised my world had rotated 90 degrees. Frantically, I found the first one, then the second, and the third. The last trickle of water ended as I fully sealed the fourth. 'That was a powerful wave,' I thought to myself. 'Thank God we didn't go fully over.' Shifting some of the bags and assessing my now very wet bed, I suddenly realised. Someone must be on deck.

Squinting through the small window in the cabin door, I could see Ewan strewn across the boat. He pulled himself up, dropped his oars and moved with speed to the stern. 'He's running to retrieve something that's gone overboard,' I thought. 'Please, not another tub of peanut butter.'

Chapter 11

Lifelines

By Lachlan

DAY 082, Thursday 3 July

LACHLAN: Song of the day – 'A Hard Rain's A-Gonna Fall' by Bob Dylan

I lie in the stern bunk dreaming of sleep. Everything from my mid-thigh down is wet. The safety lines vibrate on deck with the howling wind. I've been here for some time – 30 or 40 minutes. This is quite unlike me. Usually I'm out cold as soon as my head hits the pillow. Just as my eyelids close and the gates to another world open, I'm flipped into the wall of the cabin like a chipolata in a frying pan. After several failed attempts, I've given up. Rest will have to be as good as sleep tonight.

This was our second day of enduring a violent Pacific storm from the southeast. Huge amounts of energy push the waves forward, their momentum carrying head-over-heels as great white horses break into gallop. We've no choice other than to row downwind — the safest course possible — taking us more north than desired.

Salty, tired and bruised, we entered the final rotation of the dayshift as the sun went down. The forecast was for the wind to sustain at over 25 knots until midnight then drop off going into tomorrow.

My final dayshift concluded at 19.40 and I made my way to the stern to swap with Ewan. My hand squeezed the carabiner tethering me to the lifelines as I looked up into the darkness, waiting for a gap in the waves to clamber inside.

A gap is not what I found.

A 20-foot pyramid of water rose up in front of me off our port side. The wave was just about to crest, barrelling at 90 degrees to the boat. I grasped onto the nearest thing, a camera pole, and braced. A wall of water hit. My legs gave way under its overwhelming weight. I fell to starboard and the camera pole gave way too. The boat reared violently in a tumble dryer of salt and spray. As my legs caught the lifelines, my weight was thrown head over heels, and I somersaulted into the darkness.

Time slowed. My body became limp and disorientated; I had no idea which way was up or down. Was this a capsize? Where's Ewan? Am I clipped on?

I didn't have the time to be scared or panicked. All that was left was acceptance. Acceptance of whatever was happening. My fate was no longer in my hands.

It was then that I noticed the pressure in my right fist. My hand was clamped onto the grabline spanning the boat's waterline. I looked up. My red headtorch illuminated Mum's calligraphy handwriting on the boat's transom: *Rose Emily*. I was in the water being dragged like a doll behind the boat.

The moments that followed had a dreamlike quality. A red hand appeared out of the darkness, illuminated by my headtorch.

'Grab this,' came Ewan's voice.

Tilting backwards, he heaved with all of his might as I swung my leg towards the wave-deflecting wing like I was vaulting myself over a fence. *Rose Emily* was by now perpendicular to the wind and waves, rocking violently from side to side. We had to get her pointing downwind again. It was in these moments that she was most likely to roll. The ledge was too high, my foot too slippery. I lost my perch and slipped back into the depths below.

The next wave arrived and my timing was better. Just as the boat tilted down, I drove upwards, flopping onto the row-deck over the stowed oars like a beached salmon. It wasn't pretty, but I had made it back on board.

All sorts of detritus was strewn across the deck from the knockdown: snack packs, rowing seats, the toilet bucket. The carbon camera pole I'd taken with me was being dragged behind us by its lanyard. The only thing that had been lost overboard was another tub of peanut butter.

'It was you or the peanut butter,' Ewan said.

'A hard decision, then,' I said with a smile before clambering inside for some kip.

As I lay there in the cabin, listening to the wind howling against the thin layer of carbon, I was wide awake. My heart thumped as adrenaline pumped through my veins. A new sensation made its way up my spine like a spider crawling into its web.

Fear.

Everything had happened so quickly that I hadn't had a moment to pre-empt or rationalise. My body just reacted, my mind lagged behind. It was only now that it dawned on me how close that was. I imagined how differently those events could have gone had I not been clipped on. The sick feeling that would have formed in Jamie's and Ewan's guts as they tried to bring the boat into the wind. One pointing at the red headtorch as it emerged and disappeared in the oncoming waves, getting smaller and smaller, the other rowing with all of their might. How long would they have tried to reach to me?

I knew that my best chance would be in the first few minutes. With each minute that passed, my odds of survival would drop, like giving someone CPR. As soon as the boat was lost from view, I stood little chance. The sad reality in these conditions was that there wouldn't have been much hope. It was a reminder of the fragility of our lives out there. We didn't have a safety net; all that separated us from a desperate situation was a moment of carelessness – an open cabin door or not clipping on. Complacency wasn't an option.

We'd met a survivor from one such horrific story. A large wave had crashed over their boat, washing a 21-year-old into the darkness. They'd rowed as hard as they could, three-up, but it wasn't enough. They didn't have the power to make any forward progress into the wind. The crew stared, utterly helpless, as they watched the small light bobbing further and further towards the horizon. Then, like a candle being blown out, the light was gone and never seen again.

DAY 083, Friday 4 July

JAMIE: Song of the day – 'Feral Road' by Beluga Lagoon

I sit at the stern position, my back against the cabin door, washing sheets. It's a job I've done somewhat begrudgingly for the duration of this crossing, but it's one of those must-do necessities. Unlike on most occasions, though, I find myself weirdly enjoying this familiar process for the first time. There's comfort to be found in these mundanities as the intensities of the storm pass into memory. They might be mundane tasks. But, after the shock we've just had, anything familiar feels like welcome relief.

Before any content from our dramatic 24 hours was shared with the shore team, it was important for me to speak with Mum, Dad and Heide. I wanted to reassure them that everything was ok.

By chance, Heide had stopped at Dad's flat for some dinner after work to check in with him. I could hear the concern in their voices, but Dad quickly broke any tension with a whispered quip: 'It'll be great if there's ever a book!'

As I said my goodbyes and ended the WhatsApp call, I was happy they had one another. They were both stoic, but it reassured me to think of them eating Dad's shepherd's pie with a glass of red wine, or – in Dad's case – milk.

Next was Mum. The call rang out.

'Hello?' Her voice was tired. I'd woken her up, forgetting that (because of the International Date Line, which we hadn't crossed yet) she was now 21 hours ahead of us – she'd recently arrived in Sydney to stay with a friend, awaiting our arrival.

She was understandably upset – as any mother would be – but took it well. One of our biggest apprehensions about embarking on this journey had been the stress it could cause Mum. After her experiences during our Atlantic row, we were concerned about what could result from so much longer at sea. But she'd been dealing with it all astonishingly well. 'Clip on and keep those hatches closed,' she reminded me as I hung up.

With a favourable wind and a following current we had a brief spell of rowing one-up, giving us some much-needed time to address all the things that had been neglected over the past 48 hours. We washed clothes, dried our shoes, and attempted to dry out the stern cabin.

During the storm we'd noticed a drip coming from one of the vents to the rear cabin. By the final day, there was a layer of water sloshing about under the mattress. As waves crashed over the deck, water was gaining access through one of the Henderson hatches (the circular screw-top hatch-lids dotted across the row-deck) that had been retrofitted with a waterproof solar-powered fan.

We'd all had some pretty bad nights of sleep out here over the past 83 days, but the two nights during the storm took the prize. Truly torturous. I pulled the soggy mattress out and got to work with the deck brush and some Ecover washing-up liquid. I lay the cover out across the deck to dry in the sun and sat back with my lukewarm black coffee in hand. As I looked out upon the benign swell it was difficult to imagine the tempest that had existed here only hours ago: the shriek of the wind, the chill of the spray, the raging seas that seemed so determined to capsize our small vessel. It couldn't be in greater contrast to the peaceful ocean that surrounded us now, gently encouraging us onwards to Australia. It had been a close shave, a reminder to be doubly vigilant with safety measures, especially when conditions were big. There's no point sugar-coating it: my climbing harness and safety line almost certainly saved my life. It would be so easy to become complacent after so many weeks at sea, leaving cabin doors open and unclipping. But this wasn't a dress-rehearsal; this was it, and it was crucial that we kept our best game for the remaining miles. Three brothers left Yacht Club Peruano 83 days ago. The project's success was contingent on all three of us stepping safely off this boat in one piece.

DAY 083, Friday 4 July (log entry continued)

JAMIE

The wind continued to drop and by nightfall the surface of the sea was smooth and calm. After the strong winds of the low-pressure system we've just weathered, we anticipate some light winds as a veil of a high pressure is cast over us. This means some challenging rowing, perhaps even some light headwinds. Future problems. For now, I just sit and soak up what satisfaction I can.

Unfortunately, Jamie's suspicions were right. As darkness fell, a headwind started to build. The sad reality about rowing is that, generally speaking, the slower you're going, the heavier your oars are. The heavier your oars, the harder the rowing. Not only does your inner voice complain about the exertion you're putting it through, it also scorns the pitiful boat speed. It's a vicious circle, and as the hours ticked by into our 85th day, it finally became too much.

DAY 085, Sunday 6 July

LACHLAN: Song of the day – 'Think of Today' by Rura

Since Peru we've had at least one person – often two – on the oars, 24 hours a day, seven days a week. We've been focused – almost obsessively – on progress towards our destination. To float or, even worse, go backwards has felt unnerving. Almost wrong.

Our honeymoon of good weather following the storm came to an end overnight. The wind built from nothing into an 8-knot southwesterly. Our 2-knot limp soon became a crawl as speed over ground dipped below one knot (1.15mph) with 12 knots of headwind and some current from the southwest. We expended precious calories with almost no westward or southerly progress. Our situation was clear by morning.

For the first time in almost 6,000 nautical miles, we've spent most of today with nobody rowing. We've had to do something we've not done in over 8,500 miles of ocean rowing across the Pacific and Atlantic: deploy our parachute anchor. The headwind was too strong for making any semblance of forward progress.

The para-anchor is a giant underwater parachute that attaches onto our bowline (the rope attached to the front of *Rose Emily*). Once deployed, the pull of the boat due to wind fills the chute, creating a large amount of drag in the water. Though we'd still be swept by the ocean currents, the para-anchor reduced the boat's movement due to wind to about 0.5 knots or less.

We spent the afternoon of the 6th doing the odd jobs we'd been putting off: fixing the carbon pole I took with me for my surprise dip during the storm; arranging and organising the cabins; checking the stores hiding in the bow locker. We had some good hauls on the food front: a stray chilli chicken curry, two packs of freeze-dried chilli and half a dozen spaghetti bolognese.

A ping came in on the inReach. It was Sean: 'Hope you boys aren't too uncomfortable on para. Standing by to move off early doors: it should ease up from 05.00 boat time tomorrow. I've been thinking about Sydney—' The message cut off halfway.

'I think I know what he's going to say,' Jamie speculated as we waited for the next message.

'. . . I think we need to start looking at Brisbane as an arrival destination,' Sean continued, as the second message came in. 'It's going to be challenging to get far enough south to Sydney. Have a chat among yourselves and let us know.'

We'd seen this coming. The storm had pushed us considerably further north than desired. From where we were now, Sydney was about 2,300 nautical miles away at a bearing of 247 degrees – far further south than anything we'd been able to sustain up until this point. Brisbane was about 2,100 nautical miles away at a more manageable bearing of 256 degrees. It was a disappointing realisation. We'd had dreams of finishing under the Sydney Harbour Bridge. It felt like we'd failed ourselves and those we'd told about this aspiration.

'Australian soil is Australian soil,' I reassured us – well, myself as much as the others – as I ate my final spoonful of meat chilli. 'The most important thing is arriving in one piece and unsupported.' We only had about 60 days of food left, and trying for Sydney could mean torturous weeks of sitting on parachute anchor and rowing into headwinds as we closed in on Australia. Apart from anything else, we didn't have the food reserves for that.

The prospect of doing more boat chores faded with the light. I lay in the forward bunk while Jamie and Ewan shared the stern. *Rose Emily* jolted awkwardly as the oncoming waves ran down the hull, creating ripples of sound. The taut nylon rope a few feet away from my head yanked with each oncoming wave, a constant reminder of where I was.

I found myself with something that I hadn't had for 85 days: time. Necessity didn't dictate my actions. I had a choice – albeit limited – to do this or that. Stand on deck or go to sleep; listen to an audiobook or write my log; scoff a Cadbury's bar or save it for the next day. The prospect of a chunk of free time was appealing from the rowing seat. But now I had it, I felt slightly lost. Our purpose for almost three months had been crystal clear: get to Australia in 120 days to raise as much money as possible. Every decision was overridden by achieving that goal. There was no time to overthink in the same way that we do in normal life.

I reflected on the miles that stretched out ahead of us. From our current position, lolling on a sea-anchor somewhere west of the Pacific island of Niue, we were faced with three major challenges. Firstly, with Tonga now sitting unavoidably between us and Australia, we would have no choice but to find a route between the islands. We would need to carefully position *Rose Emily* with the prevailing conditions and pass between the constellation of islands, reefs and rocky outcrops, searching for a safe passage to reach open water on the other side. Due to weather systems in this part of the Pacific, high winds, waves and unpredictable currents would make for a difficult approach.

The second challenge was Fiji, a significantly larger and more expansive landmass. Over the next 450 nautical miles, we would need to make at least 175 nautical miles in a southward direction. If we didn't, we'd be forced to pass between the Eastern Fijian Islands, leaving international waters, legally requiring us to stop at one of the islands and clear entry in port. From what we knew, this would require going ashore. Our dream of completing the crossing non-stop and unsupported would be ruined.

Thirdly, we'd have to get far enough south so that we could round the south end of New Caledonia. If we wished to hit our new destination of Brisbane, this was essential. The risk of a northern rounding of New Cal would be missing Australia altogether. Finishing in Papua New Guinea would be quite an unexpected turn of events.

I closed my eyes for my first night of sleep in 86 days that was longer than three hours. I tossed and turned, jamming my knee against the wall beside me to brace against the waves.

After half an hour, my mind finally started to follow my eyes into darkness. But then I was awake in an instant. A hard object had fallen from the shelf above me, colliding with my face. Flashing on the light, I discovered that it was Ewan's 'mini' guitar. I placed the guitar on the mattress beside me, and went back to my sleepy purgatory.

By the time I got up, my accordion – which actually was miniature – and an underwater camera case had joined us on the mattress. They had followed the guitar's lead – much to the surprise of my poor face.

I woke every hour through the night. Our bodies had become conditioned to short, broken nights of sleep. A longer rest would need to be slowly reintroduced. The cabin bounced uncomfortably throughout the night, as the nose rose with each wave before being aggressively tugged back down by the sea-anchor.

We woke at 4 a.m. to a gentler swell. One would think that a six-hour block of rest would be rejuvenating when you've had no more than three hours for months. The complete opposite was true. After so long in survival mode, it was like our bodies had seen these longer sleeps as an opportunity to start recovering prematurely. We'd all woken up in the morning sore and stiff, much more creaky than usual, like it was the day after a physical rugby match or a rough night's sleep in a tent.

Poking my head outside, it appeared the wind had settled. Desperate to get underway, Jamie began to haul in the para-anchor while Ewan appeared out of the stern cabin. By the looks on their faces I could tell they'd both had a night of broken sleep too.

We began with two rowing and one resting, but progress was painfully slow. We'd anticipated this two days earlier, servicing all three of the rowing positions. The wheels were meticulously cleaned with ACF-50, a magic anti-corrosion spray, and the tracks were scrubbed with Ecover and fresh water. The routine for the next two days: row for three hours and make as much southwesterly progress as physically possible before deploying the para-anchor once more, then resting and eating and rehydrating for an hour. One hour on, one hour off is tough; two hours on, one hour off is punishing. But three hours on, one hour off is really quite soul-destroying. But our oars were tied. There was no other way to make progress in the desired direction and so we accepted this new level of purgatory for the time being. We desperately needed to try to make further southing to ensure a safe passage through the Tongan isles and round the south of Fiji. If we continued to drift north sitting on the para-anchor, we'd make our lives increasingly difficult. Hard miles now could save the voyage at a later date. From 5 a.m. until 8 p.m. we continued this exhausting cycle, grasping at the occasional minute here or there to eat and hydrate.

Under a moonlit sky we called it quits, dropped anchor again and checked our overall progress for the day. The sky above had the texture of goat's cheese. I made the foolish error of checking our tracker. 'Bloody hell . . . 15 hours of rowing three-up in the past 24 hours. Seven nautical miles of progress. The tracker estimates arrival on 27th December,' I said to Ewan as we crawled into the stern cabin.

'Call it Hogmanay,' he replied dryly.

A painful average of 0.3 knots of progress over a whole day and night. The day prior had seen a one-knot average. It had been two of our most exhausting days on the oars we'd ever had.

The only thing to do was laugh.

088, Wednesday 9 July

EWAN: Song of the day – 'Vancouver Time' by Leif Vollebekk

Around midday we rowed over the Tongan Trench, the deepest part of the Pacific Ocean that we will cross during our journey: 10,882 metres, over 2,000 metres deeper than Everest is high. I took a small sample of sea water as a memento inside a used olive oil bottle. Who knows if it will make it back to Scotland, or exactly what I'll do with it if it does? But it seemed like the right thing to do.

On day 89 we passed over the International Date Line. Thursday afternoon would suddenly become Friday afternoon, the following day (on the calendar, but still day 89 for us at sea). We had great plans for this. Timing it exactly, there were hopes of trying to set some kind of record for holding my breath for an entire day (in reality, maybe 40 seconds). But, alas, being distracted by one thing or another, we missed it entirely. The exact moment eluded us, and we found ourselves having time travelled being none the wiser of its happening.

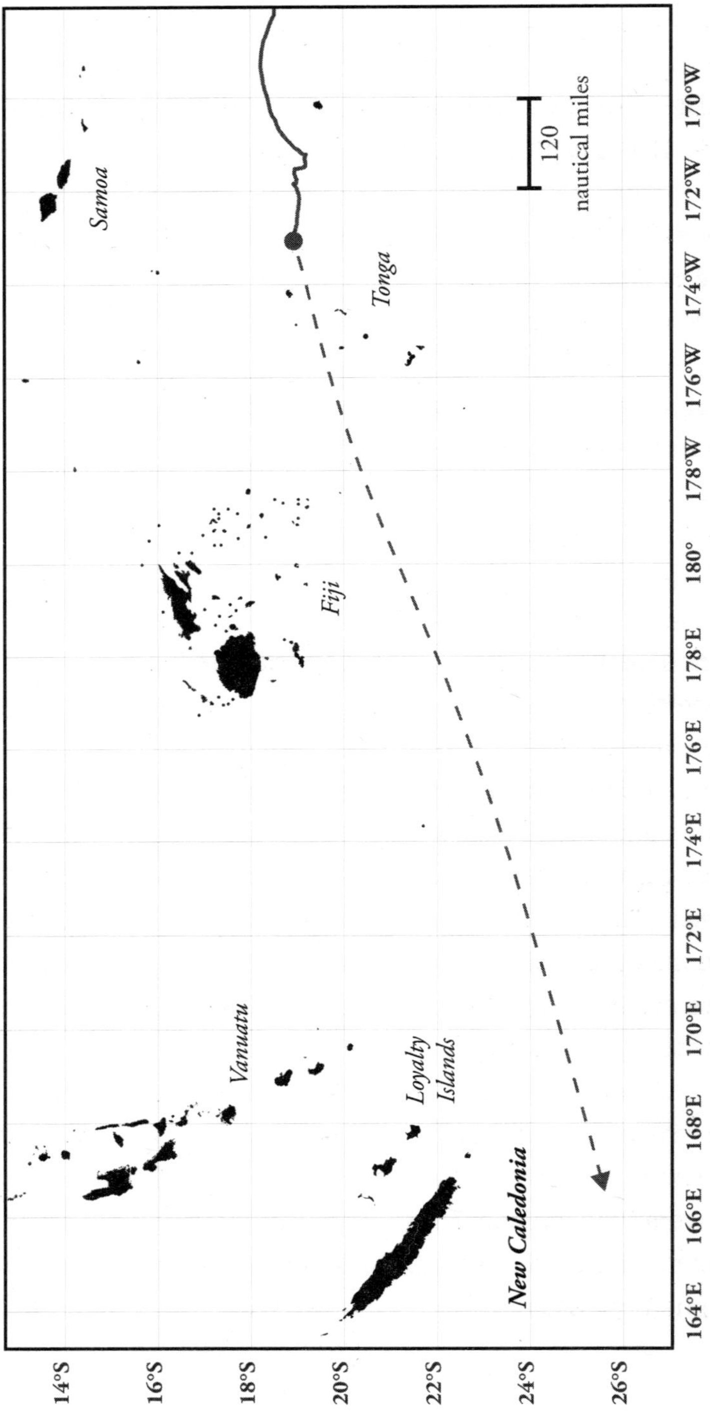

Intended route past Tonga, around Fiji and below the south end of New Caledonia

DAY 089, Friday 11 July

JAMIE : Song of the day – 'Keep Me on Your Mind' by the Bonny Light Horseman

The past fortnight has without a doubt been the most challenging period of time on our crossing to date. From flat calms to raging storms, counter-currents to headwinds, blistering heat to torrential squalls. A series of tests, a gauntlet of conditions for both us and for *Rose Emily*. Lachlan remarked earlier today: 'I feel like we've experienced what we needed to on this voyage; we've been tested both physically and mentally, and I'd happily now take fair winds and following seas all the way to Australia.' Amen to that we all agree.

I wake from my final rest as the first glimmers of dawn cast light upon the deck. I take over on the oars from Ewan, who moves to prepare some instant coffee and power up the Starlink. We have a call this morning with a childhood hero: Flea from the Red Hot Chili Peppers. We've listened to a few podcasts with Flea in preparation to figure out what on earth we should ask someone like him. He's the epitome of a rock 'n' roll legend, arguably the greatest bass guitarist that's ever lived. In truth we're all a little intimidated.

And then, just like that, as the sun rises over the Pacific Ocean and we sip black coffee out of baby beakers, we're on a live video chat with Flea. What a wonderful man. He's engaged, super interested and relaxed, which in turn relaxes us. He swears just like you'd expect a rock star to do, and like three little boys trying to impress an older sibling we in turn do the same.

As we approach the Tongan isles we've made it just below the northern islands. Once past this archipelago, we know it will be a hard push to get below Fiji. This weighs heavy on all our minds.

The island of Utu Vava'u cast muddy light into the clouds above. Light pollution. It was our first sighting of a human settlement in 6,000 nautical miles. A cleaner light shone through the clouds to the south-east like a torch shining through a dense forest. The full face of the moon raised its head for another nightshift.

It was a privilege seeing so few signs of human life for such an extended period of time. The ocean currents didn't carry with them huge amounts of plastic waste – as we had feared they would – and the skies were free of air travel and light pollution. As Australia drew closer, I suspected this might change.

As we approached the archipelago, the sea-state shifted. We'd chosen a course to take us between the island and a rocky outcrop to the south, Hakaufasi. The wave frequency increased as they became steeper and our speed over ground climbed from 1.5 to 3.5 knots. Ewan battened down the hatches and carefully monitored the changing course as the landmass interfered with strong ocean currents, shifting us this way then that. After a tense solitary hour of nightshift, Ewan successfully threaded the needle, leaving the rocks just one mile off our port side.

It had felt like we'd been crawling towards Tonga for weeks. Passing our first island of this archipelago was a big milestone, made all the sweeter by the hard-fought miles of the last fortnight. The Garmin inReach chirped as a message was received. It was Guy. He'd spent the last couple of days trying to contact someone in Fiji to get exemption from the port authorities: 'The standard process isn't looking good. The right person is away so I doubt we'll get exemption in time.'

I heaved at the oars with frustration.

Then a second message came in a minute later: 'But I've been doing some additional research on the RYA website. As long as you don't stop, don't fish and aren't there for commercial gain, you can claim the right to pass through Fijian waters with no need to go ashore. I'll confirm with the consulate asap, but it sounds promising.'

As if one, we all breathed a deep sigh of relief. We might have one less obstacle to go.

Chapter 12

Seventeen Days

By Ewan

DAY 091, Sunday 13 July

EWAN: Song of the day – Fred Again's *Tiny Desk Concert*, in full

The dark sky sketched a triangular figure in the gloom where the volcanic isle of Kao lay, rising out of the water like one of the great Egyptian pyramids. Passing within a few short miles of Tonga's highest peak – half-swallowed by cloud and the veil of night – and navigating with the shadowy shape to our starboard side, I couldn't help but glance at the GPS every few minutes as a sanity check, imagining that unseen currents might be pushing us onto a collision course. Our heading held true, yet the anxieties remained even after we were safely past.

For most of the small hours the moon was shrouded by a thin layer of mottled cloud, which formed a web of silver light shining between pillows of darkness. Rays pushed through the soft cracks, as if the moon was sitting behind a blanket of fine handmade felt. Dawn brought with it another of those moments that would have seemed impossible a few months earlier. We were due to speak to Ewan McGregor. Somehow our supporters back at home had tracked him down, shared the documentary of our Atlantic crossing, and asked whether he might be up for a mid-ocean call. He had watched it and, more generously still, followed up with a donation towards our fundraising efforts for clean water projects. He was thoughtful, warm and genuinely interested. We found common ground in the strange appeal of long journeys and life on the move, for him by motorbike and us by oar. We finished the conversation by inviting him for a row once we were back in Scotland. He sounded keen, even if it was simply politeness on his part.

For a brief spell, the morning felt improbably light. It was a welcome lift, but it didn't last. The day itself swept through in a slew of changeable weather conditions. The sliver of morning sun was eventually overcome by a thick grey lid of heavy cloud, shapeless and low-lying. The forecast changed and thunderstorms were predicted, and the atmosphere began to thicken with moisture. Almost eerily, the northeasterly breeze then died down to near flat calm conditions, and the sea moved around us in lumps, the sky spitting. It was a dank day, if ever there was one.

We needed two of us rowing to make any worthwhile progress, but even then it was heavy. Drop down to a single pair of hands on the oars and it felt like we were dragging dead weight – so 'two-up' was the required drill, and we duly settled into the grind.

A month ago this would have been brutal, but it was easier in the context of last week's relentless three-up routines. At least we weren't back to that again. It was nothing to look forward to, but it did somehow seem more manageable than it previously had. If we needed to, we could sustain this nearly indefinitely through the day – given an extra meal to maintain energy levels and enough conversation, however daft, when the mood began to dip.

By early afternoon, nothing had changed. The ambient noises around the boat were reduced to the rhythmic swish and splash of the seats and oars, and the clicking of cuffs as they rotated in the oarlocks. I swapped out with Lachlan and leant on the stern cabin, watching the water ahead. An ominous band of grey had quietly appeared, looming on the horizon before us.

Ten minutes later and we were in the thick of it. Twenty-knot winds from the southwest, a direct headwind, halted our progress entirely. The boat was forced round to the south, and then beyond as we started drifting east. We tried to turn *Rose Emily* through the wind to take the weather on the other side, but it was hopeless – the best we could do was hold a northwesterly trajectory. No good if we wanted to get below Fiji and New Caledonia. And so, much to our disappointment, the para-anchor was redeployed.

Back in the stern cabin, I sat with Jamie and stared at the compass, praying for the smallest shift, or for it all to simply blow through. It wasn't long before Jamie went on deck to see if things had improved, impatient to get moving again. They had. Wet waterproofs were pulled on and we returned to the oars in the rain and lingering headwinds, just about managing to hold a westerly trajectory. We were still drifting north, but at least we were moving, and we could make up for lost miles south later, I thought.

A good friend once shared with me some wisdom from the military. It went something like: 'When life gives you lemons, fuck the lemonade, just eat the lemons.'

Which felt about right. I'm sure there'll be plenty more lemons between here and Australia. But at least we won't get scurvy.

It took a while to accept our dismal new reality. At first, each change in the weather felt like a misunderstanding – an unwelcome squall that showed up on the horizon; an unlucky forecast that would presumably improve; a couple of hours that were lost to the para-anchor. We rolled with the punches, again and again, then clawed our way back with enough stubborn effort. But it became wearing. And as Tonga finally slipped behind us, the same sequence began repeating itself with a cold predictability.

Broadly speaking, the prevailing wind for much of our route across the Pacific should have blown from the southeast towards the northwest. That pattern originates at the equator: warm air rises, creating a belt of lower pressure, and cooler air from the subtropical highs further down south flows up to replace it. As it moves, the Earth's rotation acts to shift it off course (known as the Coriolis effect), resulting in southeasterly trade winds that are often fairly consistent, right the way across, with the exception of a few bumpy bits here and there.

For much of the journey, we had been skirting along the northern edge of big high-pressure systems, hoping to benefit from weather heading west. More often than not we had found ourselves feeling a little disgruntled by the unexpectedly large southerly component in both the wind and the waves, which resulted in plenty of tiresome beam-on seas. If nothing else, it was consistently bad.

Much further south in the wild southern ocean, deep low-pressure systems regularly spin up and then track across the Pacific in the opposite direction, starting in the west and ending further east. Rotating in a clockwise direction – as low-pressure systems in the southern hemisphere do – the strongest ones become extratropical cyclones. Mostly these exist far below the line we were trying to hold, and the trade winds carry on unaffected. But every so often, as you might expect, these monsters drift north, creating havoc and disruption in their wake.

When these systems rolled through, the change on the boat was abrupt. The eye of the storm was usually much further south, but we'd feel the effects at its edges all the same. There would be a shift in the weather in a matter of minutes, often a full wind reversal, where the breeze backs by 180 degrees. The magnitude of the disturbance would vary, but the after-effects could drag on for days. The outcome was the same: the para-anchor would need to be deployed in a hurry, then we'd wait for the weather to abate, or the wind to clock around as the system passed. When we were able to set off again, it was often in an awkward and compromised direction, until the trades eventually re-established. The miles we lost were painful, either spent tethered to that godforsaken para-anchor, or clawed back after hours of rowing an indirect course.

Before Tonga we'd spent a total of about 28 hours shackled to the para-anchor. One time had been near Palmerston Island, another after the storm that swept Lachlan overboard. From mid-July onwards, we were hit repeatedly. Not one or two rogue systems but eight separate occasions, one after the other. We had barely come back up for air before the next one smashed into us, and we watched in dismay as the hours and days bled away. Over the following three weeks, they became the bane of our existence. And as our estimated arrival kept slipping, the prospect of running out of food became harder to ignore.

By then, any darkening patch of sky was enough to sour the mood. We knew this run of bad luck was unusual, but that knowledge offered little comfort. A slight shift in the wind, a line of cloud on the horizon, and the thought came unbidden: 'Please, not again.' It was hard to hold onto any sense of progress when, every few days, the weather threatened to undo it.

Sometimes the para-anchor was out for 45 minutes, other times we spent the whole night tethered to the thing. Either way, each deployment carried the same tax: a disheartened crew, a dull nausea, a slow drift in a direction we'd spent hours fighting against. Missing days. Punishing rowing. And as if to add to the misery, it rained through almost all of it.

It wasn't dramatic in the way the storm was. It was wet and relentless and thoroughly depressing. In the small hours, I often found myself locked in an internal battle, simply trying to stay awake on the oars as the rain came down. I'd breathe deeply and squeeze the oar handles hard in my palms, trying to pull myself back from the edge of sleep. There was a weary inevitability to it all. As the days rolled past, the same grim sequence played out again and again: an eerie stillness, then an unwelcome gale, often at night and accompanied by cold thrashing rain. We'd be drenched in an instant and the boat would be going backwards until we managed to sling the hook. The torrential downpour and blustery wind would make for painfully slow progress as we battened down the hatches and stowed away the oars. Headtorches glaring, hands fumbling, fabric flapping, lines becoming crossed . . . eventually the underwater parachute would be in, and the boat would pull round. But even that was a bleak ordeal.

Each time the bowline came taut, the boat would be jerked around, forced into an unnatural pitching motion as its nose was repeatedly yanked into the sea. Hollow, insistent crashes shuddered through the cabins as the hull slammed into the water with each passing wave. Jamie hid in the forward berth, feeling each impact through the thin damp mattress, and Lachlan and I crammed into the stern, waiting for it to be over.

After the Pacific had decided we'd had enough, we'd pull on damp layers and step back out into the night to try again. Sometimes the wind had eased enough to make worthwhile progress – maybe a day or two of reprieve, if we were lucky. Other times it hadn't and we were back on the para-anchor not long later.

DAY 094, Wednesday 16 July

EWAN: Song of the day – 'Bòcan' by Beluga Lagoon

As we approached the Fijian border, having spent weeks trying our level best to get below the islands and remain in international waters, there was an air of mild anxiety aboard *Rose Emily*.

The status quo for pleasure craft entering the country is to gain clearance in port – something we have been eager to avoid. The non-stop and unsupported aspect of our attempt will, of course, become void should we make landfall. Unfortunately, weather has driven us north and we are faced with no alternative but to pass between the southerly islands of Fiji.

A few days ago, campaign manager Guy found a clause. It appears that we can claim a right of passage called an 'innocent passage' through Fiji's territorial sea and its archipelagic waters provided our passage is 'continuous, expeditious, and innocent (no fishing, no research, no stopping except as allowed)'.

Having no need to stop is the key thing. Armed with this knowledge, we have positioned *Rose Emily* on a more favourable course to maximise miles towards Australia.

Given the short notice, no confirmation has been received yet from Fiji, so we've decided to just go for it anyway and see if we can make it to international waters on the other side without the coastguard turning up. Although we are relatively sure that our right of passage will be granted, it still conjures up an amount of anxiety, despite the wide open sea and little sign of life around us. We've got about 60 nautical miles to cover over the next day or so to get clear. Let's hope we make it.

Back in Peru, we watched a video of an ocean rowing team being attacked by a marlin. Its spear-like bill and powerful body smashed a large hole in the side of their boat, crumpling the fibreglass as if it had been hit by a car.

This is unfortunately not uncommon behaviour. The year that we rowed across the Atlantic, two other teams met a similar fate. In one case, I saw photos of the potentially lethal bill protruding a few inches into the cabin, right between a rower's legs, where he lay resting during his off-shift. What a way to wake up.

Taking this into consideration, our boat has been designed with an additional layer and a ten-centimetre gap beneath the berths, to avoid any of us being skewered. We saw a marlin briefly out on the Atlantic, and one a number of weeks ago on this journey, however neither of them had seemed particularly interested in coming that close to the boat. That was until today.

Cutting through the water a few metres behind the boat, two fins appeared, tracking us with serpentine motion. We gave a yelp as we spotted the fish behind the boat. From my rowing seat I heard Jamie cry, 'There's two big fins – maybe a pair of sharks?!'

Reaching for the camera, he thrust it into the water, trying to get a good shot of the following animals. Jamie's excitement increased as he yelled, 'It's an absolute tank.' Wide-eyed, he turned round: 'It's not two fish following the boat, Ewan. The fins belong to the same fish, and it's an absolute monster.'

The marlin followed us for a few minutes, seemingly deciding whether a 30-foot rowing boat was appropriate prey. It was absolutely huge, moving with muscularity like a bull, powerfully gliding through the water with its sword for a face. A fearsome-looking beast. Marlin have been known to reach weights of up to 750 kilograms, which is utterly terrifying. I'm not sure how big this one was; the way it moved in the water gave an indication to its size – maybe 749 kilograms, at a guess . . .

Even the double layer of high-strength carbon fibre reinforcing the hull suddenly started to feel a little flimsy when faced with this monster of the deep.

I glanced at the fishing rod, imagining the fight that would ensue if we hooked it. If it swam the right way, we'd be in Australia in no time. But then I remembered: we're not allowed to fish while in Fijian waters. The marlin was safe, if not for its ginormous size then at least through the laws of the Fijian sea.

Then, with a flick of its huge tail, it was gone, disappearing off into the blue. 'Until next time, Mr Marlin,' I thought.

The excitement of the sighting was a brief reprieve from the grim drudgery that had otherwise plagued us. In our hearts we already knew that our position after the storm meant that an arrival in Sydney was no longer realistic. The route we had originally planned should have taken us below Tonga and then far below Fiji, but the weather had forced us north again and again, conceding hundreds of miles in latitude just to gain westward ground. From where we were now, getting as far south as Sydney would have required a miracle. Brisbane was fast becoming the more likely destination. This was hard to accept. We had imagined arriving in the throng of the big city, and believed it would have brought more attention to the expedition and, in turn, helped with the fundraising.

But the incessant weather seemed determined to push us back from whence we came, back towards South America. The repetition of it all was probably the hardest part. It was a battle with the elements, one that we fought tooth and nail. Two and a half more days spent on the para-anchor, setback after setback, a time where hope was diminished.

DAY 095, Thursday 17 July

JAMIE: Song of the day – 'Bangor Town' by Foy Vance

Today was just one of those days that you desperately want to end as soon as it begins.

The clouds had drawn in at dusk and by the time I started my first nightshift the heavens had opened. It poured for the full hour and 40 minutes that I rowed, saturating my lower body and leaving me with cold shivers and my hairs standing on end.

With a southerly wind progress is slow. Changeovers are always tricky in weather like this. In an attempt to keep the cabins as dry as possible, we agree that all wet clothes need to be taken off outside. The issue with this is there's a brief moment when those precious few remaining dry spots are exposed to the elements. By the time you're in the cabin and the door is shut, everything is a little wet. I toss and turn in bed until the alarm goes off. I wake and listen, barely able to distinguish one noise from another in my weary state. But it's still there, the sound I prayed had stopped: the drum of rain bouncing off the cabin, louder than ever.

I don my wet shorts and damp base-layers, and as quickly as possible open the door, step out and grab my wet foulies. They are cold and the fabric clings to my skin. I'm eager to start rowing to simply warm up a little.

We repeat this process as the rain persists throughout the night. The moisture in the cabins progressively gets worse, and with only a handful of dirty t-shirts to dry off the mixture of perspiration, condensation and salt water that has found its way in, dripping down the walls and from the ceilings, the battle is lost before it's even begun.

I wake to a grey sky with thick clouds as far as the eye can see. Ewan and Lachlan are on the oars. A gentle spit of rain ensures that everything is still very wet. Tipping the water out of my shoes and wringing out my socks, I replace Lala on the oars as the rain starts to tumble down.

Rowing two on, one off, the brief break we get is cold and uncomfortable. The driving rain soon saps any heat from your body and you wish to be back on the oars swiftly in an attempt to warm up. Going into the cabins isn't really possible; each time the doors are opened our bedding and mattresses get wet and electronics are put at risk.

There's no music as we are down to one Bluetooth speaker – the other one died due to water ingress at the charging port, which eventually stopped it from recharging – so we're being cautious and avoiding using the remaining one in the rain, even though it claims to be waterproof. Our snacks are soggy and our porridge cold. In truth, it's really quite bleak. Silence comes over the boat as we slide backwards and forwards.

I constantly look towards the horizon, praying for a break in the clouds. It doesn't come. For eight long hours we endure, progressively getting wetter and wetter as the hours pass. It's difficult not to question why we are here on days like today.

We are unable to use any sat comms today due to our battery levels, and making water is a push. As a result we eat wet rations: all-day breakfast and veggie curry. I'm not convinced this is necessary, but Ewan and Lachlan overrule me. I struggle to get the wet rations down; they taste artificial and processed and lacking in good calories and nutrients. Feeling unsatisfied, I return to the oars.

There isn't much conversation today, our thoughts turning inwards. The occasional mutter breaks the silence: 'Well, this is quite miserable isn't it.'

DAY 096, Friday 18 July

LACHLAN: Song of the day – 'Guiding Light' by Mumford & Sons

Some days out here it all just feels a bit much. One thing leads to another and, before you know it, your thoughts are lost in a negative spiral.

Our first mistake was getting our hopes up. The forecast suggested pleasant rowing conditions and good southwesterly progress before some nasty weather rears its head next week. The further south we can get over the next few days, the less time we'll need to resort to the para-anchor next week. The reality, however, has been wind and waves from the south/southeast – not the forecasted easterly – making a course of anything below 280 degrees painfully slow. Expectation has certainly been the thief of joy.

We resort to the toolkit that we've picked up during this crossing to cheer us up: hydrate well (it's astonishing how much this generally helps) and eat some frogs – i.e. do the things we've been putting off.

A few frogs slipped down nicely: fixing a selfie pole, cleaning some storage bags out, drying bed sheets in the cabin, locating the charger for our GPS tracker.

Next, a gas check. I rummaged in the awkward forward Henderson hatch for the canisters. The last check was around the Marquesas, and exactly how many we have left has been a slight unknown since. Digging through the locker, filled with some equipment and lots of stored rubbish, I come across 15 canisters . . . but, to our dismay, only two of them are full. At our usual consumption, two cans will last us 15 days. We're going to have to start eating half of our meals cold going forwards, and hot drinks will be rationed to every other day. The frog turned out to be a can of worms.

We received the most touching message from two strangers today. Messages like this are keeping us going, more than anything. It reads as follows:

> Dear Lachlan, Jamie, Ewan,
>
> We are following from Australia and are so invested in your journey.
>
> Since the birth of our son, two years ago, my husband has struggled through episodes of profound depression. Sometimes

it feels like there's a whole world between us, and even though we are reaching out, we cannot reach each other.

We've been sitting down at the end of each night, with a cup of tea, and reading your log. It has brought us together, it has inspired us, and it has helped immensely with [his] mental health. I am so grateful for you sharing your journey. You are making the world a better place in more ways than you know. Thank you, from the bottom of my heart.

We live in Adelaide, SA. And we're really hoping to come and see you at the finish-line, whichever part of the coastline that might be.

Sending you all the good vibes and good weather.

Sophie and James

I was the first to go. My voice wavered as exhaustion and emotion took its grip. I finished reading and looked up. Jamie and Ewan were welling up, holding back the tears. 'Just three brothers in a boat, out in the Pacific, having a wee cry,' I said, with a smile.

DAY 099, Monday 21 July

JAMIE: Song of the day – 'The River at Night' by Beluga Lagoon

The crescent moon is my companion this evening. A sickle of white light that slices through the clouds. A blanket cloud covers most of the sky, perforated here and there to create small windows into another world. The stars seem perfectly positioned within the voids, framed by the cloud, as if on display in an interstellar exhibition.

I plunge through the silvery grey surface of the ink blue sea. It's been over two weeks now since we cleaned the hull of the boat. The last time was pre-storm, pre-para-anchor, pre-man overboard.

I wouldn't say we have been avoiding it, it just hasn't seemed necessary as the marine growth has been slow to build these past few weeks.

In fact, ever since the Marquesas Islands, we've seen a dramatic decline in the amount of growth on the bottom of the boat each week. Perhaps a change in water temperature is to thank, although sadly with less growth there has also been noticeably less marine wildlife swimming up to say hello. I hold out hope for more dolphins and whales as we approach the coast of Australia. If we can get over to the Queensland coast within the next few weeks then we may have timed it perfectly for the migration of minke and humpback whales from the waters of Antarctica up to their breeding grounds near the Great Barrier Reef. What an escort that would be.

I'm on shark and jellyfish watch today. It's a very calm and quiet day, a gentle current nudging us in the direction we wish to head. I tentatively poke my head over the side of the boat and peer into the bright blue depths below. I can't begin to comprehend the depths that stretch out down there. The coast seems clear.

With the anchor rope firmly tied around my waist, I dive off the side of the boat. Ewan and Lachlan shortly follow. As my momentum carries me down I pause for a moment, suspended in the turquoise waters. Rays of sunlight illuminate the silhouette of *Rose Emily* as I notice the shoal of little fish that have made her shadow their home. It's breathtakingly beautiful. I become weightless in the water and pause for a moment of motionless serenity.

One of the small black and white fish swims right up to my camera, as if curious to understand the creature responsible for their new home. I yearn to stay here for longer but the pressure of carbon dioxide within my lungs forces me up. I surface near to Lachlan, who lets out a surprised shriek: 'Ya bugger, I thought I was done for!'

DAY 105, Sunday 27 July

JAMIE: Song of the day – 'Deep In Love' by Bonny Light Horseman

Two steps forward, one step back. We always knew that this part of the crossing would be the most challenging. And yet part of me still held out hope that we might have a favourable last run with fair winds and following seas.

For a couple of days, I thought our prayers had been answered. A strong northeasterly wind allowed us to cruise downwind, building momentum and racking up consecutive days of 75 nautical miles and more. Two or three more days of this, we reasoned, and we'll reach New Caledonia; the final major milestone in our non-stop Pacific row! If the weather holds, it will then be only 17 days until Australia. There's light at the end of the tunnel – at last.

Then I'm woken by the thunder of rain against the roof of the cabin. It's incredibly loud and must be a heavy squall passing through. I hear Ewan f'ing and blinding as he struggles on the oars. I drift back off for the remaining 20 minutes of sleep. The alarm goes. I pull on my foulies and step out into a different night.

I can tell by the look on Ewan's face that he's had a rough time. The favourable northeasterly from yesterday evening has vanished during his shift. An ominous black wall of weather has rolled in and flipped the wind 180 degrees again. With the heavy deluge he's been unable to check or change course, blinded by the lashing rain that had woken me. He suggests attempting to maintain course, but if the southwesterly wind continues there will only be one option . . .

I pull on the oars for a heavy 40 minutes, but I'm pushed backwards on an easterly course. No matter how hard I try, every attempt to push west, or south, or even north, is in vain. At 23.00 the para-anchor is deployed.

We bob around for the next five hours, slowly being pushed

northeast and losing the precious miles that we'd worked so hard to gain. At 04.00 Lala lifts the anchor and we are on our way again, albeit on a course more northerly than we wanted.

The adverse weather continues into the next day, forcing us to row two-up during daylight hours. Ewan supplies his full account of the weather front that flipped the wind, concluding that it had been his worst nightshift yet. He looks exhausted today.

There's a ping from a satellite message arriving. Our weather routers have been studying some concerning weather travelling up from the south. A large and powerful low-pressure system is forecast to make its way out of the southern ocean, building in momentum and complexity as it moves up the east coast of Australia. It is due to collide with New Caledonia in approximately a week's time, on the very stretch of water we intend to cross.

We've reached a fork in the road – presented with two options, neither of which are ideal.

Option 1: outrun the storm. Subject to us being able to push far enough south over the next two days, we may be able to get low enough to use the storm to our advantage. If positioned well, the high winds and following seas will propel us westward, catapulting us towards our destination. The risk is obvious: if the storm tracks in a different direction, we could be exposed to the full brunt of it, sent backwards, or pinned against the lee shore of New Caledonia.

Current predictions set the wind speed at somewhere between 40 to 60 knots, with 12- to 14-metre seas. To put this into perspective: that's over double the strength of the last storm, where Lachlan was washed overboard. It sends shivers down my spine. If we're caught in that, we'll need to batten down the hatches, secure the oars, put on our helmets, and brace for impact. We'll need to trail a rope astern to steady the boat in the writhing seas, and pray we aren't rolling and need to abort.

Option 2: the Coral Sea and the Great Barrier Reef. We've tried our best to avoid this area of the Pacific, awash with atolls, coral reefs and lagoons. However, the low-pressure system may force our hand, leaving no other option but to pass to the north of New Caledonia – which will all but erase any chance of Sydney. Brisbane, too, will likely slip away. The price will be hundreds of extra miles, and a much later arrival, with the added complexity of navigating the reef-strewn waters beyond.

We expect to reach the southeastern end of New Caledonia in a few days' time. But, sooner or later, subject to the progression of the inbound storm, a decision will need to be made. For now, we wait for the tempest to deal the cards.

DAY 106, Monday 28 July

LACHLAN: Song of the day – 'Raglan Road' by Luke Kelly

Forty-eight hours ago we were cruising at 4 knots with a generous tailwind. Southing New Caledonia was likely, and an arrival in Australia within three weeks on the table.

How things change. We crawl along with a knot of counter-current, rowing two-up, doing in two days what we'd done in one not long ago. The forecasts haven't settled yet, and there's no point pretending we can make the call before they do. Safety is the guiding light. We must have patience. I'd be lying if I said that our spirits hadn't taken a bruising. We foolishly got our hopes up about how close we were.

There have been many lessons in finding peace in not knowing these past months. Out here, we live in a state of uncertainty. Weather dictates everything, and reliable predictions of what's to come span only a week or so ahead.

We like to think we have a large amount of control in life. Whether it's career progression or personal relationships, we find comfort in the idea of having a grasp on things — being at the helm, in a sense — as we travel on a linear path from A to B. The reality is, I believe, that life is more like rowing across the Pacific.

It's a funny thought that we might at any point receive a piece of news that will change our lives for ever. Life leading up to that moment and life afterwards might be completely different. Whether it's a phone call, a doctor's checkup or the breakdown or formation of a relationship, plans might be derailed at any time. The narratives we tell ourselves about what's to come might be smashed into tiny little pieces on the ground in front of us.

Life is like walking along a path at night. We can only see as far as the illumination of our headtorch. But surely that's half the fun? We never know what's around the corner. If we did, our lives would be robbed of all sense of agency and spontaneity. It would be like watching a film and already knowing how it ends.

DAY 107, Tuesday 29 July

EWAN: Song of the day – 'Raineach' by Beluga Lagoon

The decision to go north has finally become clear.

Weather conditions are always changeable and fraught with uncertainty, but a sound approach to gaining higher confidence in the forecast is to check for discrepancies between the various forecast models that exist – one being the Unified Model from the UK Meteorological Office, another the Global Forecast System from the US. Various others exist from countries and organisations around the world, each using different datasets from satellite, marine and terrestrial sources. If they disagree, you treat everything with caution. If they begin to converge, you pay attention.

The reason for delaying the decision to go north and avoid the storm until today is because of discrepancies between these different models, making the forecast unclear. However, the various models have started to agree and show that a weather system of significant magnitude is developing ahead of us. It is due to stretch across the entirety of the water between our current position and the shores of Australia, over a thousand nautical miles. Its genesis is forecast somewhere above Brisbane, tracking towards New Caledonia on the very route we had hoped to cross. Near the eye of the storm, where the weather is at its strongest, winds of up to 65 knots are now predicted. On the Beaufort Scale, this could be a Force 12 storm: the highest classification, a severe tropical cyclone. Not something to be caught in while rowing in a small boat like ours. And definitely not something to be caught in while on a lee shore, as we might have found ourselves had we continued to push south.

So we've done the sensible thing in abandoning the hard-won miles and swallowing our pride. It's no exaggeration to say that, had we known this would come to pass, we would have followed a different course for the past 5,000 miles, taking a much more direct route and likely avoiding more of the rough weather in the south. It feels crushing.

Our new route will take us in a northwesterly direction, where we aim to seek refuge behind the Loyalty Islands until the weather passes. In doing so, however, our fate is sealed. Regaining the lost miles south to round the lower end of New Caledonia will no longer be feasible. Instead, we must now pass above the territory, adding many hundreds of miles to our journey. It's hard to describe the frustration, having fought so hard to maintain a southerly course over the past weeks and months.

We must then navigate onward via the part of the Coral Sea to which it owes its name. The Great Barrier Reef lies here, where the shallow sea on the coast of Australia is studded with thousands of small islands, reefs, rocky outcrops and partially submerged protrusions.

It is hugely disappointing. We had started to feel the presence of Australia, as if it were just over the horizon, but it's now slipping away again. More than that, we had told our loved ones that we might be only two and a half weeks away. And now we have many hundreds more miles to row.

But safety is not an area we are willing to compromise. And so, with heavy hearts, we turn our boat north.

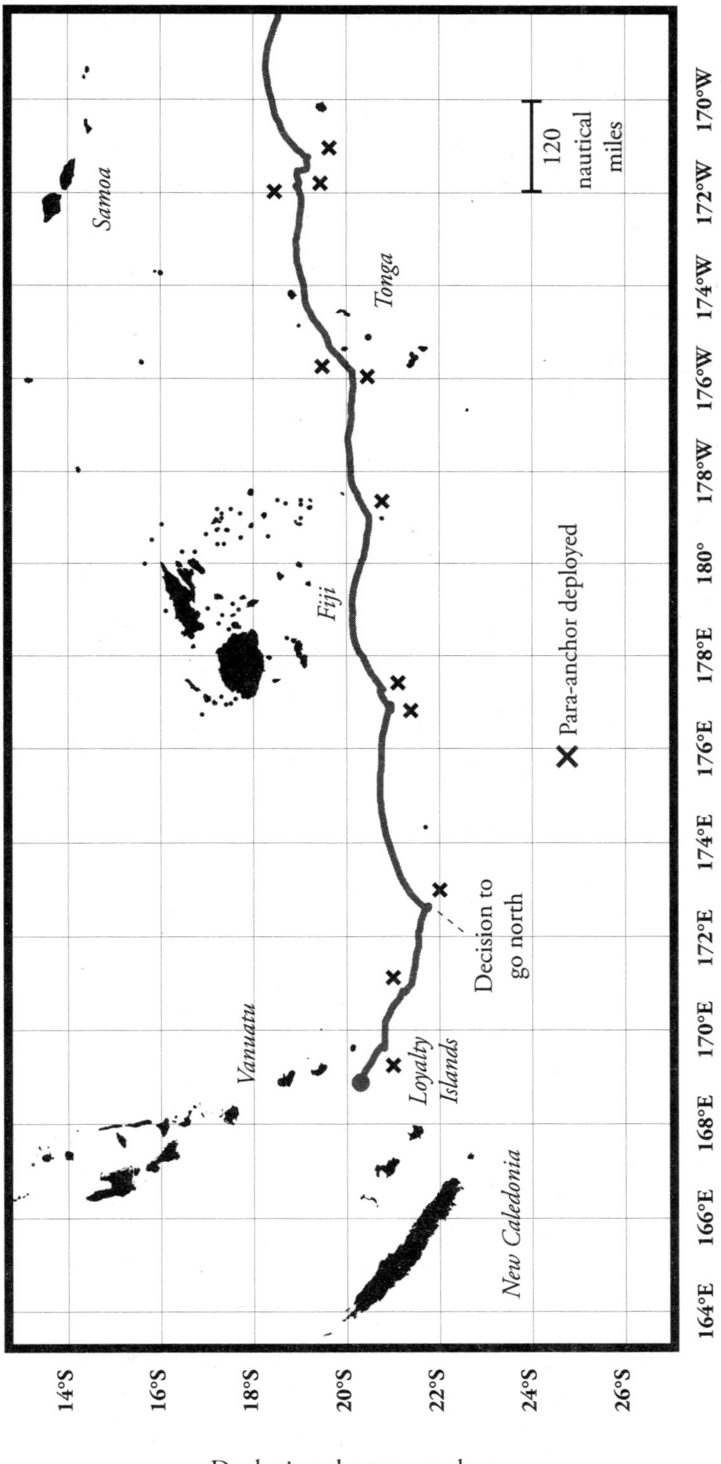

Deploying the para-anchor

DAY 109, Thursday 31 July

LACHLAN: Song of the day – 'Stuck in the Middle with You' by Stealers Wheel

Sandwiched between a cyclone and a tsunami . . . what's next, I wonder?

We left Ewan on the oars to start the nightshift, waiting for a bump caused by an earthquake off the Russian coast to reach us. 'Have a good shift, Ewan . . . and give us a knock if there are any 20-foot waves on the horizon.'

'Will do,' Ewan's voice came back with a tone that I knew to be humour with a tinge of apprehension.

My head rested on the pillow. I imagined a solitary wave marching south, spanning the vast body we've almost crossed.

In the end, the wave went unnoticed during the night, swallowed by the swell from the south. Counterintuitively, the middle of an ocean isn't a bad place to hide from a tsunami. Our thoughts went out to the people who would actually be impacted on the fringes of this mass of blue.

Most nights, if the weather permitted, I made a voice note for my partner as I rowed alone in darkness. I'd set my phone to record and just talk, sometimes for 30 minutes or more, until the words ran out. Without fail, Francesca would send one back. It became our ritual, and in these last few weeks it mattered more than ever. Her messages were always filled with brightness, and she told me about home: the engagements and marriages and children born to friends – life continuing on without me, and the life I'd return to soon.

In reality, I knew she found it tough most days. But she never made the sadness obvious. It wouldn't have helped, and she knew that. Even on the days when life was cruel, I rarely knew.

I still remember the excitement in her voice when the forecast suggested we were only two and a half weeks from Australia. Seventeen days. She was looking at flights and accommodation – after nearly five months apart, we'd finally see each other again. It felt like years of build-up would finally be behind us. Sometimes the row had seemed a barrier of my own making, a wall I'd placed between us and the life we looked forward to: a front door we both had keys to, the chance to start a family together.

So when we turned the boat north, I felt like I'd let her down. It would be another six and a half weeks at sea, and it weighed heavy on each of us.

And it wasn't just us. Lachlan's partner, Heide, had already booked her flights. And Jamie's partner, Em, had been in Australia for weeks already. She had committed long before the delays in Peru, when the flights were still affordable, staying in the spare rooms of friends for longer than she'd ever planned. The cost was mainly emotional, but it wasn't only that. The delay had practical consequences, too, carrying a financial cost for the people we loved most.

Out here, the consequences of a decision don't just stay on the water. They ripple across kitchens and calendars half a world away. Turning north was the right call, we all knew that, but it didn't make it any lighter. That night, listening to Francesca's voice in the dark, I could hear the strain behind her words. And I realised the weeks we'd added weren't only ours.

DAY 113, Monday 4 August

EWAN: Song of the day – '1990' by Valtos

Since leaving Vanuatu behind, we have made a leap of faith by making a dash for the Loyalty Islands in the hope of seeking refuge there before the storm.

To cover the distance westward we had to make a gamble on the wind, rowing around 40 nautical miles to the north and then praying that the building weather would bring us round and down towards the gap of water between Lifou Island and Ouvéa Atoll, around 150 nautical miles to the west.

This route didn't come without a fair degree of trepidation. Misjudge the distance or have the wind change early and we'd be forced to weather the storm on para-anchor in the middle of the channel between the island groups, where the weather would likely be at its strongest. Or worse, we might fall short of the gap and find ourselves uncomfortably close to land with a northerly gale forcing us onto a lee shore. Helplessly sitting on para-anchor and drifting towards the rocks at a rate determined by the weather gods.

But by nightfall we were quietly confident we could make the gap between the islands. The wind had remained consistent with the forecast and we had managed to cover the required mileage over the previous days, positioning our approach perfectly.

Arising for my second shift of the night, I took over from Lachlan, who had spent his shift navigating the final few miles towards the island. He was a little slower to retreat into the cabin, knowing how crucial the next few hours would be. I could sense the mixture of nerves and excitement that was keeping him from his sleep: 'We're about to clear the reef near the mouth of the bay. It's pretty wild, just try your best to get as close to land as possible once we're past it.'

I nodded, feeling more alert than I usually did so soon after waking, grunting a few words of confirmation in reponse.

'At least the moon is out tonight, to guide you in.' With that he swung the hatch shut and climbed into bed.

Rowing past the outlying reef, I began the dash for the mouth of Santal Bay on the northwest side of Lifou and the promise of safe haven. There should be a few areas that would remain calm throughout the storm, and we had identified several anchorages that were protected from different aspects if the wind changed direction.

Taking the reef on this side was the safest option. However, it meant we now had a three-mile gap to close before reaching shelter. The wind and waves had built in strength and the boat was absolutely flying, running with the tailwind. But having rounded the reef, and pointing eastwards and into the bay, I now had the weather bearing down onto the port side of *Rose Emily*, driving her south.

If we were to drift too far, the low-lying island would offer little protection and we'd be blown across the bay with little hope of fighting our way back up to the protected shore on the northern side. So, digging deep, I spent a nerve-racking hour holding the boat as high into the wind as I could, cutting the corner towards the coast to where I knew the water should be calmer.

Finally, I reached the shore and the wind began to die down. With land now lying upwind of *Rose Emily*, the waves and swell of the ocean fell away and the tension that had built dissipated.

And then, under the light of the setting gibbous moon, the smells of land filled my lungs: exotic and earthy, with burnt spices and rich sandalwood. After so many months, and having become totally accustomed to the scents of the sea, I hadn't for a moment anticipated how overpowering this sensation was going to be.

With Jamie and Lachlan now on deck, we found a cove that would offer shelter from the storm, and for the first time put out the anchor into flat water and the comfort of a quiet bay. The sounds of trees blowing in the wind and waves washing over mangrove roots filled our ears.

I thought of Dad, many miles away back home in Scotland. With his voice ringing in my ears, I heard him say those familiar words – 'safe harbour after storm doth greatly please' – and I knew what he meant now more than ever.

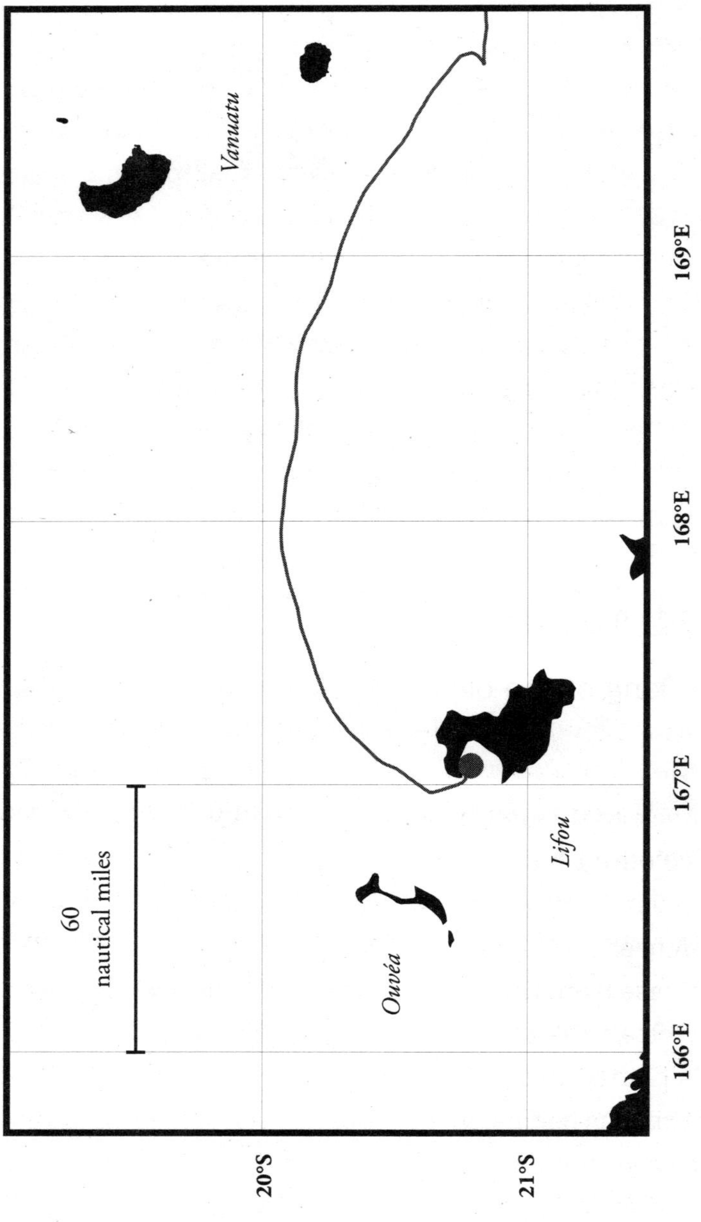

Entry to Lifou

Chapter 13

New Caledonia

By Jamie

DAY 114, Tuesday 5 August

JAMIE: Song of the day – 'Unknown Air' by Duncan Chisholm

I am on deck as the night turns to day. The dawn sky is filled with a peach-coloured haze, and the headland reveals itself: the dark outline of land with the silhouettes of trees standing like tall, slender figures on the horizon, backlit by the moon and the stars. Low cliffs rise from the sea; a small patch of white sand and dense greenery cloak the shore. I recognise the distinct smell of moist air that's drifted over the morning dew of vegetation. And then the dawn chorus begins. As the creatures of this distant land begin to waken from their rest I hear for the first time in 114 days the chatter and warbling of little birds.

Somewhat by chance, we have found ourselves in a Pacific paradise: crystal-clear waters, white sandy beaches, coral reefs teeming with fish; an abundance of marine life like we've never seen before. Bright yellow and blue fish swim in shoals around the boat, and, as we tuck into our afternoon curry, a whale breaches 20 metres to our stern. Medium in size, we suspect it's a minke. It appears to be feeding, swimming back and forth, breaching for sustained periods as its weathered back reflects the sun. A pod of dolphins is spotted on the horizon; these waters are exploding with life.

We decide to lift anchor and move as the wind shifts round to the west, creating swell and disturbance at our current location. Entering a more sheltered cove to the east, the dark cobalt waters of the deeper bay give way to aquamarine as we approach the shore. Fifty metres out, where the coral bed is dotted with patches of sand, the waters burst with cerulean blue like the vibrant feathers of a peacock.

The volcanic coastline is punctured by coves where the gentle lapping waves have eaten away at the stone. Directly above, the dense greenery of the tropical undergrowth shrouds every inch of land. We drop anchor in the late afternoon, as a giant turtle slowly floats by. Briefly poking its head above the surface, it's startled to see us there and swiftly dives down to the safety of the reef.

We notice a small cluster of buildings hidden among the trees by the shore. We're uploading some media and so the Starlink is on. Curiosity gets the better of Ewan as he zooms in on Google maps for a closer inspection. As he moves over the buildings a pin on the map pops up: 'Boulangerie Gaölöl'. There's a bakery less than 200 metres from where we are anchored. It's painfully close. We've been obsessing over baked goods for many months now. I wonder if the smell of fresh bread will waft over us at dawn? We might have to tie Lala down.

As we count and reorder our food stores, I look up to the shore. For the first time since leaving Peru, I see another human being who isn't Ewan or Lachlan. I'm quite grateful that we are a little too distant to communicate with them. I return to the task at hand, confirming that we have enough freeze-dried rations to last 28 more days. It seems we have just enough, plus perhaps ten days' worth of emergency wet rations in case of another delay. I feel a slight surge in anxiety around the food, one that takes me back to those long days of meal preparation back home in Edinburgh. We're well into the final quarter of this crossing and the food has been such a highlight to date, but what if we still run out short of Australia?

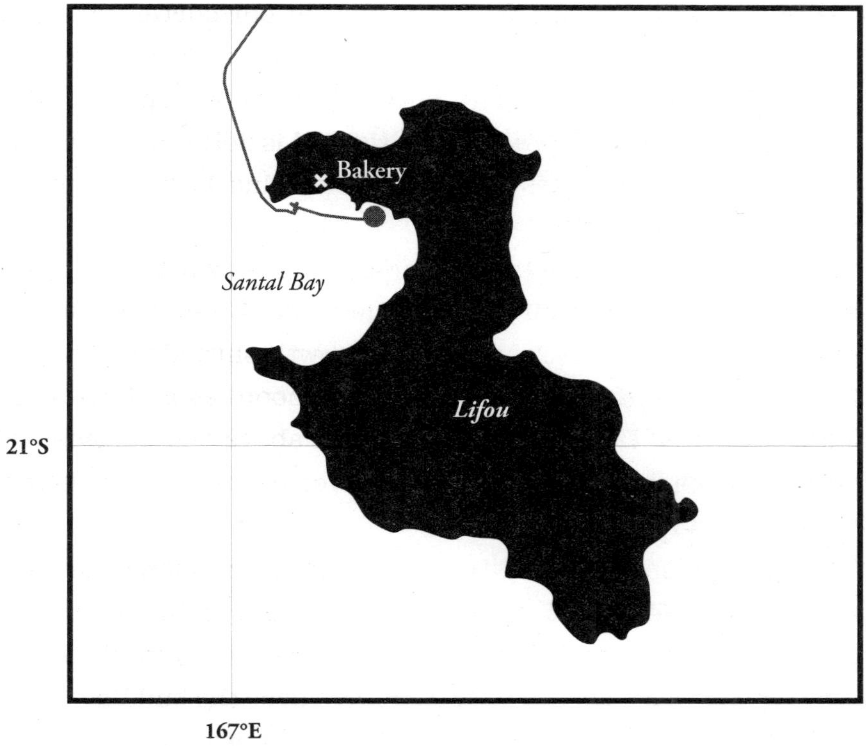

Bakery at Lifou

I glance back up to the beach; the person is gone. As I scour the headland, I suddenly realise they are in the water, swimming directly towards *Rose Emily*.

I notify Ewan and Lachlan of our impending visitor. I don't think any of us have prepared ourselves for this. Ewan waves hello as the swimmer stops 3 metres short of where we float. The man attempts to communicate with us in French but soon realises the limitations of our understanding.

In a very broken response, Ewan says, 'Hello. We are rowers. Peru to Australia. Here for two days.' The swimmer looks very confused. He points at our fishing rod, which is strapped to the stern, makes an X with his arms, and says, 'Reserve.' We nod, and after we confirm, 'No fish, no fish,' he seems satisfied and swims away.

My body is a bit confused as to what is going on. We're suddenly no longer in survival mode. And with time to rest and sleep, our bodies have gone into recovery. Sores have begun to heal, blisters on hands have hardened. The small cracks and cuts created by calluses that have caused issues these past few months have almost instantly healed over and disappeared. And with it all, I've got a hunger like never before. It reminds me of when we landed in Antigua after our Atlantic crossing. That feeling of never truly being full. We had thought we might be able to save some rations over these next few days, but that's not looking very likely. We know we will have to wait here for at least 36 hours, perhaps more like 48, before the strong westerly winds from the storm pass us by. Tucked in close to the land, you wouldn't be able to tell that a tempest was raging out on the open sea. We're all eager to get going as soon as possible; every day we wait is another day apart from family and friends. My partner, Em, has been in Australia now for nearly four weeks, using the trip as an opportunity to see the country and visit her brother. I think of her, sitting on a headland in North Queensland, looking out towards the Great Barrier Reef and beyond. Waiting for a small rowing boat to appear on the horizon.

As the sun sets over this magical place we decide to move once more, across a sheltered bay and into a southerly protected position. The winds will increasingly move from due west to southwest over the next 24 hours and we don't want to find ourselves being blown towards a lee shore. We head across the bay, to the north-facing coastline. Singalong PAC sounds on the speaker. It feels good to be rowing again.

As the wind settled in the southwest, we arrived at our third anchorage late in the evening. Dark clouds whistled by overhead, backlit by a half-crescent moon. The sound of the ocean echoed out from the shoreline to where we nestled between two lumps of coral. We slept with cabin doors open to an elemental soundtrack of water and rock.

Dawn arrived to reveal another chiselled coastline, with ribs and coves carved out of the stone. A torrent of water gushed out from one of the grooves. These caves went further than the eye could see. I imagined a complex network of tunnels – half water, half air – travelling under the headland. It went against our curious nature not being able to go ashore and explore.

Upon the limestone shelf perched a thick mass of green. Small bushes fringed a thicket of shrubs, palm trees and larger trees, some of which looked like hardwoods. Peculiar-looking evergreens soared above like rockets that had been paused mid-flight. There's no sign of anything touched by human hand here – a perfect tropical paradise.

We took it in turns to wear the goggles and explore the coral bommies that surrounded us. In the turquoise crystal-clear water, we discovered a land below the waves that bustled with life. Purples, blues and greens dotted the seabed. Swimming close, I saw the mushroom, finger and brain-like coral formations in more detail. Streaks of oranges, yellows and blues darted as tiny multicoloured fish went about their business, unfazed by my presence. Sleepy sea-cucumbers sat on the seabed below. A brightly coloured streak passed over as a bright blue and white sea-snake slithered along. I watched as it coiled into a small ball, waiting for some poor fish to stray too far from its home. I thought of Mum, an avid snorkeller, and how much she would have loved it here.

The previous 24 hours spent sheltering from the storm forced us to accept that some things are simply out of our control. With westward progress off the table for now, we were trying our best to rest, eat, hydrate and enjoy the situation we now found ourselves in.

We thought we'd have a lot of time to think and reflect on these past few months while crossing the ocean, but when you remove the act of rowing from the equation, the days seem to have no real start nor end. We meandered from one job to the next, endeavouring to maintain some aspects of our routine. Other than eating, cleaning, repairing and reordering, we were somewhat at a loss of what to do. Even in a paradise like this, we started getting itchy feet. Staying still is difficult. The journey ahead started to feel overwhelming as I divided miles to go by daily predicted mileage. There was nowhere to go and clear my head. The empty shoreline looked appealing. I wanted to sit under one of those trees and have space – a luxury we'd not known in a very long time.

By early afternoon, the forecast predicted that the southwesterly would drop off to 7 to 9 knots, potentially allowing us to make some headway. It was time to make our move. On the afternoon of the 118th day, the anchor was lifted and we set a course for the mouth of the bay. Onwards we rowed to the lagoons of New Caledonia.

By nightfall we had made it beyond the headland and into the exposed channel between the island of Lifou and the neighbouring atoll of Ouvéa. Dropping down to one on the oars, we began the nightshifts. Ewan continued to row through the growing headwind alone. The ocean currents that normally travel from east to west across the Pacific were against us, flowing instead in an easterly direction, pushing our boat back from whence we came.

My alarm went off and wearily I climbed on deck. The moon hung in the sky, illuminating our passage. A tanker rumbled by, the unfamiliar sound of engines drifting across the water until it disappeared again over the dark horizon. The forecast had been unclear as to what we would find beyond the bay. But, alas, it became increasingly apparent that the currents would remain and headwinds only grow.

By midnight the parachute anchor had to be deployed. We'd been losing progress and the oars were heavy in our hands. Perhaps we had left safe harbour on Lifou prematurely? Another night on anchor and we may have been met with more favourable conditions upon leaving. But the forecast ahead had suggested a limited window available to round the north end of New Caledonia, and we had made peace with the fact that the first night would be challenging.

We diligently continued the shifts, watching for the weather to die back and waiting for the moment where we could resume. Three hours passed and two nautical miles were lost as we drifted backwards with the currents. In the early morning, the wind shifted a little and Lachlan retrieved the underwater parachute. We plodded on. The swirls of bubbles from the blades of our oars floated obstinately away at a snail's pace, refusing to part beyond the aft quarter of the boat. We were moving at less than half a knot, sometimes a complete standstill. But at least we were no longer losing ground.

As the light returned, the island we had left behind us 14 hours prior lay less than ten miles away.

It never ceased to amaze me how quickly our experience could change out here. Reflecting on my last log entry – 'It feels good to be rowing again . . .' – how remarkably fast that passed. I hadn't voiced it yet, but I was growing increasingly concerned at our dwindling provisions on board.

DAY 117, Friday 8 August

JAMIE: Song of the day – 'Rapa Nui' by Ross Ainslie

With at least three to four weeks left on this voyage, our food supplies are beginning to wear thin. Upon inspection my findings are as follows:

- 312 freeze-dried main meals: 50 per cent homemade, 50 per cent off the shelf; 24 days' worth of main meals, at four meals each per day. If all goes to plan these should last us till the end of the voyage. Just . . .
- 38 snack packs: Just over two weeks' worth, with a couple of stragglers. We have some spare oats and loose bags of chocolate-covered honeyberries which, combined, will

make up another 21 packs – three weeks' worth in total. In any case, the snack packs have been getting progressively pitiful over the past few weeks. We're down to oats, some seeds, a chocolate bar and four electrolyte sachets. It's better than nothing but hardly a bounty of calories.

- 3 Tony's chocolate bars: these will be divided into thirds and are being saved to mark the three remaining major milestones: 7,500 nautical miles, 8,000 nautical miles and just before arrival.
- 12 packets of jelly sweets: a packet each every 250 nautical miles.
- ½ large squeezy honey bottle: 1 drizzle each on our oats. I anticipate this will maybe last 14 days at best.
- 1 900g tub of crunchy peanut butter: this morning Ewan jokingly claimed that this was his.

Having not wanted his initial share of peanut butter during the first few weeks of the crossing, he was attempting to explain that the remaining amount was his: 'It's only fair. You two have squandered your portions and I chose to save mine. I would like to enjoy this final tub without worry that Lachlan is going to "accidentally" dip into it on his nightshifts.'

'You must be joking?' Lachlan laughed out loud. 'You're a funny wee man sometimes.'

'This is outrageous. You opted out of the peanut butter before. You sacrificed your share knowing all too well that it wasn't going to be "saved" for later in the crossing,' I chipped in. 'This is a ridiculous conversation to be having.'

'I'm just saying, I think it's only fair. You guys have eaten at least one additional tub each, and now, with the new set of circumstances, I would like to enjoy a tub to myself,' Ewan continued.

'Ha ha ha. Next you'll be laying claim to all the drinking water because you "repaired" the water bladder,' Lachlan exclaimed.

'It's two on one, Ewan, and you may be small and feisty, but you'll be swimming alongside us before you know,' I said with a smirk on my face. 'He can't actually be serious,' I thought.

'Fine, but I'll remember this if there's a next time,' Ewan ended, with a wry smile showing. The cheek of it.

The ration was decided at one teaspoon each on our morning oats. It might last three weeks, at a push.

- 1 large Jetboil gas canister: these normally last us ten days, but we're now eating half our meals cold and the other two with a 50–50 mix of cold and hot water, which results in a lukewarm meal, but it means we should just about make the gas last. We have cut down hot coffees to a once-a-week treat; we abandoned hot tea weeks ago. I was almost certain we had at least one more gas canister on board, but with all our rubbish now filling the compartments in which the food and canisters used to be stored, it was impossible to get access to the very bottom of these areas of the boat. The prospect of pulling the bins out was just too overwhelming. Each drybag (now bin bag) was stuffed to the brim and unable to fit through the round Henderson hatches on deck. We would have to empty the bins out, digging through old bags of filthy meal packets, snack wrappers and used baby wipes awash with stinking bin juice. It was better to keep these drybags shut tight until we arrived in Australia.

We couldn't ignore the evidence in front of us. We had, at a push, one more month of supplies. Depending on our progress across the Coral Sea, we would need to start rationing in approximately two weeks' time.

In hindsight, we would've packed things a little differently. But I don't know where we would have stowed anything extra. With the boat loaded to the gunwales and bags of food strapped on deck when we left Peru, we were in many ways already over our limit. Our fate now lay in the hands of the weather. On the eve of day 119, Ewan had announced: 'Well, fellas, it all ends tomorrow. Day 120, the day we had estimated we would arrive in Australia.' We all let out a little snigger and then one by one joined in.

Lachlan: 'It's funny, the coastline of Australia is much more mountainous than I anticipated, and it appears to be only a few hundred miles long.'

'I'm just amazed at how few boats we've seen. And no houses either. And we didn't even notice the Great Barrier Reef,' I chipped in from the bow.

Of course we weren't arriving tomorrow, or the next week, or the next. But it was the best and only way to deal with the fact that Australia still lay 1,500 miles away, a good three to four weeks' rowing depending on conditions. We soon dropped into our night routine. My parting words to Ewan as I closed the cabin door: 'Second to last nightshift, big man, I hope you make it count.'

He laughed and replied, 'You know by the time you wake I'll have probably dropped anchor in Cairns marina.' We both chuckled and I went off to bed.

The peaks of New Caledonia towered off our bow. We peered up at the impressive ridges, the highest reaching over 1,600 metres, that span most of its northeastern coastline. The hills reminded me of Loch Lomond's wild east coast, with forest giving rise to toothy cloud-topped peaks. Streams and rivers snaked their way down the mountainsides like wrinkles in a weathered brow. The warm sweet air of land wafted seawards, evoking fond memories of hot heather and Scottish hills.

There were so few signs of human life on this coast. For many miles there was nothing. Then the fleck of a remote dwelling was spotted; then another – and another several miles along. Then nothing again. New Caledonians are either quite antisocial or very respectful of personal space.

The sky burned with mango yellow behind the northernmost headland as the sun drifted towards the horizon. A full moon rose into a lilac sky above our stern. As evening approached, we planned to enter the reef and get into the lee of the lagoon before the wind shifted to the north overnight. A line of standing white breaking waves stood seven nautical miles off the shore. The reef below was invisible, but the chart showed a shipwreck beside our chosen entry point, Passe de Pouébo – always a reassuring sign. As the nautical-mile opening came alongside, I shifted the autohelm 50 degrees to port. We pulled hard on the oars, bouncing along at 3.5 knots, as *Rose Emily* swayed from side to side in the awkward swell.

Nothing and everything changed. We passed through the invisible gates and the sea-state flattened out. We'd made it into the lagoon.

DAY 120, Monday 11 August

JAMIE: Song of the day – 'Orange Sky' by Alexi Murdoch

We arrive at the south end of the island of Paaïo in the great northern lagoon of New Caledonia. It's late afternoon and the sun has begun to set over the western edge of the reef, filling the sky with streaks of peach and blood orange. There is a strong breeze but the shallow water is almost flat. For miles in all directions the depth doesn't drop below 12 metres, resulting in a bright turquoise sea. The occasional turtle breaches to say hello, its small bald head briefly bobbing above the surface. The water here is slightly opaque, a bright milky blue caused by the sandy sediment of the seabed below.

Although the storm has passed, a strong wind still lingers in the south so we tuck ourselves as close into the cove as the reef will allow. Paaïo shares many of the traits found on most of the islands in this lagoon: white sandy beaches; dense green undergrowth dotted with coconut palms; a backdrop of triangular peaks that rise to create a jagged horizon.

Some of the islands are inhabited, but the majority show no signs of human life; they are fragments of land that have broken free, untouched and idyllic. It makes me consider the beauty of nature when left to its own devices, undisturbed by our intervention.

Even though there's a decent breeze there is no swell. For the first time in many months *Rose Emily* lies flat and still in the water. It takes me a while to drift off; it feels strange for everything to be so calm.

I sleep for 13 hours, waking every two hours to reposition my body or check that we haven't started to drift and drag the anchor. I'm woken properly by the heat of the sun as it begins to warm the cabin, its bright light piercing through the small window in the door. I stretch off my back, which is surprisingly stiff after such a long rest. Simple oats and honey for breakfast – we're saving the final tub of peanut butter to mark our departure from the reef. Periods spent on anchor or para-anchor are always strange: land is a mere stone's throw away and yet we endeavour to keep our lives and routine the same. We need to maintain the conditioning that we've worked so hard to gain over the past four months at sea and the previous 12 months of training. We eat and hydrate well and our bodies thank us for it. We need to be going into the final leg of this journey with our best foot forward, and that means replenishing our energy levels.

We do what we can on board to keep ourselves busy. Decks are scrubbed, solar panels cleaned, oats are counted (again!), damaged sponsor logos/vinyls are replaced. We touch base with Mum, Dad and our respective partners, reassuring them that the storm has now passed and we are needing to wait out the strong southerly winds before making any progress. I can tell Em is upset, her voice a little shaky on our call. We've accepted the fact that it's impossible for us to make any headway in the current conditions, but it's more difficult for people on land to properly understand the delays.

We do some tests rowing directly into the wind, but we make little progress. Had these gone well we were geared up for a departure from the waters of New Caledonia today. However, with the wind still sitting in the south to southwest, and the hours of daylight fading, it would be reckless to leave now. We move anchor once more, looking for a sheltered spot that is marginally closer to the gap in the reef through which we will travel tomorrow.

But the wind has picked up and, even in the sheltered lee of a large island, it gusts and dances across the lagoon. Carefully navigating through patches of reef, we drop anchor in the shallow water, but it doesn't want to hold. We move further up the shore to a slight inlet in the land but, again, we drag along the seabed. Third time lucky and thankfully she holds. We set the anchor alarms and agree the rota of watches.

As we scoff down our final meal of the day, a lukewarm chilli chicken, we hear a rattling rumble in the night air. It's pitch black and the howling wind confuses my senses. I grab the nearest torch and shine it into the darkness. Travelling at great speed and showing no signs of slowing is a metal-hulled fishing boat with a roaring outboard engine. There's no lights on board, just the faint silhouette of a figure and the small glow of the end of a cigarette.

We drop our curries and grab every light we have on board. Pointing all the torches towards the oncoming vessel we shout and wave. But the rattle of the engine doesn't cease. They are hurtling towards us at speed and we have no ability to get out of their way.

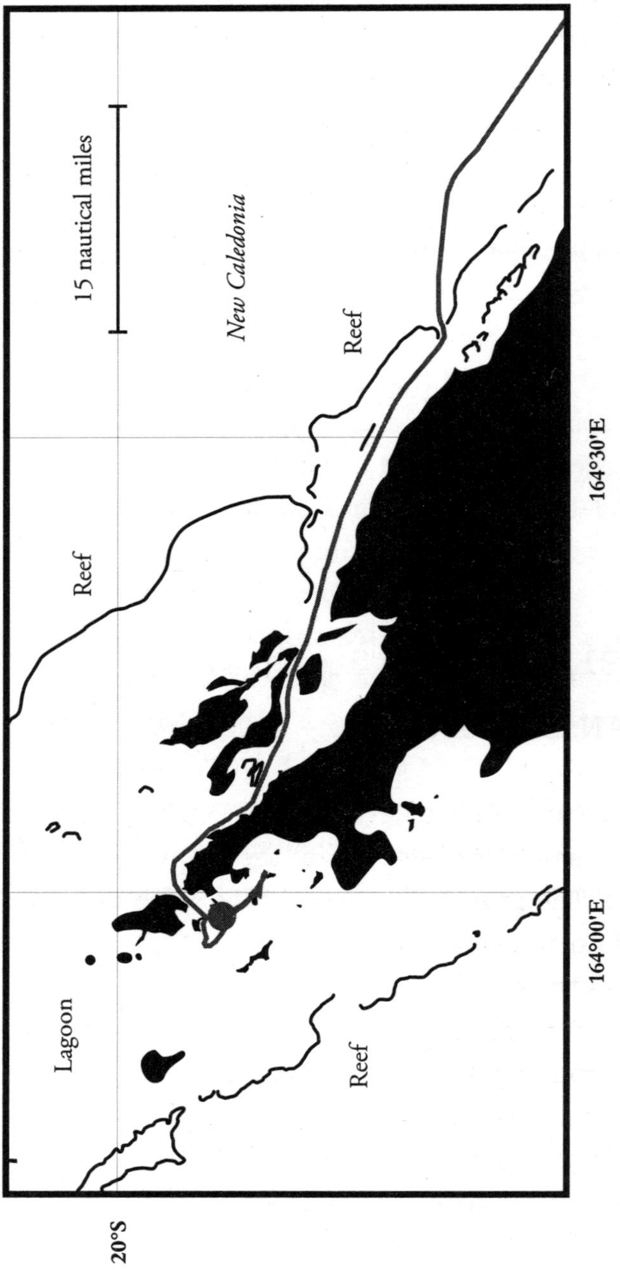

Entry to New Caledonia

Chapter 14

Reef Roulette

By Lachlan

DAY 121, Tuesday 12 August

LACHLAN: Song of the day – 'Laid Bare' by Beluga Lagoon

'Oi! Hello! Stop!' I shout into the darkness, waving my flashlight. The boat hurtles towards us over the reef we had just so carefully navigated. The previously silent anchorage fills with the gravelly sound of an unhealthy petrol engine. These people know these waters like the backs of their hands. But have they seen us in the pitch black? I have a sinking feeling in my stomach. After all of this, over four months of toil, this is how it will end. I glance to my left, checking the water where I will dive in to escape the collision of aluminium and carbon.

At the last moment, the boat swerves sharply to starboard, grinding to a halt less than ten metres from *Rose Emily*.

'*Bonjour!*' comes a cheerful voice. We watch as a figure rustles around in a rucksack to produce a light. To our complete surprise – and relief – our headtorches reveal a man, his wife, three young children and a baby. The children look at us with wide open eyes like we are wild animals in a zoo.

I explain in my terrible French what we are up to. '*Pendant cent vingt-trois jours*,' I say, gesturing a rowing motion. They beckon us into their boat and point ashore: '*Manger et boire*.' We decline apologetically, struggling to explain with what limited vocabulary we have that, for our row to be unsupported, we have to stay on the boat, and can't allow anyone to help us. How much they understand, I don't know, but they seem to get the gist. The man yanks on the outboard engine, and moments later they are careering back over the reefs.

We finish the chilli chicken and laugh at this memorable encounter and are in our bunks by 20.00. We need all the rest we can get for what is to come in the morning.

Our progress across the lagoon has been good, so the decision is clear: we will set off through and beyond the reefs; Cairns, Australia, our destination. We row three-up, heading almost due west to make the small gap. Though there is a larger gap slightly to the north, we choose the smaller southern opening, only a hundred feet wide. With the strong southerly breeze, this gives us an out. If the conditions become too big and the wind too strong, we'll turn *Rose Emily* about and duck back into the lagoon through the northern entry point.

We hug close to the south side of the opening. To the north, the jagged coral pokes four nautical miles westward. We need to row like hell to avoid being caught on a treacherous lee shore. The first breakers come into view about two nautical miles out. Barrelling waves march in walls on either side of the gap as a three-metre swell collides with the reef. Some waves curl around the lip, travelling perpendicular to the others, creating a tangle of foaming white wash. We've checked and rechecked the forecasts, but have accepted that it is impossible to know in advance what it will be like out here.

I stand at the bow on navigation as Jamie and Ewan pull on the oars. Ewan calls out the readings from the depth sounder: 'Ten metres, nine metres, eight metres, seven . . .' The crystal-clear water magnifies sand changing to rock on the seabed. Though we've timed our departure with slack water, I can feel *Rose Emily* tremble and shudder as strong currents interfere with our rudder. I look back and forth at the reefs on either side.

'Seven metres . . . still seven metres. I think we've stopped moving,' says Ewan.

I turn astern to check the Garmin deck repeater, our on-deck speedometer: 0.0 knots. Ewan is right, we've stopped in our tracks. 'Give it all you've got, boys,' I shout up to them as they pull harder and increase their stroke-rate. I gaze at the middle of the narrow gap ahead. We are neither moving forward nor back. The power of the current matches that of Jamie and Ewan. For not the first time in this journey, we are utterly at the mercy of Mother Nature.

I look to my right. Then left. Then right again. A horrible sinking feeling fills my stomach. Slowly but surely, *Rose Emily* is being sucked into the north side of the opening. Only 150 feet of water separates us from a truly desperate situation. Have we made the wrong call here?

Something had to change. I slipped my feet into the foot position and slid the carbon oars through the gates to join my brothers. Large swirls rippled from every stroke.

'Twenty big ones . . . ten more . . . and another,' Jamie shouted from the middle position. Our strokes were fast and efficient. After so many days on the ocean, we were rowing as one, our strokes altered unconsciously to match one another's. Facing astern, I glanced over my left shoulder again, transfixed by the rocks we'd been moving towards. There was movement. Inch by inch, the reef off our starboard side started to move, edging its way down the boat. We were, slowly but surely, moving forwards. Speed over ground climbed to 2 knots. We still had a long day ahead of us, but we were through the worst of it. I flicked on our small speaker.

'Only one tune for it,' I said with a sigh of relief. '"Rose Emily" by Duncan Chisholm and Ross Ainslie.' Two of our favourite musicians had written a tune to help with the fundraising, a fusion of the Fijian Cibi – akin to the New Zealand haka – and Scottish trad music. It was just the song for that moment.

We rowed three-up for the next 12 hours, snatching small breaks for hydration and food. We'd pre-made our meals for the day. It was full-on, but clearing New Caledonia and keeping a good course was the priority.

We clocked nearly 14 hours of non-stop rowing before Jamie eventually kicked off a delayed and shortened night routine. Ewan and I remained on deck, maintaining the forward momentum as best we could, pinching up into the wind, away from the sharp reefs to the southeast.

I was approaching 15 hours on the oars, snatching small breaks here and there to do the essentials: eat, drink, pee. My back and hands ached from their continual use. An egg yolk-coloured moon rose above the horizon in front of me as I took the last bite of my Snickers bar. I was mesmerised by that moon. It had been our friend in the sky for thousands of miles, lighting up the darkest of nights. The bioluminescence was magnificent that evening. I hadn't seen it this bright in such a big sea-state. As the waves broke around me, the surf was illuminated from within. The specks of shimmering plankton cascaded through the waves, changing the jet-black landscape into a brief series of glowing hills. Sometimes a handful of plankton stuck to the blades of my oars, glowing away as it was carried along on our journey for a brief moment of time. I felt utterly exhausted, but I couldn't remember feeling that satisfied at any other time in my life.

Stillness.

Nothing was on my mind. No niggling thoughts or concerns, no reflections on time past or worries about time future. Where I was at that moment was the only thing that mattered; the only thing that was.

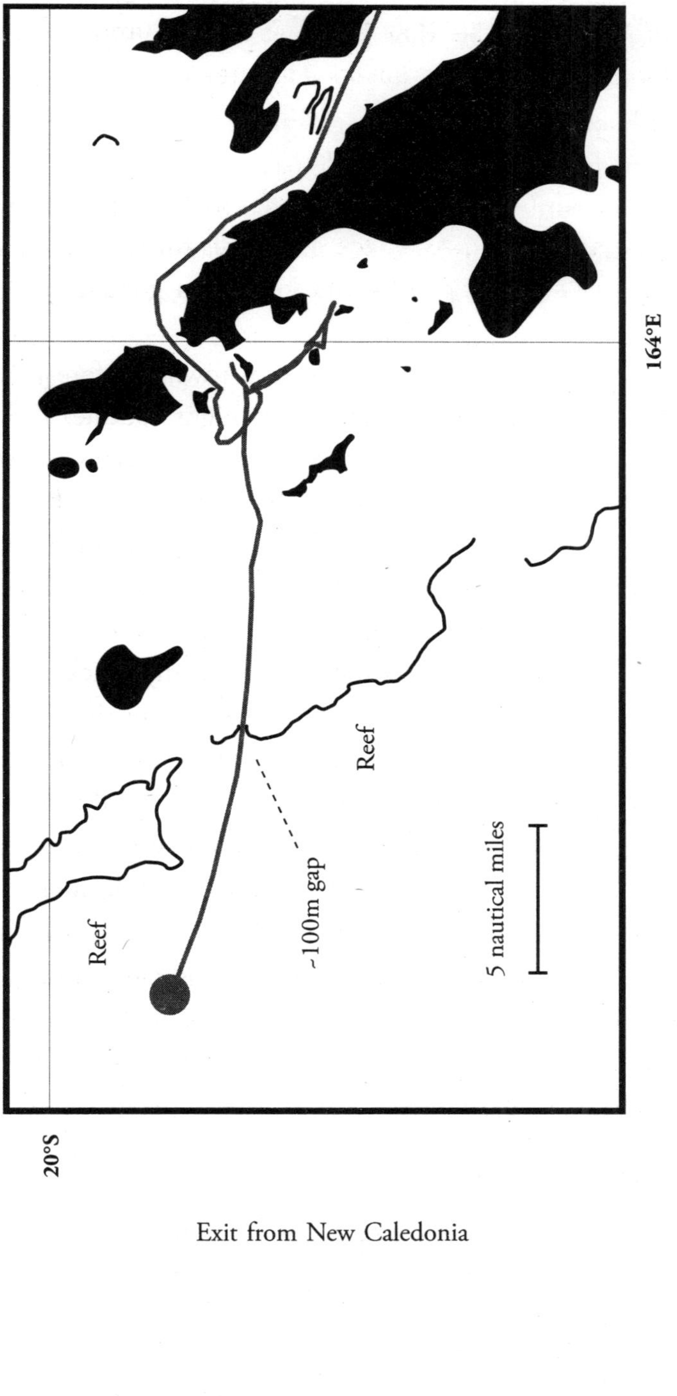

Exit from New Caledonia

My body knew the drill. I scooped the water effortlessly with each stroke, doing not thinking. I looked up. A cloudless night sky with billions of stars sparkled like coal dust on dark velvet, the vast peaceful galaxies disturbed only by shooting stars streaking silently by.

And then it was my turn to put down the oars, and Ewan was left alone to hold our course into the nightshift. The weather had slowly crept round in our favour to make a single oarsman tenable. But only just.

At long last, Jamie's alarm clock sounded from behind the hatch door of the bow cabin, waking him from his 90-minute slumber and signalling the end of Ewan's longest day yet: 16 hours on the oars. He crawled into the bunk and shut his eyes for what felt like a few seconds, conscious of the ache in his hands. Then, before he knew it, three hours had passed and the alarm was sounding again, calling him back outside for yet another solo shift. His watch told him that he'd slept for two hours and 50 minutes. By daybreak, we'd each rowed for 18 ½ hours over the previous 24. It was our biggest day yet, but we were into the final leg: the Coral Sea and the Great Barrier Reef.

After leaving the lagoons of New Caledonia, we endured two days of the type of weather that Scots describe as being 'dreich': thoroughly depressing. It was that fine but heavy rain that's relentless and soaks you to the skin. With the wind predominantly coming from the south we rowed hard – two on, one off – trying to maintain some sort of western progress. The currents appeared to be changing every couple of hours, at one moment pulling us south, the very next sending us north.

DAY 124, Friday 15 August

LACHLAN: Song of the day – 'We Grew Up at Midnight' by The Maccabees

I squeeze on my soaking-wet waterproof Atacama smock. This

fantastic piece of kit, designed specifically for this crossing, had kept my body bone-dry when I was washed overboard, but even this isn't enough to keep out the relentless downpour. Saturation squeezes through the Velcro seals around my wrists, neck and waist, determined to crawl its way in, in search of every dry fibre. It's difficult not to take it personally.

When you're in 36 hours of weather like this, it feels like it will never end. It's hard to imagine ever being warm and dry again. The thick dark cloud that stretched all around was all-engulfing. Our hands were cracked and sore from the heavy rowing of the past few days. A combination of salt sores and the rashes on our backsides had got progressively worse with the salt spray. There wasn't much hope of anything healing until we got to the other side of the Great Barrier Reef.

But that wasn't the only sense of urgency on *Rose Emily*. As the days climbed past 120, snack packs were progressively getting worse: a sachet of oats and a Snickers bar if you were lucky. We were doing everything we could to avoid a calorie deficiency, scouring the hatches for any loose snacks. I'd started eating raw chia, pumpkin and sunflower seeds – we had excess for our morning oats – for extra calories.

DAY 126, Sunday 17 August

JAMIE: Song of the day – 'Beeswing' by Christy Moore

With our arrival at Cairns estimated somewhere between 27 August and 3 September, it's touch-and-go whether we'll have enough freeze-dried food, so we've started rationing to four meals per day. The gas for the Jetboil is set to run out within the next seven to ten days. Most of our meals are being eaten cold – we're saving our final gas for the other side of the Great Barrier Reef. Any fish caught will have to be eaten raw – a last resort, but one we're willing to take. There's not much room for error.

Just as the sun dipped below the horizon, I had a realisation: '23rd of August. It's Dad's birthday.' We flicked on the Starlink. Usually we would only use it in direct sunlight, but the battery levels were unprecedentedly high. As we got closer to Australia, the ozone layer had become noticeably thinner. Our exposed forearms had become accustomed to the sun but were now burning in the strong UV.

Jamie made the phone call, Ewan and I rowed. It was early morning in Scotland. I could see Jamie straining to hear Dad's voice down the phone. The laryngitis hadn't improved at all in the time we'd been away, even with periods of silence. If anything, his voice was worse than it had been, a faint whisper of his usual self. Dad was due to be flying out to New Zealand in a few days to stay with his brother, David, before coming over to Cairns. Though he hated long-haul travel, the last time we spoke he'd seemed excited to see us arrive.

After five minutes of chitchat, Jamie's expression became concerned, his ear angled towards the phone. Dad was evidently telling him something that was difficult to hear, for more reasons than one.

'Ok, thanks for letting me know. I'll have a chat with Lachlan and Ewan and we'll be in touch with Uncle Jamie.' They said their goodbyes and Jamie put away his phone.

'Everything ok?' I asked, as Jamie took his perch against the stern cabin.

'Sort of. Well, not really. Dad had a biopsy on his larynx. It's throat cancer.'

All of us had been secretly contemplating this as a possibility, of course. But we had all been hoping and praying it would not come true. We'd spent some time in the months leading up to departure digging into the things that scared us most about the journey ahead of us. It was part of our mental preparation with Chloë. Talking through and pinpointing the things we were most apprehensive about was helpful, and allowed us to introduce measures in training to make those fears less of an unknown. An example of this was the man overboard. On Chloë's advice, we'd finish some longer rows by jumping overboard and swimming behind the boat then scrambling back on board. The idea was to become familiar with being tired and in the water then getting back on board so that if it happened in real life – as it had – we wouldn't start panicking.

There was no shortage of nightmarish scenarios we could dream up that might immediately affect us on board *Rose Emily*. Knockdowns, capsizes or pitch-poles. Losing power or the watermaker breaking down. Sharks or marlins attacking the boat or whales breaching onto us. But they were all to some extent within our control, or at the very least we were in a position to know how to react in the right way: fix or combat whatever problem had arisen. Our greatest fear about this trip was something happening far from the boat – illness or a bereavement of someone close to us. We'd feel completely helpless out there if that did happen.

'How does he sound?' I asked, tentatively.

'His usual stoic self. He seems relieved that they're getting to the bottom of it,' said Jamie.

Dad was still intending to fly out to New Zealand, but would need to return on 29 August for an appointment with the throat specialist. We talked it through as dusk settled over the water. We didn't think it was a good idea for him to fly out. Though we were excited to see him, getting the ball rolling with his cancer treatment was much more important, especially when there was a good chance that he'd miss our arrival. There would be a big gap in whatever crowd would be there when we got in, but it was the right call. We sent a message to Uncle Jamie, Dad's brother, an orthopaedic surgeon, and made our position clear.

A quick reply came back: 'Righto. I think that's the right call. I'll call your dad in the morning. Keep it up, boys. UJ x'

As I entered my first nightshift, under a clear sky, a wave of emotion hit me. Tears streamed down my cheeks as I reflected on the situation, considering Dad's mortality. In many ways, I was grateful that we'd heard the news now rather than on arrival. I felt like I could process the situation properly out here in this environment – there was no hiding, and I had time to feel what I needed to feel. As soon as we left *Rose Emily*, it would inevitably become overwhelming and hectic.

I remembered lying in my bed as a small child. I must have been barely five years old. It dawned on me that Dad wouldn't live for ever. He was almost a decade older than Mum and drank and smoked. Though I was young, I knew these things weren't good for longevity. That must have been the first time I'd grappled with the idea that people didn't live for ever, even Mum and Dad. It was funny to think that I'd be doing the exact same thing over 20 years later, bobbing somewhere just off the Great Barrier Reef after crossing the Pacific.

Despite all of this, it was important that we didn't take our foot off the pedal. We were gearing ourselves up for what would be the final and most critical leg of this journey. All our bodies were feeling the fatigue, but our backs and bums were taking the brunt of it. We just needed to keep it up for a few more days until the weather turned more favourably in our direction. And if it didn't turn in our favour – it wasn't the first time in this crossing we'd held out this sort of false hope – then we'd just need to cling on and pray that things didn't go catastrophically wrong.

As we approached the Great Barrier Reef, the final major obstacle ahead of us, the South Pacific Equatorial Current – which we'd been riding west – reaches the Queensland coast. At this point, it forms the East Australian Current (EAC): a strong southward current that travels down the east coast. It is the largest ocean current close to the shores of Australia. Where we hoped to enter the reef, the current would be gathering strength, pushing us away from our destination. We needed our best game for the final round – the pinnacle of this voyage – before we could truly relax for the first time in more than four months.

Australia was almost within our grasp as we kept as far south as possible to round the south of the Flinders Reef, southeast of Holmes Reef. From there, it was 112 nautical miles to pass below Raaf Shoals then onwards to the Noggin Pass. Two on, one off was our bread and butter, punctuated by a treat of three on to punch through the stickier patches.

DAY 133, Sunday 24 August

EWAN: Song of the day – 'Eoghainn's' by Ímar

Rowing has been a wet business today. Not due to rain, but rather waves breaching the boat. Wind-whipped foam and spray carried over the gunwales added to our discomfort and, after a time, we simply succumbed to the salt, giving up the usual rinse with fresh water after each drenching. I questioned my life decisions as my backside crawled with irritation. I can also confirm that cold chicken tikka masala with an added cup of salt water isn't exactly palatable.

Sometimes it's best to accept one's fate.

On day 135 I wearily settled down into my first nightshift, flicked on my headtorch to locate my water bottle – and noticed an unfamiliar object on deck. We had a stowaway. A South Pacific booby sat on our port-side wing, balancing impressively like a gyroscope in the swell.

I decided to let it stay. I'd never seen a bird looking so tired. It was black and white and looked like a gannet – an exhausted gannet, one which seemed to be enjoying some respite from the waves. We'd recently passed two shipping lanes. 'Maybe the gannet can be on shipping-tanker watch,' I thought to myself. My mind drifted elsewhere.

Thirty minutes later I looked once again to see how our guest was holding up. The bird was fast asleep, its beak tucked into its neck, its face covered with a wing. It had shat all over three of our deck solar panels. I considered chasing it away, but concluded that it would only return and potentially land somewhere even more inconvenient. Our guest continued to disgrace itself until the sun came up, requiring two chase-aways and three deck cleans.

'What the hell's happened here?' Ewan asked, as he swung open the cabin door.

There was bird shit everywhere. When it took flight for the final time and set off over our bow, I couldn't help but feel envious. I imagined the bird gliding over the miles that we had ahead of us. We were so close, yet so far. If only we weren't affected by current, wind and reefs.

DAY 137, Thursday 28 August

EWAN: Song of the day – 'Rose Emily' by Ross Ainslie and Duncan Chisholm

The water became increasingly heavy overnight, and no matter how hard we pulled, we had to watch with dismay as our speed dropped off. We had met the East Australian Current, which was pushing us south – and away from Cairns.

There was little choice but to summon our last remaining scraps of energy to give one final Hail Mary, rowing three-up from the first light of dawn. Our hope was that on reaching the Great Barrier Reef, the powerful current would largely die away where the continental shelf rises out of the seabed to disrupt the flow. The only problem was that the reef was still 25 miles away. And travelling at less than a knot, it would take us over a day to reach it.

However, with three on the oars, the boat began moving faster again. And so we slogged away under the hot sun, gradually making ground, every metre taking its toll. We listened to *The Old Man and the Sea*, rapt by the tale of Santiago, the protagonist of Hemingway's classic, and reminisced about our Atlantic crossing. We had listened to the same story at a similar stage on the Atlantic. What a memorable way to have concluded each journey.

'Channel your inner Santiago, lads,' Jamie motivated us as we heaved in the glassy heat.

'Feels like we're dragging a fucking marlin . . . where are those sharks when you need them?' I added.

If we could harness one per cent of Santiago's fortitude we'd be across the East Australian Current in no time.

At that very moment, there was a flurry of commotion off our stern. As if we were being listened to, a pair of sharks, both over two metres in length, breached out of the water, their serpent-like bodies slinking across the surface. We watched in silence, mesmerised by the beauty of these creatures.

'Best to leave that hull-cleaning for a bit, then?' Ewan remarked with a chuckle. We planned to give *Rose Emily* one final scrub before entering the reefs. We needed to pull out all the stops for the final straight.

After 13 hours of three on the oars, we were approaching our entry point to the south of Raaf Shoals. Birds dived around us catching the bait fish that had been driven to the surface by the predatory yellowfin tuna. The shimmering golden bullets breached the sheer surface, homing in on their prey. Before we lost the light, I plunged into the blue expanse, floating like a spaceman on the threshold between two worlds for the last time. A line attached me to our boat – my umbilical cord to forward progress. Legs kicked and arms flailed. The sun cast bright turquoise-blue rays, taking my gaze downwards. The blue deepened the longer I looked. I didn't know the depth – one or two miles? A shimmering shoal of fish were followed by a string of otherworldly jelly. They, like us, were at the mercy of this current. We were all visitors in this great mass of moving blue.

'I wonder where those sharks are?' I thought to myself as I floated there.

As I squeezed my final blob of shampoo onto my palm – I'd made this 50ml bottle last almost 8,500 nautical miles (10,000 ordinary miles) – I reflected on how my relationship with hull-cleaning had changed. For the first half of the journey, I'd dreaded getting in the water; it was now something I looked forward to. I'd done the thing that scared me until it no longer did.

Our hull free of growth, we were ready. Rowing into the night – three-up through the Noggin Pass – we took it in turns to study our carefully plotted charts. Accidents most often happen in the final leg of any journey, and we were determined not to take our eyes off the ball. We made Yogi tea to pep ourselves up as our energy flagged – a welcome reminder of home. This was our first hot drink in over a week.

We dropped down to one on the oars for a brief window overnight, but then got back on. My watch told me I'd had only two hours and 50 minutes' sleep in total. Pretty abysmal, even by our standards. But there was no time to spare. *Rose Emily* was hardly moving with one on the oars, and we were eager to reach safety as soon as possible. It wasn't the downwind jaunt we'd hoped for, but we were making progress. If we kept this up, we'd reach the inside of the reef by sunrise.

DAY 138, Friday 29 August

LACHLAN: Song of the day – 'Still' by Beluga Lagoon

A storm petrel bounces around *Rose Emily*, scooping water with its shovel-like feet. These joyful birds have joined us for the duration of this journey. Disturbance on the surface, a boat's length away, indicates life. The golden figure of a mahi mahi leaps out, silhouetted by a warm mango-coloured sky behind. A tern squeaks like a children's toy as it swoops like a conductor's arm, elegantly plucking a sand eel from the water's surface. The tern's motion looks effortless, but I've come to appreciate just how tough their lives are – the true endurance athletes of this ocean.

I hold my hand close to the Jetboil burner to check it's not been blown out. This morning we have a treat: lamb saag curry – our last three freeze-dried meals. We've saved our very final drop of gas for this moment. I flick on the speaker to listen to our singalong playlist. Sitting back, I look out over our bow. I remember doing this shortly after leaving Peru. It felt then as if the blue was never-ending, our boat so small and progress so slow that viewing anything more than a day ahead gave me a nauseous feeling in my stomach.

A dark cloud hugs the horizon in front of us. 'Odd,' I think to myself. 'There hasn't been any rain forecast for today or tomorrow.'

Then it dawns on me. My gaze narrows on the slug-like shape. I am fixed on it, using my neck to stabilise against the motion of the boat.

This is no cloud.

I turn off the speaker and look at Jamie and Ewan. They raise their gaze with bland expressions. I can see the tiredness in those weathered faces, and the salt from dried sweat staining their t-shirts. Their beards have made them almost unrecognisable, but they've never looked more themselves. How lucky I've been to have had their company for these months at sea.

'Look over there.' I point over our bow. 'That's Australia. We've done it, boys.'

I bless the night that nourished my heart
To set the ghosts of longing free
Into the flow and figure of dream
That went to harvest from the dark
Bread for the hunger no one sees.

All that is eternal in me
Welcomes the wonder of this day,
The field of brightness it creates
Offering time for each thing
To arise and illuminate.

I place on the altar of dawn:
The quiet loyalty of breath,
The tent of thought where I shelter,
Waves of desire I am shore to
And all beauty drawn to the eye.

May my mind come alive today
To the invisible geography
That invites me to new frontiers,
To break the dead shell of yesterdays,
To risk being disturbed and changed.

May I have the courage today
To live the life that I would love,
To postpone my dream no longer
But do at last what I came here for
And waste my heart on fear no more.

—John O'Donohue, 'A Morning Offering'

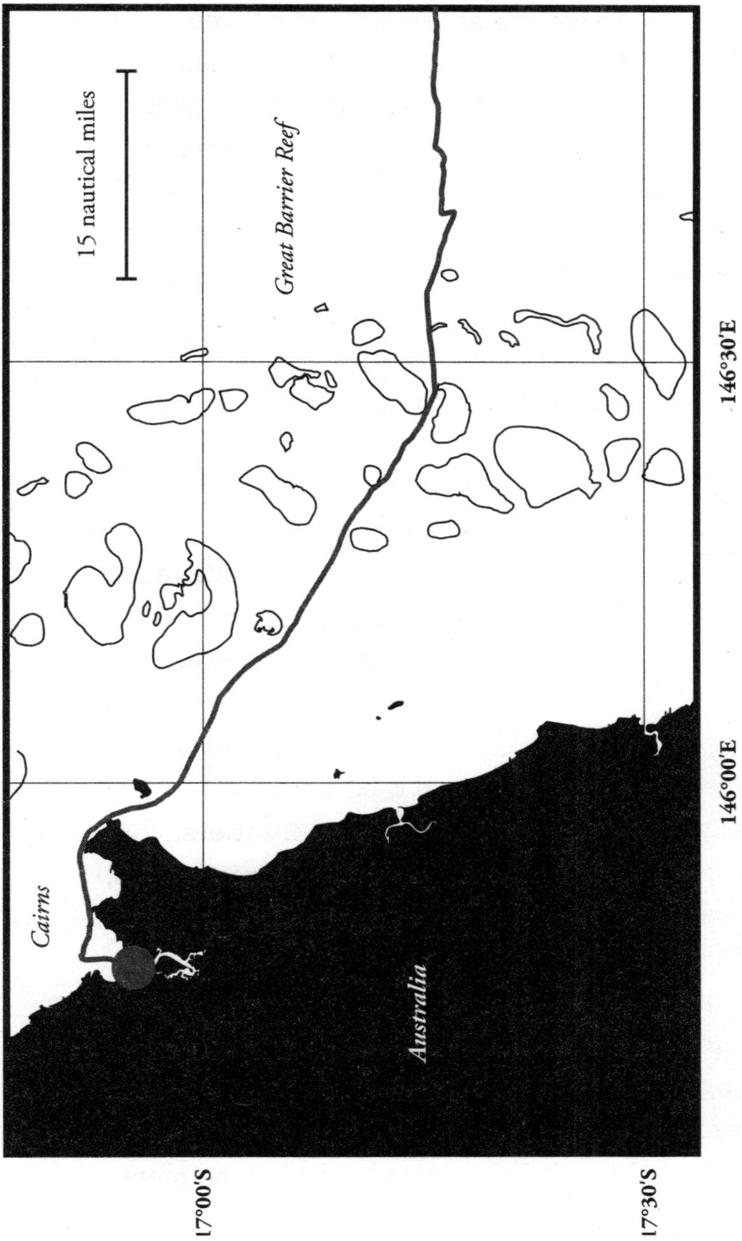

Arrival in Cairns

Chapter 15

One Million Strokes

By Ewan

DAY 139, Saturday 30 August

JAMIE: Song of the day – 'Catriona's' by Rura

With less than a mile to go, we eased the pace, letting the oars run a little lighter, savouring the last remaining moments aboard *Rose Emily*. I couldn't quite believe it was all about to end.

As we approached, the clock struck 11.30 a.m. and I heard the distant sound of bagpipes. More than one. I knew who it would be, but still I didn't want to let my expectations get ahead of me. The sound drifted across the water and we made our final turn, pointing directly for the harbour mouth. I rowed in the mid-position, Lachlan at the bow, Ewan standing at the stern and steering with the hand lines, the way forward visible from his vantage point.

It brought me back to the end of our Atlantic row – my back to the oncoming crowd, reading the moment in the face of our helmsman. Ewan beamed, tears gathering and rolling down his salt-worn cheeks. He tried to describe what lay ahead, the scores of people who had come. But there was no need. His expression said it all.

As we passed the harbour walls I caught sight of a few of my closest friends – Nick, Matt, Alex and Angus – all with pipes in hand, having travelled halfway around the world to welcome us into Cairns to the sound of 'O Flower of Scotland'.

The sound sent a shiver down my spine. Then one came in at the wrong moment, missing the group cut-off and playing a wayward note – our music teachers would have been dismayed. I laughed out loud. Some things will never change.

The marina opened ahead of us and I saw the pontoon for the first time – only 50 metres to go. Less than a stone's throw away.

Cheering, shrieks, whistles and horns came from the shore. And then . . . there was Mum. She'd made her way to the end of the nearest jetty and was waving frantically to make herself seen. She was holding her phone up awkwardly, the screen turned towards us. And then it hit me. She was on a video call, and Dad was on the other end of it. I let out a shaky exhale – a breath I hadn't realised I'd been holding. Of course, she'd hold him up like that.

It would be about three in the morning back home in Scotland, and though I couldn't make him out, I pictured him alone in his flat in Edinburgh, in his dressing gown. All I wanted to do was hug him.

The unmistakable voice of our cousin, Guy, crackled through the radio – the signal we'd been waiting for. Oars down. It was now or never. I lifted my pipes, flares strapped to the drones, and struck them up. Lachlan yanked at the ripcords and they burst into brilliant red flame. Moving quickly, he lit two for himself, and held them above his head. Ewan followed suit. Smoke swirled around the boat, and I could feel the heat on the back of my neck. These Peruvian flares were intense. One of Lachlan's began to pop and splutter and he ditched it into the bucket on the deck, half-filled with sea water. It fizzed away, and I thought, 'That had better not put a hole in our boat – imagine sinking this close to shore.' Then I felt the tassels that held my bagpipes in place begin to give way, and as I reached the final part of the tune, I realised they were on fire. Not figuratively, quite literally. For a brief moment I wondered if we'd taken it too far, the acrid smell of fireworks and burning plastic in the air.

But the flares died down. The cheering swelled. Ewan pulled on the hand lines and 50 metres became five. And as the smoke thinned, it all began to feel very real.

DAY 139, Saturday 30 August

EWAN: Song of the day – 'Rose Bay' by Ludovico Einaudi

A passing boat shouted encouragement as we rowed towards the harbour. I tried to answer them, to thank them for their kindness, but nothing came out. My throat tightened and my vision blurred with sudden emotion.

We waited for port clearance in the bay, pausing as we signed our names on the entry documents. The pen felt so strange and unfamiliar between my stiff and clumsy fingers that had become so conditioned to the oars. I pressed too hard at first, the signature wavering across the page, as if it belonged to someone else.

Then came the last few metres on the water, steering *Rose Emily* towards the place where it would end.

I'd imagined that moment a hundred times before, but still couldn't quite believe that we were here. My heart was pounding as faces came into focus. Some I recognised, many I didn't, all of them watching us.

I suddenly felt out of practice with the steering lines, having rowed almost entirely with the autopilot at sea. Now, with the boats lining the marina and the pontoon waiting, my hands didn't feel as sure as they should be. To add to the pressure, a catamaran yacht appeared and drifted into our course, watching the spectacle unfold.

But riding the wave of encouragement from the onlooking crowd, we eased in. *Rose Emily* gently kissed the pontoon. And the clock finally stopped.

With tears streaming down my face, I turned and hugged my brothers. We steadied ourselves on each other for a moment, holding onto that euphoric haze. We then turned, hand in hand, and stood for a moment before stepping ashore.

With one deep breath, we stepped off the boat and our feet met dry land for the first and final time.

For a long time, I had imagined that moment. The vibrant colours and sharp, exotic sounds. We had lived those first unsteady steps so many times before in the refuge of our imaginations, when our minds had drifted during months of living with an oar in each hand. Holding the thought of arrival had given us a thread of hope – it had pulled us forward over the infinite horizon. Those dreams had served their purpose. Yet, as is ever the case, the reality was different. The imperfect edges and flooding emotions prevailed, our senses were saturated, struggling to keep up. We swayed on the narrow pontoon, muscles compensating for an imagined swell that no longer lay beneath our feet, our brains wobbly and unsure how to handle stationary ground, which was now so unfamiliar. *Rose Emily* had been as steady as a rock. Terra firma felt buoyant and untethered.

It all felt slightly dreamlike. We moved through the crowd like children seeing the world afresh, pulled between people we loved and people we had never met, not knowing quite how to be with either.

The body arrives before the mind does, and although the physical recovery begins almost immediately, I'm sure that the ocean has claimed a part of me for good. It's somewhere out there with the waves and the spray. But I came back carrying something, too.

Today, my memory of our time out there is patchy at best. There are large stretches of the row that I can't access clearly, no matter how hard I try. Whole weeks have been erased, and when I try to step back into them, I find only fragments. Sleep deprivation must have played its part, but I think the mind also protects itself by letting certain things go. I can remember the broad shape of the journey, and a scatter of razor-sharp moments that appear when my eyes close. But much of the detail has dissolved away.

After reading back the words I shared in our logs, that much has become clear. Putting this account together has made me realise how much has already left my memory. It's a disconcerting discovery to make. I've continually found myself thinking: 'Did that really happen?' It's an odd thing, reading my own account – primary source material, written by me – and not being able to place myself fully within it. As if the person who lived that experience was me, but also someone else. I'll be forever grateful to Jamie for insisting we write a daily log. This book wouldn't exist if not for that decision.

We've tried to keep the story focused on what it felt like for us: three brothers rowing an ocean together. That was the experience we lived, and it's the experience we wanted to share. We've tried to avoid slipping into a catalogue of everything that happened around it, but there is a great deal we haven't told: the unseen work of friends and family, the years of planning and preparation, the people who supported from afar, the motivation that arrived in messages and donations and practical guidance, the full complexity of lives continuing on shore while we lived a distant floating existence.

I don't want to romanticise our return within these final pages too much. Much of it was more basic than you might imagine. Simple things, in the ensuing days and weeks, that we no longer took for granted: a hot shower; clean sheets; fresh clothes; fruit and bread; the ability to drink water without rationing or trying to make it last. Things that are so normal, they become almost invisible in everyday life.

And then there were the people. I saw Francesca as we came in, smiling through tears. I stepped off the boat and, for a moment, a few metres still stood between us. Three unsteady steps down the pontoon and I was holding her, my arms tight around her shoulders, my face tucked into her neck, the heat of the Australian sun on our backs. Only afterwards did I realise that, until I embraced Jamie and Lachlan a few moments earlier, it had been over four and a half months since I'd embraced anyone – and nearly six for Francesca.

It's part of the reason to do hard things now and again: they let you return to ordinary life with clearer eyes. And though I know the clarity will fade, I hope some of it remains. As time passes, the shine of these experiences will diminish. Ordinary life will quietly slip back to comfort and routine. Small irritations will begin to regain their old size; minor frustrations will recover their old power. That's part of being human, I think.

I hope I can remember, when that happens, how easily the most basic gifts become invisible. Clean water from a tap. Fresh food to eat. A safe bed. The arms of people you love. None of these are guaranteed, though it's easy to move through life as if they are. And I don't confuse the discomfort that we chose with the hardships so many people do not choose. Whatever the row demanded of us, it was never that.

As for how we've changed, I'm not sure anyone can see that clearly in themselves, not at first. Our beards got chopped and our bodies healed. Much of what shifted may only reveal itself later, though, in the decisions we are yet to take. But I do know the Pacific stripped life back to a few simple truths.

You can't bargain with weather or negotiate with a storm. You can't predict a flat calm or a cyclone. And you can't force life to be fair. The ocean is oblivious to the hopes and dreams of humans.

But you can control a few honest things. Whether you show up for the next shift. How you speak to the person beside you when you're tired and raw and not at your best. Whether you meet hardship with bitterness or with humour. Whether you keep moving in the direction you chose, even when progress feels slow. That distinction, between what can be changed and what you must accept, is one I'll keep trying to remind myself of back on land.

The row didn't magically make us better people. It didn't fix our flaws. If anything, it put them in a sharper light. We are just three ordinary brothers with an unlikely dream – naïve enough to believe we could do it, and stubborn enough to see it through. We've got plenty of failings. I'm impatient, perfectionistic, controlling and intolerant of indecision. We all take on far too much, and it spills over into the edges of our relationships. Between us, we don't even nearly make up for one another's blind spots.

But maybe that's the point. Until seven years ago, I'd never really rowed before. I'm below average height and don't exactly look like the sort of person built for rowing oceans. When we weighed in at the start-line of the Atlantic rowing race, the larger guys were over twice my weight. A betting man would have looked straight past the three of us.

Writing was similar. I hadn't written much in my life before rowing across the Pacific. That's an odd thing to write in itself. English was probably my worst subject at school, and I scraped through at 16 before moving on, convinced that words didn't belong to me in the way they belonged to other people. I never felt especially good at it. My exam results did little to suggest otherwise. If I was harbouring any promise, it did a very good job of keeping out of sight. If you'd suggested before this adventure that the three of us would one day write a book about it, I don't think we'd have believed you.

The thing that changed wasn't a hidden gift. It was starting. And then it was continuing. Putting in the hours.

We've tried continually to be good beginners. Not in the sense of being naturally gifted at something from day one, but in the sense of being willing to admit we don't know but are eager to learn anyway. We've made plenty of mistakes but have kept showing up and doing the work. A long series of ordinary decisions made in the right direction.

But we certainly didn't do it alone. If there's one skill that I'm proud of us for, it isn't heroic grit or superhuman resilience. It's that we learned to surround ourselves with exceptional people. People who gave their time, expertise and belief. People who supported us, built with us, trained us, carried parts of the load we never even had to see. The whole is greater than the sum of its parts. This dream happened because other people helped make it happen.

It's easy to look at the world and assume the worst is the true nature of things. But this journey was threaded through with kindness. It gave some hope. Messages from strangers. Donations from people who had no reason to care. Friends showing up in all sorts of ways. Small acts of generosity arriving like lights on difficult days. There is kindness in the world. And we're all better off if we refuse to let the loudest, bleakest parts of the news define what we believe about people.

Before we even made it back to Scotland, our fundraising had crossed a line that I still struggle to believe. One million pounds. It's a number that's incomprehensible to me. But reaching that milestone wasn't the ultimate goal of this campaign – that was never the point. The point is what it represents: illness prevented; time saved; kids staying in school; parents being able to work; the simple dignity of clean water, and how unfair it is that something so basic can still be out of reach for so many.

Out on the Pacific, we kept moving forward by breaking everything down into the next rowing stroke. On land, the same principle holds. Big changes rarely come from one grand gesture. It's usually lots of small actions, repeated, supported and sustained. The oars have now stopped, but the work continues.

If this book leaves you with anything, I hope it leaves you with a few practical truths.

You don't need to be good at something to start. You just need to begin. And then be consistent and intentional about taking the next step.

Surround yourself with people who make you better. Let your dreams be shaped by community, not just willpower. The world is full of people who can help, and you might be one of them for someone else.

Don't give up on hard things too early. Most difficult goals aren't conquered in a single act of bravery. They're conquered by showing up again and again, by ordinary people.

And if you can, help yourself by helping others. Do something, however small, that improves the life of someone you'll never meet. The world could use more of that. Refuse to succumb to greed or to the idea that the current state of things represents being human at our best.

Times will be hard sometimes. That's part of the deal. But search for humour, and kindness, and beauty where you can find it. Have gratitude and a greater purpose. Dare to hope.

Then hold onto your thread and let it pull you over the horizon.

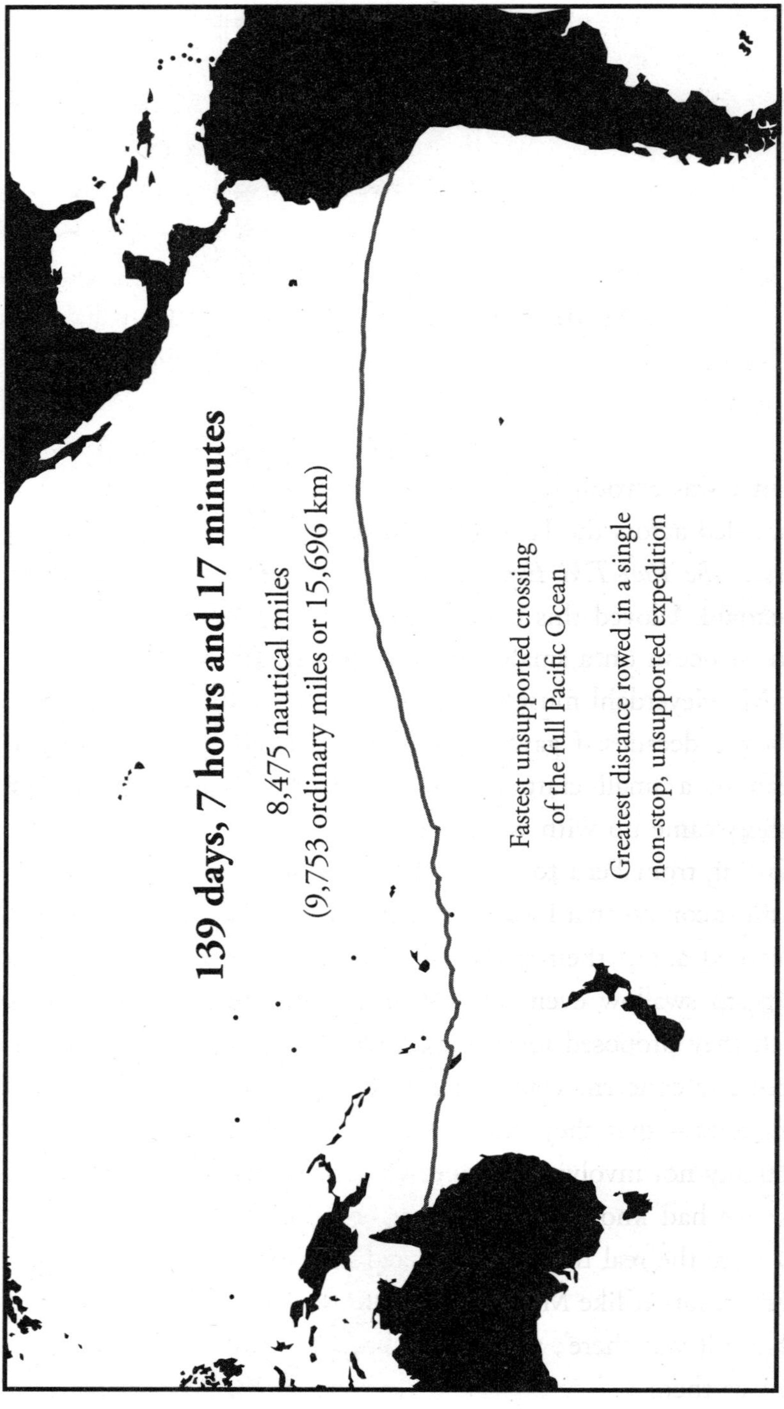

Crossing the Pacific

Afterword

By Sir Alexander McCall Smith

When I was a young boy, aged 12 or so, I had a book about a man who sailed across the Pacific Ocean on a balsa-wood raft. This was, of course, *The Kon-Tiki Expedition* by the Norwegian adventurer, Thor Heyerdahl. I loved this book. I remember thinking that to set out to cross an ocean on a small boat was an extraordinary thing to do, and that Mr Heyerdahl must be a man of unbelievable bravery. Thereafter, for many decades, I gave little thought to the crossing of the Pacific Ocean in a small craft, until suddenly my godson, Jamie, and his brothers came up with what I felt was the completely unrealistic idea of rowing from Peru to Australia.

I must confess that I was distinctly lukewarm about the project, being concerned about their safety on an ocean known for its vastness and ability to swallow even much bigger craft than the rowing boat on which they proposed to embark. Other friends of the Maclean family shared my concern, voicing the wish – not mentioned to the rowers themselves – that they might decide to do something else altogether, preferably not involving small rowing boats and wide oceans. No such luck: we had known the Maclean boys all their lives and knew that they were the real thing – they liked nothing more than an adventure and that, rather like Mallory, who said that he wanted to climb Everest 'because it was there', they felt inclined to cross the Pacific because it, too, was there.

And so their adventure began, and day by day even those who had misgivings over the daunting scale of the undertaking were drawn into the unfolding story. The regular dispatches from the boat, the ship's log, proved to be as addictive as they were informative. Day by day their audience grew; day by day armchair rowers all over the world expanded their knowledge of maritime matters and came to appreciate the sheer enormity of the task that Ewan, Jamie and Lachlan had taken on. With hearts in mouths we waited for the latest bulletin that would bring news of winds, waves and currents. And as the boat drew nearer and nearer to Australia, we rushed off to atlases to acquaint ourselves with the position of various islands that might provide sanctuary if the need arose, or that might be obstacles to be avoided by a bit of skilful navigation.

And what a marvellous account the ship's log proved to be. Not only were these three young men intrepid rowers, they revealed themselves to be accomplished and at times lyrical writers. Few voyages since that undertaken by Odysseus on his journey back to Ithaca have been so beautifully recorded. The body of prose that is the ship's log is, I think, a very profound and moving piece of maritime writing.

They arrived, and across the world we watched the moment when these three brothers stepped ashore in Queensland and, putting their arms about one another's shoulders, stood in silence. It was a magnificent moment that I think many of those who watched it being broadcast will never forget. This was a moment of triumph not only for three rowers who had made it against all the odds – it was also a significant moment for certain values: for brotherhood, for determination, and, of course, for the compassion that inspired the donation of a million pounds of aid to those whose life sentence was to endure a shortage of fresh drinking water. What a story – what a gift.

All of this – this whole endeavour – took place at a time of uncertainty for the world. The last year or two have been a period of conflict and confrontation – a period when the values of courtesy and co-operation, of civility, have been gravely threatened. Amidst the wars and suffering of our times, amidst the selfishness and seediness, a wonderful story was enacted before our eyes, and is now recorded in this gripping narrative. This book is a beacon in the darkness, beaming out the message that obstacles are there to be overcome, suffering and need are there to be assuaged, oceans are to be crossed; friendship and co-operation, positivity and hope have not faded from our world, but insist on making their presence felt.

I finished reading this manuscript and thought: 'Yes!' I did not feel the need to think anything else – just, yes!

Mum's Reflections

By Sheila Maclean

I stare out at the expanse of the Atlantic Ocean exactly where my sons rowed into Antigua over five years ago, and say this mantra as I meditate on the image of a tiny boat on a vast ocean:

The waves of the sea have spoken to me
The wild birds have taught me
The music of many waters has been my master

– (Translated from *The Kalevala*)

I think of my three sons voluntarily harnessed to a giant floating playpen named *Rose Emily* (after the sister they never got to play with), now bobbing across the biggest ocean in the world. 'They are doing something they love, with a sense of purpose, and they have each other to look after. For once I know exactly where they all are and, quite frankly, they are safer at sea than on land,' I say to myself, and, 'They're also having the adventure of a lifetime.' Having survived years of ski jumping, hiking, free climbing, mountain biking, cycling across continents and contact sports, this seemed like a pretty safe activity.

This new feeling was quite different from the overwhelming fears I had felt when they tackled the Atlantic. I had consciously set out to find a new mindset that would keep me on the rails; my mental health had suffered badly last time they rowed an ocean. How best to deal with this epic challenge? I was drawn towards finding a spiritual route, and, like my youngest son, had in recent years developed an interest in exploring Buddhism and other mind-opening practices. By following such a path, I could hopefully prevent a momentous wave of anxiety from washing me 'out to sea'. I began to look out daily at the horizon of the Atlantic from a rocky height in Antigua, trusting the universe to look after them. To put it simply, I had no choice but to hand their safety over to a power much greater than myself. The Great Outdoors. A simple realisation and practice, but once I had got there, how much easier it was then to face the repeated question of, 'How do you feel about your three sons in one small boat rowing across the biggest ocean on the planet?'

'They'll be fine,' I would answer, spieling off the playpen story, trying to calm friends' and neighbours' palpable fears and make light of it. To drown myself in anxiety would have been no help to anyone. I could now also see clearly that this was the purpose *Rose Emily* had served, to keep her brothers safe. After leaving us she was followed by the arrival of Lachlan into the family, my second insurance policy attempt for his brothers, and, ironically, it was he who initiated the crazy idea of rowing across an ocean. Lala's adventure, but Ewan and Jamie were quick to join in – it was a surprising new step up in the hierarchy of their brotherly bond! So, post Atlantic, they chose their moment. While casually chopping vegetables with me in the kitchen in Assynt, Jamie slipped into the conversation, 'How do you feel about us doing another row, Mum?'

I paused. I've always encouraged them to follow their own holistic path in life, and may have been more than a little responsible for encouraging their sense of adventure. I couldn't say no. My instant reaction was to offer the suggestion of a few extra safety precautions (double harness and rigorous handovers) and the die was cast, little knowing that Sudocrem should have been on the list as well. And it was to be the strength of this bond that would hold them together when Lachlan was washed overboard – on hearing of this terrifying episode it was the only time I allowed myself to cry during the crossing.

It is strange how in the face of adversity we often unite, and this was to be the case with us as an extended family in general, so by the time they rowed into northeast Australia I was holding the phone for a live video call directly to their father back in Scotland. Years of separation had not damaged the family bond, and it was a reminder that often our best times had been spent adventuring on the sea around the rugged coastlines of Assynt. This new challenge required a united front. It's not only their lives that were to be changed for ever; this latest adventure could benefit so many living in less fortunate circumstances, and hopefully give inspiration to others to follow in their steps.

Epilogue

16 April 2026

By Lachlan

Warming golden light wafts through the half-closed shutters. A handful of children, girls and boys, play football in the red clay square outside with a ball formed out of paper and Sellotape. The sun is rising out of a luscious landscape, and these children are squeezing in a game before school starts. Verdant valleys, tiered with vibrant green rice paddies, are connected by rolling hills. Paths snake their way down the hillsides, joining the constellations of palm-thatched houses. Though it's 6.25 a.m., the town is already busy with the hustle and bustle of people getting ready for their day.

On all of our four visits to Madagascar, we've visited Ambohimahamasina. It has a special feeling, and it's comforting on our return to see familiar faces that we've known for years. Haja, a local farmer and walking guide, welcomed us with open arms off the bus. We crammed into his living room with his young family, ducking below the door-frame, and enjoyed fresh lemongrass tea and rice pancakes with crushed peanuts. Peanut butter isn't really a thing here, but Haja knows how much we like it. Unlike in Scotland, he grows his own peanuts, which he and his wife, Arline, grind into a paste with oil and salt. It might be the best I've ever tasted.

It's an important day. It's a year and four days since we left the coast of Peru, and today marks the official launch event of Feedback Madagascar's clean water initiative in the rural municipality of Ambohimahamasina. This four-year project in the southeast of Madagascar will be funded entirely by our Pacific row.

The goal is to ensure sustainable access to clean, safe drinking water for a population of around 40,000 people who live in the municipality, including every village, every school and every health centre. When all is said and done, it could be the first municipality in Madagascar with 100 per cent access to clean water. The programme will dovetail into the wider web of Feedback Madagascar's longstanding work in the area – school-feeding, agroforestry and reforestation, livelihood and health initiatives, to name just a few – catalysing a groundswell of positive change that will go far beyond just water.

We've done a lot of reflecting and storytelling in the eight months since we docked into Cairns marina. We've relived the story told in this book many times, sharing the highs and lows at schools, universities, care homes, conferences, energy summits, film premieres, dinners, TED talks and more. We've been invited to present the match ball at a Scotland rugby match, sat between Ewan McGregor and James McAvoy at the Scottish BAFTAs and even been given some awards ourselves. There's been an overwhelming amount of praise for what we've achieved, which has, at times, been uncomfortable for three Scottish lads who aren't good at receiving compliments.

But that's not the only reason for this uneasy feeling. As flattering as the acknowledgement has been, it's also felt, in part, undeserved. As I hope has become clear by reading this book, there have been far more than three people at the heart of the project's success. There's been so much sacrifice, hard work and commitment from so many others around us.

Our first thanks must go to the people who made this book happen. Thank you to Jamie Byng and his team at Canongate: Helena Gonda, Jenny Fry, Francis Bickmore, Brodie McKenzie, Caitriona Horne, Lucy Zhou, Valeri Rangelov, Louise Tyler and Karen Stretch. A massive thanks must also go to our editors, Robert Collins and Ian Preece, for being so patient and compassionate, and for taking on the challenge of editing a book written by three non-writer brothers . . . some might argue that this was a more daunting task than rowing the Pacific. Finally, thanks to our dad, Charlie Maclean, and David Spaven for their writing mentorship.

Canongate wouldn't have heard about our story had it not been for our agent, Cathryn Summerhayes at Curtis Brown, reading our log to her daughter over Weetabix and cups of tea and thinking, 'There could be a book in this.' A huge thanks to her and the exemplary Elliot Prior who has gone over and above at every step of the way.

One of our most frequently asked questions is: 'Three eggs in one basket . . . how did your mum and dad cope?!' We can't imagine how many sleepless nights we've caused our parents over the years. From falling out of trees to bike touring, from rugby injuries to rowing across oceans, we've definitely not been the easiest boys to bring up. Without your unconditional love and support, we would have lacked the foundation required to dream of rowing the Pacific. Thank you for teaching us to always pursue the things we love, not being afraid to stray from the conventional path.

After a month of radiotherapy treatment shortly after we got back to Scotland, Dad was given the all-clear from his throat cancer in December 2025. He's weathered the storm in his usual stoic way: gracefully, cheerfully and without a word of complaint. Mum returned with us for a short spell in Scotland, then went back to Antigua to continue her life as a full-time artist. She continues to inspire us with her adventurous spirit, spending any spare moments bobbing off the coast with her snorkel and flippers.

Our next thanks go to our partners, Fran, Em and Heide. The stress of these projects is felt most keenly by those closest to you. Thank you to each of you for your support, through thick and thin. From cooking over a thousand meals in three days to doing all-nighters helping us pack, sharing our ship's log each day and sending encouraging voice-notes for those darker nightshifts, you each contributed so much in your own way.

The same goes to our family – both old and new – and friends. The support was diverse: from banging the drum to teaching us how to tourniquet; sending amusing thoughts for the week from Assynt to writing poems and songs; 24-hour rows to ultra-distance relay runs. We're indebted to you all.

We've mentioned on several occasions our one superpower of surrounding ourselves with exceptional people. We were extremely lucky to have the shore-based team that we did, sharing our story to aid the fundraising: cousin Guy managing the team; Gregor, Scarlett and the team at Story Shop on socials and PR; Graham, Calum and Andrew at Lost Clock Productions on the YouTube channel; Jack Macaulay on social videos, website and anything else we could throw at him; Calum Fraser for medical support; Sean, Tom and Mark for weather routing; Nick, Sarah, Annabel, Jamie and Johanna on fundraising. If it weren't for this team, we might not have reached Australia at all and wouldn't have come close to our fundraising target – we're eternally indebted to all of you.

When we first spoke to Chloë Lanthier about preparing to row across the Pacific, she said that she was going to prepare our bodies and minds to be able to perform for over five months at sea. The goal was to be able to accumulate energy – not fatigue – through the crossing, finishing stronger and fitter than when we started. This seemed out of the realms of possibility, but we can now confirm that it wasn't. During our 12 months of training, Chloë prioritised physiological and metabolic adaptations, building strength and power for the distance, and rewiring our brains so we could perform, in any given conditions, for months at sea. We did not lose weight, we gained in strength and endurance, and we all came away injury-free. That is testament to Chloë. She's like a big sister to us, and we feel so lucky to have worked with her.

A massive thanks to Mark Slats and The Ocean Rowing Company for building a boat that was up to the task of crossing the full Pacific non-stop and unsupported. Thanks also for allowing us to come out to the workshop and get in your way for a couple of weeks and try – but fail – to keep up with you on the rowing machine. Your work and support have been second to none at every stage of this journey.

Ocean rowing is an expensive sport, and we couldn't have dreamed of embarking on this venture without all of the individuals and companies who supported us. A huge thanks to our two top-tier sponsors: Kai Einheuser (Nepa Group and M Yachts) and Mike Bain (Rare Whisky 101). It's no exaggeration to say that this whole project would not have happened were it not for these two individuals. In addition to making the row possible, their support enabled us to share the story and build awareness that has translated into life-changing funds for people in Madagascar.

Many thanks also to David and Janet Maclean (FLXMAT), Clarus Networks, Jayson and Helen Woodbridge, Carol Swift, the Bridges family, Sam Mayall (Zelim), Matt Chapman (Contagious), V Group, Formlabs, Arbuckle's Farm, Better Beer, Menzies Aviation and last but certainly not least James Jarvis and the team at ClearRoute, for their ongoing support of our charitable mission.

A special mention must go to the people who created our clothing and footwear. Jamie and Angus Morrison, the father-and-son duo behind Atacama Performance, together with the talented Jenny, designed every garment from scratch – custom-made to a demanding specification and on a tight timeline. They produced ten bespoke items over multiple iterations, from hats to jackets, that stood up to the full variety of conditions we encountered. Then Nick and Willa Martire, the power couple behind Norda, completed the outfit with a shoe that proved equally suited to the harsh environment and the brutal repetition of rowing millions of strokes. We look forward to our next adventures together.

There are many others that helped in so many ways that we wish we could recognise in these pages – we'll be forever grateful for each and every input; you know who you are. Without all of you, this project would have remained a dream – it was your belief that made it become a reality.

A number of sportspeople, actors, musicians and celebrities were extremely generous in helping us get the word out during the crossing. Thank you to them all: Ewan McGregor, Lorraine Kelly, Mark Wahlberg, Sam Heughan, Flea from the Red Hot Chili Peppers, Ben Fogle, Danny MacAskill, Nedd Brockmann, Jessica Watson, Blair Kinghorn, Ally McCoist, Mark Beaumont, Rob Wainwright, Leif Vollebekk, the Stoltman brothers, Jim Hamilton, Donncha O'Callaghan, Kenton Cool, Greg Hemphill, Pierre Schumann, Jimmy Nicholson, Danny Campbell and SHOTY.

Thank you to Duncan Chisholm and Ross Ainslie for writing us a tune, 'Rose Emily', which will forever more transport us back into the Pacific. Thanks also to Anthony Garratt for bringing our logs to life in a series of beautiful artworks.

There's one final group of people we must thank. Later today, we will give a presentation in the village of Ambohimahamasina. We will tell the people living here about how we rowed from Peru to Australia in 139 days. As we rowed, people around the world started tracking our dot, reading our logs and following our social media. Many people – over 15,000, to be precise – donated their money to support clean water projects in this municipality. It's thanks to those people – not us – that we will fund clean water access to the people living here.

To everyone who donated to this campaign, you are the unsung heroes of this story. Raising £1 million was a pie-in-the-sky idea, an abstract goal we pinpointed at the beginning of our journey. In many ways, it was more daunting than crossing the Pacific when we set out, and has been our North Star. It gave us direction when the going got tough, motivated us to keep on going. We wouldn't have stood a chance to get there without you. Every donation – big and small – will make a difference. You may never meet the people that you've impacted, but on behalf of the people of Ambohimahamasina: *misaotra*. Thank you.

If you are able, and this book has inspired you, please consider donating towards clean water projects. Visit themacleanfoundation.org or scan the QR code to help continue the story and support the future charitable work of The Maclean Foundation *(Registered Scottish Charity No. SC051703).*

Glossary

Anti-foul – a protective coating on the hull to prevent marine growth
Autohelm/ autopilot – the very important electronic arm that keeps us on a course by controlling our rudder
Automated Identification System (AIS) – an electronic tracking system that allows visibility between vessels (i.e. us and tankers . . .)
Beam on weather – a side on wind and waves
Bilges – the lowest parts of the internal sections of the boat
Bilge pump – a water pump that removes bilge water
Boat speed – our speed through the water
Bommies – isolated coral outcrops/coral formations that rise from the seabed
Bow – the front of the boat
Bowline – a line attached to the very front of the boat
Capsize – when a boat rolls upside-down
Centreboard (daggerboard) – a retractable fin to maintain course and increase stability
Chart-plotter – a mapping device that combines location data with electronic charts
Course – our intended direction of travel
Daggerboard (centreboard) – a retractable fin to maintain course and increase stability
Deck repeater – on-deck screens showing information from the chart-plotter and autohelm
Desalinator (watermaker) – a mechanical device that makes salt water potable (drinkable) through reverse osmosis
Emergency Position Indicating Radio Beacon (EPIRB) – a locating device for *Rose Emily*
Following sea – waves travelling in the same direction as the boat
Footplate – where our feet are secured on the boat
Foulies – waterproof clothing used in stormy weather
Garmin InReach – a satellite communicator
Grab line – a line on the hull just above the waterline for grabbing or clipping onto (important if you're swept overboard)
Gunwales (pronounced gunnels) – the top edge of the boat's side
Head wind – a wind that blows against the direction the boat is travelling in
Henderson hatch – a round, screw-top waterproof hatch
High pressure – high atmospheric pressure – often calm winds and flat seas
Hull – the main body of the boat
Knockdown – when a boat tips onto its side
Knot – 1 nautical mile per hour (roughly 1.15mph on land)
Land anchor – an aluminium anchor and chain for use in shallow water (<20m)

Lee shore – a coastline that's downwind from a vessel
Life raft – a self-inflating raft deployed if things go wrong (*Rose Emily* sinking or on fire)
Low pressure – a low atmospheric pressure – often strong winds and big seas
Nautical mile – a distance of 2,025 yards – 1.15 times the distance of 1 statute (ordinary) mile*
Oar blade – the end of an oar which dips into the water
Oar collar – a protective sleeve on the oar close to the handle
Oarlock – the thing that holds the oar in place
Ordinary mile (statute mile) – an ordinary land mile is 1,760 yards*
Parachute anchor – an underwater parachute deployed to slow us down when the boat is being blown backwards
Pee bottle – a bottle for peeing in (we each had our own)
Personal Locator Beacon (PLB) – a locating device on our harnesses and in the grab bag
Pinch – steering a boat close to the wind
Pitchpole – when a boat somersaults end-over-end
Port – left hand side of the boat when facing forwards (the bow)
Retrieval line – line used to reel in the parachute anchor
Rudder – the rotating fin that steers the boat
Safety lines – four lines that run between the cabins for clipping ourselves onto and stabilisation
Shit bucket – our bucket for number 2's (we left with two . . .)
Speed over ground – the speed we travel over the sea bed
Statute (ordinary) mile – an ordinary land mile is 1,760 yards*
Starboard – right-hand side of the boat when facing forwards (the bow)
Steering lines – two lines that manually control the rudder
Stern – the rear of the boat (opposite the bow)
Stern bridles – two lines attached to the back of the boat
Swell – waves caused by weather far away, often lower frequency and consistent
Transom – the surface that forms the stern (rear) of *Rose Emily*
Waypoint – a planned point on the route
Weather system – the pattern of atmospheric pressure and wind circulation at a given time and place that determines the weather

** When 'miles' are referred to in the book, this is always 'nautical miles', unless specified.*